ENDORSEMENTS FOR MARRIAGE IN AND iWORLD BY DR. DAVID MCCLAIN

David McClain has written a roadmap for fulfilling marriages in a selfie world. The map is interesting, insightful, compelling, and extremely helpful. I came to the end of every chapter with fresh insights. This is a book to read cover to cover, and apply cover to cover.

—*Dr. Dave Gibson, Author, speaker, missions executive*

As an ordained Minister I tell couples today that I have the last say on their marriage vows. There is so much wrong thinking about marriage today even among Christians. It shows up in their vows. Full of sweet romantic sentiment they promise, "You will always be the light of my life!" No, someone else already has that job. Your spouse will fail you over and over again. Jesus will not. Marriage is important. Marriage starts in the Garden Genesis 1-2 as a picture of the eventual uniting of Heaven and earth Revelation 21-22 . Jesus called Himself the "Bridegroom".

For this reason David McClain's book, "Marriage in an iWorld", is a breath of fresh air for the contemporary Church. In an obsessively "iWorld" where marriage has become a contract, rather than a covenant, where self becomes the central tenant of marriage, McClain plows rough ground making sense of the current state of marriage in the West and declares afresh a Biblical path forward.

David is many things, but first a pastor-teacher. A shepherd of God's people. This motivation is seen in every chapter. Each chapter is an exposition of God's Word with very practical pastoral counsel offered on many real-world realities in marriage. People may say McClain's book on marriage is just a repackaging of an old paradigm. A Biblical view of marriage that harkens a bygone era. But marriage is in trouble and his book provides sound answers and solutions to the problem. Be assured that you can't be on the wrong side of history if you're on the right side of Jesus."

—*Steven Jones, President, The Fellowship of Evangelical Baptist Churches of Canada*

From Pastor Mark Paulsen dated April 10, 2018

My friend Dave has done his home work. Having read many marriage books myself, this one separates itself from the masses by an abundance of wise quotes and enough humor and wit to make it very enjoyable to read. Dr. McClain brings years of biblical learning and study down to a quick yet powerful read. I was hooked about two chapters in. Every pastor, counselor and married person can learn from Dr. McClain's easy but impactful message. Marriage in an iWorld has taken its rightful place on the top shelf of my bookcase.

—*Pastor Mark Paulsen Rexburg Calvary Chapel*

Marriage in an iWorld

Restoring God's Design for Marriage

Dr. David H. McClain

EQUIP PRESS
Colorado Springs, Colorado

Marriage in an iWorld
Restoring God's Design
for Marriage

Copyright © 2018 Dr. David H. McClain

Scripture quotations marked (ESV) are taken from The ESV® Bible (The Holy Bible, English Standard Version®) copyright © 2001 by Crossway, a publishing ministry of Good News Publishers. ESV® Text Edition: 2011. The ESV® text has been reproduced in cooperation with and by permission of Good News Publishers.
Unauthorized reproduction of this publication is prohibited. Used by permission.
All rights reserved.

Scripture quotations marked (KJV) are taken from the King James Bible. Accessed on Bible Gateway at www.BibleGateway.com.

Scripture quotations marked (NASB) are taken from the New American Standard Bible® (NASB), copyright © 1960, 1962, 1963, 1968, 1971, 1972, 1973, 1975, 1977, 1995 by The Lockman Foundation, www.Lockman.org. Used by permission.

Scripture quotations marked (NIV) are taken from the Holy Bible, New International Version. Copyright © 1973, 1978, 1984, 2011 by Biblica, Inc.® Used by permission. All rights reserved worldwide.

Scripture quotations marked (NKJV) are taken from the New King James Version®. Copyright © 1982 by Thomas Nelson, Inc. Used by permission. All rights reserved.

Scripture quotations marked (NLT) are taken from the Holy Bible, New Living Translation, copyright © 1996, 2004, 2015 by Tyndale House Foundation. Used by permission of Tyndale House Publishers, Inc., Carol Stream, Illinois 60188. All rights reserved.

Scripture quotations marked (NRSV) are taken from the New Revised Standard Version Bible, copyright © 1989 the Division of Christian Education of the National

Council of the Churches of Christ in the United States of America. Used by permission. All rights reserved.

First Edition: 2018
Marriage in an iWorld: Restoring God's Design for Marriage / Dr. David H. McClain
Paperback ISBN: 978-1-946453-25-9
eBook ISBN: 978-1-946453-26-6

ACKNOWLEDGEMENTS

When I multiply my years by the number of books I have read each year, the numbers add up. In light of that, I doubt I have an original thought of my own. For that reason there are the figurative fingerprints of many authors all throughout this book. But there are some authors who stand out in their influence. Ronald Allen, in his book *Liberated Traditionalism,* was one of the first people to help me grasp the importance of the Genesis account in understanding God's design in the relationship between married couples. If the goal of interpretation is to discern the one intended meaning of an author, I believe Allen's position better fits that objective than many of the alternatives.

Another author is Tim Keller. His book *The Meaning of Marriage* influences several chapters of this book—even if he is not directly quoted, some of his ideas are evident. The same could be said for John Piper, Andrew Walker, Ryan Anderson, Robert George, Serif Girgis, Linda Waite, and Richard Rohr in other chapters.

I would also like to acknowledge the apostle Paul. I think Paul unfairly gets a bad rap in today's iWorld. His epistles have probably done more to exalt the status of women and slaves in Western Civilization than any other single source. His words in Galatians 3 have greatly influenced Christianity for two millennia, where he says there "is neither Jew nor Gentile, neither slave nor free, nor is there male and female, for you are all one in Christ Jesus" 27–28 . But it is the same Paul who gives instruction on how couples should relate to each other in marriage, and it is for these passages he is condemned as misogynistic. I do not think Paul found these two teachings to be in conflict nor do I find any inconsistency with Paul. I believe this book will explain that.

I would like to acknowledge my congregation who interacted with this material as it was presented as a sermons series with the same title. Several of them recommended I make this into a book. Finally, I would like to acknowledge my wife, from whom I have learned more about marriage than any book could ever teach me.

MARRIAGE IN AN iWORLD[1]: RESTORING GOD'S DESIGN FOR MARRIAGE

Steve Jobs was a marketing genius. By adding a simple *i* before his products, he summarized what seems to be the central obsession of the modern Western psyche. Because of our obsession with self, we have managed to turn something as basic and central to our lives as marriage into something divisive and controversial. The simple complementary nature of this union between a man and a woman has come under attack in the last fifty years as a result of this pervasive worldview that places the individual at the center. The modern "human potential movement" even sees marriage as a threat to individual fulfillment and argues that our greatest human needs are autonomy, independence, and all choices are of equal value. In contrast, traditional views of marriage are seen as oppressive and a threat to the human rights of women, gays, and more recently, transgenders.

We can argue that the iWorld is a natural result of the modern democratic experiment that places supreme value on

---

1   The term "iWorld" comes from Dale Kuehne's book *Sex and the i orld*, Michigan: Baker Academic, 2009 . I will be using the term somewhat differently than Kuehne, who distinguishes an iWorld from a tWorld, which is traditional in its focus, and an rWorld, which places the emphasis on relationships that characterize a postmodern world.

autonomy and equality. The freedoms that are intrinsic to these values have some wonderful benefits and provide a context for remarkable creativity and productivity. Most of us enjoy these benefits, which come out of the biblical principle that we are all equally created in the image of God and out of the Protestant Reformation, which promoted the priesthood of the believer and teaches that all of us equally have direct access into the presence of God. But I would argue that these values are only viable if they are grounded on the religious foundation on which they were rooted. To remove that foundation is to create an environment for radical individualism which ultimately leads to hedonism and radical egalitarianism which ultimately leads to tyranny .[2] Yet these beliefs and values are so firmly entrenched in the American psyche that many are unable to see its weaknesses, and this is no more evident than in what has happened with marriage and sexuality.

The contemporary egalitarian worldview paints a picture of the past in which marriage was patriarchal, and that can be described in one simple phrase: contempt of our ancestors.[3] Past marriages are viewed as oppressive where women were little more than property. For example, recent comments by Canada's minister of foreign affairs, Chrystia Freeland, explains why she believes it is better that we are moving away from our "ignorant and stupid

2   Robert Bork, *Slouching Toward Gomorrah: Modern Liberalism and American Decline* New York: Harper Collins, 1996 , 11.

3   Jonathan Van Maren, "Our ancestors would weep to see how progressives have smeared their good reputation," *Life Site News* blog, Feb. 15, 2018. https://www.lifesitenews.com/blogs/our-ancestors- would-weep-to-see-how-progressives-have-smeared-their-good-reputation.

past." She says, "It's important for us to remember that the arc of history is pretty positive." Asked to explain her statement she responded, "I'm a woman. I'm a wife. I'm a mother. One hundred years ago I would've been beaten by my husband. That's what happened to pretty much all women."[4]

Her simplistic and cynical perspective on past marriages summarizes the basis for our modern contempt for the historical biblical view of marriage. The problem in responding to her contempt is that history is messy and complicated. There were good men and bad and some with a mix of both—just as we have today. Citing cases of abuse and insensitivity are possible within both eras. But inherent in her view is a "chronological snobbery" that C.S. Lewis describes as "the uncritical acceptance of the intellectual climate common to our own age, and the assumption that whatever has gone out of date is on that account discredited."[5] This idea that we are so much better than the men and women who went before us paints a distorted picture of both the past and the present. It has blinded many of our contemporaries from seeing the flaws and shortcomings of their own ideologies. Flaws that are progressively being exposed as we consider the present state of marriage and relationships.

The position of this book is that this iWorld view has wreaked havoc on the stability and longevity of marriages. For those who

---

4   Simon Lewson, "Chrystia Freeland Wants to Fix the Twenty-First Century," 2018, *The   alrus.* accessed February 14, 2018. https://thewalrus.ca/chrystia-freeland-wants-to-fix-the-twenty-first-century/.

5   C.S. Lewis, Surprised by Joy: The Shape of My Early Life New York: Harcourt, Brace & World, Inc., 1955 , 207-208.

view marriage as society's most basic and essential institution, the trends are seen as tragic in that the state of marriage in a society impacts its social environment for good or bad. And the state of marriage in North America is not good—as we will argue. To cite one example, in the 1930s there was one divorce for every forty marriages—and one was expected to be married if they were to be sexually involved. In the decades following we began to see an exponential increase in the number of divorces and the number of people who cohabit because they see no value in the marriage covenant—if it threatens the autonomy of self. The relation between sexuality and marriage has all but been abandoned. By 2018 marriage has lost its central role as society's most fundamental institution, and the signs show this trend will continue unless something happens to change it.

The attack on marriage in Western culture is historically unprecedented and is not just coming from groups lobbying to redefine and undermine it. It is also coming from people who claim to value traditional marriage. Even among Christians who claim to uphold a biblical view of marriage, the numbers of stable marriages are declining. The iWorld has permeated into the church and is disrupting the very marriages that God chose to be models of the relationship between Christ and the church. As Paul tells us in Ephesians 5:31–32, "'For this reason, a man will leave his father and mother and be united to his wife, and the two will become one flesh.' This is a profound mystery—but I am talking about Christ and the church."

Can we reverse this trend and restore the ideal of marriage to God's good and original intent? The answer to that is far more complex than this book can address—if we could even offer an answer. But at a minimum, we must address the problem at its core—the obsession with autonomy. We will see that the problem ultimately finds its origins in the fall when Eve questioned God's motive to desire her greatest good. She chose instead her own path by rejecting God's design and pursued her own misguided quest to be "like God"—a futile, hopeless quest that leads only to the destruction of relationships.

Complicating the discussion of the issue is our propensity toward confirmation bias. As much as we would like to think that we are intelligent, reasonable people who are willing to go where the evidence leads, this is clearly not the case; otherwise, we would have a more intelligent discussion on the topic and more consensus about its value. As believers in Jesus Christ, we should all agree that there is such a thing as objective truth and that truth originates with the person of Jesus Christ who claims to be the Way, the Truth, and the Life. Yet there even seems to be confusion among believers on this issue. This iWorld philosophy has caused many well-meaning Christians to buy into its values, and scripture is often reinterpreted through its lens. The desire to accommodate our Christian faith in order to make it more acceptable and understandable to a culture that is often hostile to it has a place, but our first priority must be faithfulness to God's Word. We must, therefore, seek out the one intended meaning of the biblical author as we interpret scripture before considering how that meaning is applied in a given culture. The position of this book is that the traditional basis for Christian marriage, and the roles within it, more accurately reflect the intended meaning of the biblical authors than much contemporary commentary on the topic.

The problem of confirmation bias is addressed in a book by self-identified liberal atheist Jonathan Haidt titled, *The Righteous Mind: by Good People are Divided.*[6] Haidt is a psychologist and professor specializing in moral psychology, but his book has a bearing on the topic of marriage. His book is an attempt to understand why the liberal and conservative sides have reached an impasse when it comes to public discourse. He acknowledges most liberals as leaning toward atheism, some with a near disdain for religion, and most conservatives have a bent toward Christianity or religion in general. He, like most liberals, could not understand how Christians could be so judgmental, closed-minded, uncaring and closed to reason. That is, at least, as he and others like him have perceived it. So, he began to research what was happening.

In his quest, he provides an illustration to describe the issue of confirmation bias. He used an elephant with a rider on its back in which the elephant represents intuition and the rider represents logic and reason. He argues that intuition, whether right or wrong, is the dominant basis on which people determine their values—not reason. Instead of using reason as the first avenue to determine their values, most people think intuitively and then try to find reasons to support their intuition. So, he asks, "How does one change ones view on something if not through reason?"

A trip to India for research purposes was a turning point for him. He started off in shock and discomfort with some of their cultural dogmas he encountered, but within weeks he

---

6   Jonathan Haidt, *The Righteous Mind: by Good People Are Divided by Politics and Religion* New York: Pantheon Books, 2012 , Kindle edition.

became more comfortable with them as he began to understand how the society worked. He writes: "It only took a few weeks for my dissonance to disappear, not because I was a natural anthropologist but because the normal human capacity for empathy kicked in. I liked these people who were hosting me, helping me, and teaching me. Wherever I went, people were kind to me. And when you're grateful to people, it's easier to adopt their perspective. My elephant leaned toward them, which made my rider search for moral arguments in their defense. Rather than automatically rejecting the men as sexist oppressors and pitying the women, children, and servants as helpless victims, I began to see a moral world in which families, not individuals, are the basic unit of society, and the members of each extended family including its servants are intensely interdependent. In this world, equality and personal autonomy were not sacred values."/

That is the nature of the problem we face when we try to address the issue of marriage in our culture. So much of the "scientific studies" are so tainted with confirmation bias that it is often hard to sort through legitimate research and agenda-driven research—research that seeks to undermine more traditional views of marriage and sexuality. What more obvious example could there be than the research by Alfred Kinsey on human sexuality. No one who has a basic understanding of proper research methodology would find his methods and conclusions legitimate. Yet the impact of his study is still felt. He had an agenda before he began the research and his conclusions reflect that.

/   Haidt, 119.

The Bible clearly was written with, and I believe supportive of, a very different view of marriage and the individual than what our culture espouses. Judged from our contemporary cultural norms, Paul comes across as misogynistic and chauvinistic. Yet if we can see marriage as he did, I believe it makes sense and is much more conducive to building more stable marriages—and, consequently, a more stable society.

The topics addressed in this book were addressed by the author in a sermon series with the same name as this book. It addresses the common problems in marriage and looks at the core underlying causes that eat away at the foundations of the marriage covenant. It will address the issue from the firm conviction that God Himself designed marriage for our good and is the best path to human flourishing for those He chooses to join together.

Each chapter will be centered on a question that is drawn from the text for each topic. Each question will have three primary responses that are drawn from the text as well. All commentary that follows is intended to support the text or expound on it.

Following are a list of topics that we will address:

Prologue- *The State of Marriage in North America*
Big Idea: While marriage was once considered a comprehensive union suited for procreation and the sharing of family life, it has become a private matter, an affair of the heart between two adults, in which no outsider, not even the children of the marriage, should be allowed to interfere. The effects of this dramatic change have become evident over the last fifty years.

Chapter 1- *Revisiting God's Design for Marriage: Lego vs. Painter Views of Marriage:*
Text: *Genesis 2:18–24*
Big Idea: Marriage is God's construct designed for companionship, procreation, and permanence. If we approach marriage as an inviolable covenant that models Christ and the church, we must seek whatever avenues are necessary to restore them when damaged.

Chapter 2- *Knowing What is Good for You*
Text: *Genesis 3:1–7*
Big Idea: Marriage is threatened when we question the goodness of God's design. Sin and disobedience is the result of believing that God is withholding something from us and we know better than Him what is good for us—so we pursue our own path.

Chapter 3- *Broken People Produce Broken Marriages*
Text: *Genesis 3:8–19*
Big Idea: We cannot fix relationships until we first realize we are broken, sinful people that God loves and wants to restore. The self-obsession of broken, sinful people creates a self-awareness that seeks to hide our flaws and blame others for them when exposed.

Chapter 4- *The Evidential Case for Marriage*
Text: *Proverbs 5*
Big Idea: The Bible and evidence overwhelming shows that the emotional, economic, physical and sexual benefits of marriage between a man and woman are essential to the well-being of any society.

Chapter 5- *The Divorce Decision*
Text: *Matthew 19:1–12*

Big Idea: The marriage covenant is to be a permanent bond that is created by God Himself. Jesus responds to the disciple's surprise at His stringent view of divorce and remarriage by stating that only those willing to abandon everything for the sake of kingdom of heaven can accept it.

Chapter 6- *God's High View of Submission*
Text: *Ephesians 5:18–24, Philippians 2:1–11*

Big Idea: The one-flesh union of a man and woman requires mutual submission with the woman specifically called to that role. In her marriage, the wife needs to follow the example of Jesus, who demonstrates that submission is a noble act that ultimately benefits everyone, including herself.

Chapter 7- *A Tough Act to Follow*
Text: *Ephesians 5:25–33*

Big Idea: A husband needs to follow the model of Jesus by providing selfless, loving servant- leadership with his wife.

Chapter 8- *Fairy Tale Marriages: The Hidden Dangers of Romantic Love*
Text: *Song of Solomon*

Big Idea: Love must be more than romantic love. When romance supersedes covenant as the central bond of marriage, the stability of that relationship is subject to our emotional whims.

Chapter 9- *Unwritten Contracts*
Text: *Romans 7:1–8:4*
Big Idea: There is a potentially destructive tension when our expectations of our spouse do not match our reality. We reduce the tension when we create more realistic expectations and identify and agree to the terms of our unwritten contracts.

Chapter 10 – *Conflict Management*
Text: *2 Samuel 14:1–15:37*
Big Idea: We reduce destructive marital conflict when we identify and address the source of desperation that drives it. Conflict is driven by a desperate feeling that leads to a drastic action and produces a highly predictable response. We reduce conflict when we identify and reduce the threat that underlies the desperate feeling. The problem becomes easier when we deal with underlying fear.

Chapter 11- *Our Secret Fears*
Text: *Philippians 4:4–13, Matthew 6:25–34*
Big Idea: We overcome the deepest fears that negatively impact our marriages by learning to be content in Christ alone. Anxiety is an undefined belief that something tragic is about to happen to our self-worth and well-being. The seven areas we are most vulnerable love, acceptance, loss of control, etc. can all be addressed when we place our complete trust in Jesus. Until we identify and address them, we will have unhealthy conflict.

Chapter 12- *How to Handle Betrayal and Rejection*
Text: *Matthew 18:21–35*
Big Idea: Anger at a spouse who has betrayed or rejected you can only be resolved by loving confrontation and letting go of the account you hold against him. Anger and resentment destroy the person harboring anger and can only be addressed when we accept the unfairness of this present life and that the sinful nature of others is something we cannot control.

Chapter 13- *The Myth of the Greener Grass*
Text: *2 Samuel 11*
Big Idea: Being committed to God and our spouse protects us from inappropriate relationships. The addition of a third party almost always damages or destroys the relationship of a married couple. It is one of the few reasons Christ grants divorce— because of a foundational betrayal of the marriage bond. While forgiveness is always needed, trust is seldom easy to restore. Time and a complete abandonment of the third-party relationship are essential for recovery of the relationship.

Chapter 14- *Cohabitation: Building a Relationship on a Shaky Foundation*
Text: *1 Thessalonians 4:1–12*
Big Idea: Building a healthy lasting relationship requires both parties to commit to a permanent relationship with God. The current dominant practice of cohabitation builds relationships on distrust and impermanence that assure couples will remain insecure in their commitment. The overwhelming number of cohabiters end their relationship within two years and

reduce their ability and willingness to commit to long-term relationships.

Chapter 15- *I Think I Married the Wrong Person*
Text: *Hosea*

Big Idea: The bond of marriage is grounded in the covenant—not in the ideal person. The popular notion of a "soulmate" that God, or fate, has out there for you to simply discover has no basis in reality. A search for a soulmate is counterproductive to the real work of building healthy, lasting marriages. Better to seek out common faith and values. But if left with what seems an unsatisfactory partner, then the real work of building begins.

Chapter 16- *Married to a Fool*
Text: *1 Samuel 25*

Big Idea: Being married to a fool requires great wisdom and maturity. People who are married to a person who has severe personality and character flaws requires a high level of maturity and wisdom from the spouse. Two fools together create a disaster. An ongoing tendency toward bad, impulsive decisions, control issues, and insecurity add extra stress to a marriage.

Chapter 17- *Life Crises That Impact Marriages*
Text: *Psalm 51, 1 Samuel 12:13–23*

Big Idea: When dealing with a major life crisis, only God can deliver us. Major crises put huge strains on marital relationships. Things like miscarriages, job losses, and financial collapse add an emotional stress that limits our partner's capacity to support and encourage us because we are dealing with the same anxieties.

We must look to God alone for the strength we need. The issues include: miscarriage, job loss, relationships with in-laws, and boredom.

Chapter 18- *They May Not Break Bones, But Words Can Still Hurt*
Text: *James 3:1–12*
Big Idea: Taming the tongue is vital to healthy communication in marriage. The words we use to say and hear things can strengthen or damage those we claim to love. Couples must learn that they cannot use hurtful words with their spouse to manipulate to get their way. And they must learn skills to communicate their concerns without directing blame.

Chapter 19: *Money and Marriage*
Text: *Matthew 6:25–34*
Big Idea: Money issues in marriage are resolved when couples put the kingdom of heaven first. Finances become a major issue in marriage when one or both members of a marriage get too wrapped up in accumulating things, or they worry too much about financial matters. They are resolved when both parties trust God for their needs.

Chapter 20- *The Addictions That Destroy*
Text: *Romans 7*
Big Idea: The Spirit of God frees a person from the addictions that destroy marriages. Addictive habits can destroy marriages by causing behaviors that drive a wedge between the couple.

Chapter 21- *Parenting: Training Up a Child in the Things of God*

Text: *Ephesians 6:1–5, Deuteronomy 6:1–8*

Big Idea: Parents must agree on the values and principles for childrearing. Each parent brings a needed perspective to a child's life, but parents must communicate and agree on the core values and beliefs that give the child the things they need to know God.

THE STATE OF MARRIAGE IN NORTH AMERICA

If we start with the assumption that there are no utopias, even in marriage, then it affects how we approach the contemporary discussion on marriage. It means we recognize that there has never been a time in history when there was a utopian era for marriage and family. In other words, the only time it was perfect was before the fall in the garden. So it is easy to identify flaws in the traditional views of marriage. In our contemporary attempt to remove the flaws we have sought to change the nature of marriage and sexuality. But in trying to eliminate one set of problems related to the older view of marriage, we have introduced another set of problems that may be just as bad, or worse. The position of this book is that the problems intrinsic to our new views on marriage and sexuality far exceed the set of problems intrinsic to the older view. So let us consider what they are by contrasting the two views.

What are the two views?

The Old View Conjugal View : Marriage is a comprehensive union inherently suited for procreation and the sharing of family life. It calls for permanent and exclusive commitment. It is also a moral reality with an objective structure, which is inherently good for the couple and society at large. In this view the state has an interest in marriage for this reason: society needs children who become healthy adults capable of contributing to the common good and stable marriages are best suited for that. The state has a vested interest in preserving lasting marriages.[8] This view is consistent with Christianity.

The New View Revisionist View : The view now most advocated by our culture says that marriage is essentially a private matter, an affair of the heart between two adults, in which no outsider, not even the children of the marriage, should be allowed to interfere. Marriage is primarily valued by how well it benefits or satisfies the adults' individual emotional need and is primarily for and about adult happiness. It is essentially an emotional union, merely enhanced by whatever sexual activity the partners find agreeable. If the benefits are absent for one or both parties e.g., I don't love him anymore, we have grown apart, etc. then divorce becomes a valid and even recommended option.[9]

At the heart of the unacknowledged war on marriage is the attempt to demote marriage from a unique public commitment—supported by law, society, and custom—to a private relationship, terminable at will, which is nobody else's business. This demotion is done in the name of choice, but reimagining marriage as a purely private relation doesn't expand anyone's choices. For what it

---

8   Andrew T. Walker and Eric Teetsel, *Marriage is: How Marriage Transforms Society*, Nashville: B&H Publishing, 2015 .

9   Ibid., See also Sherif Girgis, Ryan Anderson and Robert George, *hat is Marriage? Man and oman: A Defense*, New York: Encounter Books, 2012 , Kindle Edition, 7off.

ultimately takes away from individuals is marriage itself, the choice to enter that uniquely powerful and life-enhancing bond that is larger and more durable than the immediate, shifting feelings of two individuals.

Why does this matter? Among other reasons, when we compare the results of the new with that of the old, some alarming evidence stands out. This new view is wreaking havoc on families and society at large. All the signs are that it will continue to do so unless we change to a more realistic view. What is this evidence?

Divorce rates: It has become a well-known fact that the divorce rate increased exponentially from 1930 to 2005 when it leveled off in part because more people were cohabiting, and many are just not pursuing committed, lasting relationships at all. In 2011 StatsCanada temporarily stopped tracking divorce and marriage rates reflecting the prevailing attitude about marriage. The negative effects of divorce are numerous and are a key cause of many societal ailments to be noted here.[10]

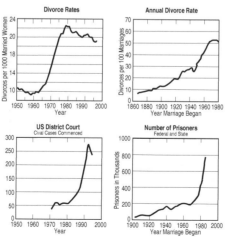

10   Richard Swenson, *Margin* Colorado Springs: NavPress, 1992 .

Cohabitation: While the exponential growth of divorce has flattened out over the last decade, much of that is due to the fact that fewer people are getting married. They have seen the exponential rise in broken marriages and in response have created a "trial period" to see if the relationship will work. It is a failed strategy. We now know that people who cohabit before marriage are far more likely to divorce if they get married and far less likely to have a permanent relationship. It affects the children born of these unions. The problem it was intended to solve created another, more severe set of problems.[11]

Millennials have abandoned both marriage and cohabitation. The millennials, ages 18-32, are the least marrying group in known history. Just 26 percent of this generation is married. When they were the age that millennials are now, 36 percent of Generation X, 48 percent of baby boomers and 65 percent of the members of the Silent Generation were married. Most unmarried millennials 69 percent say they would like to marry, but many, especially those with lower levels of income and education, lack what they deem to be a necessary prerequisite—a solid economic foundation. While they are sexually active and value marriage, they are afraid of commitment.[12]

---

11   https://www.theglobeandmail.com/news/national/statistics-canada-to-stop-tracking-marriage-and-divorce-rates/article4192704/. See also, www.stateofourunions.org and www.americanvalue.org.

12   Elizabeth Landau, "Commitment for Millennial: Is it OK, Cupid?" last modified February 8, 2016. https://blogs.scientificamerican.com/mind-guest-blog/commitment-for-millennials-is-it-okay-cupid/

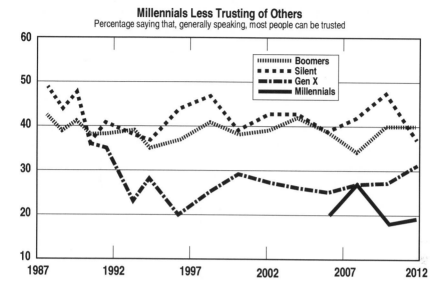

Question wording Generally speaking, "would you say that most people can be trusted"
or "that you cant be too careful in dealing with people?"
Source: General Social Servey data, 1987-2012 PEW Research Center

Source: Data for 1980, 1997 and 2013 from the March Current Population Survey,
1960 data are from the 1960 Census. PEW Research Center

Fertility Rates: Canada has a fertility rate of 1.6 children per couple and the trend is moving downward. At a ranking of 177, it has one of the lowest birth rates out of 233 countries recorded. The U.S. is only slightly better at 1.9, placing it at 150 on the list.[13] If we

---

13   "Birth Rate: Country Comparison, accessed March 8, 2018. http://
www.indexmundi.com/g/1.aspx?v=25.

consider the fact that it takes around 2.3 births per couple for a country to maintain its population numbers, then Canada is heading in the wrong direction. Historically, no culture in history has been able to sustain itself with those kinds of numbers.[14]

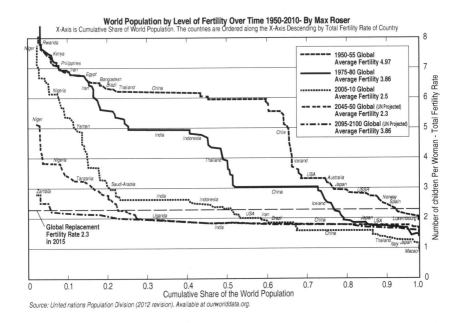

World Population by Level of Fertility Over Time 1950-2010- By Max Roser

X-Axis is Cumulative Share of World Population. The countries are Ordered along the X-Axis Descending by Total Fertility Rate of Country

Source: United nations Population Division (2012 revision). Available at ourworlddata.org.

Immigration: To fill the population void that low fertility rates are creating, it will require aggressive immigration to counteract the loss. They will most likely come from countries with much higher birth rates and which do not share American or Canadian values. They will change the fabric of our culture. The major negative consequence this creates will be when the aging population is out of the workforce, and the younger generations

14   Centers for Disease Control. *National ital Statistics Report* 61, no. 21 2012 .

will have to "foot the bill" as all past societies have done for their elderly.

Nonmarital births: The percentage of children born to unwed parents has increased to 43 percent, meaning most of these children will have no father present throughout most of their life. Note: Canada quit keeping records distinguishing nonmarital births form marital births in 2011.

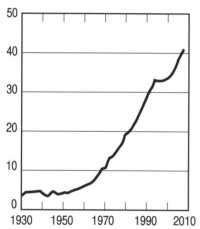

Growth of Unwed Childbearing 1929-2008
Percentage of Children Born Out of Wedlock

Source: US Bureau of the Census and the National Center for Health Statistics.

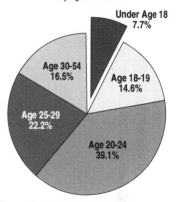

Few Unwed Births Occur to Teenagers
Percentage of Out-of-Wedlock Births by age of Mother

Source: Centers for Disease Control, National Health Statistics, National Vital Statistics Report, "Births: Preliminary Data for 2008" April 6, 2010. Table 7, at http:www.cdc.gov/nhs/data/nvsr/nvsr58 /nvsr58_16.pdf (Sept 13, 2010)

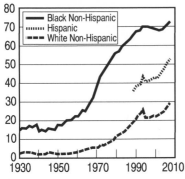

Growth of Unwed Childbearing by Race, 1930-2008
Percentage of Children Born Out of Wedlock

Source: US Bureau of the Census and the National Center for Health Statistics

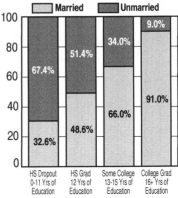

Less-Educated Women are More Likely to Give Birth Outside of Marriage
Percentage of Births Outside of Marriage

Source: Centers for Diease Control and Prevention, 2006 National Health Servey data

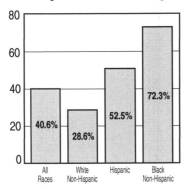

Unwed Birth rates Vary Strongly by Race
Percentage of Births Outside of Marriage

Source: Centers for Diease Control, national Center for Health Statistics, national Vital statistics Report "Births Preliminary Data for 2008" April 6, 2010 table 1

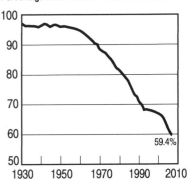

Death of Marriage in the US 1929-2008
Percentage of Children Born to Married Mothers

Source: US Bureau of the Census and the National Center for Health Statistics

Fatherlessness: Fatherhood is a social role that obligates men to their biological offspring. It is society's most important role for men. More than any other activity it helps men to become good men and it significantly benefits children. The growth in fatherlessness is directly tied to the increase in some major social ailments. Two significant works make a very strong case that it is a major crisis in North America.[15]

Forty years ago, 17 percent of all children had no father living at home. Today, around 75 percent of American youths will live without their fathers at some time before they turn 18. Fatherlessness is also the leading cause of many of our most urgent social problems:

> 80% of all adolescents in psychiatric hospitals come from father-less homes.
> 90% of all homeless and runaway children are from fatherless homes.
> 85% of all youths in prisons grew up in a fatherless home.
> 80% of rapists motivated with displaced anger come from father-less homes.
> 72% of adolescent murderers grew up without fathers.
> 71% of all pregnant teenagers lack a father.
> 63% of youth suicides are from fatherless homes.[16]

1. Poverty: Families headed by single women with children are the poorest of all major demographic groups, regardless of how poverty is measured. In *Poor Support,* David T. Ellwood concludes that "the vast majority of children who are raised entirely in a two-

15   David Blankenhorn, *Fatherless America: Confronting Our Most Urgent Social Problem* New York: Harper Perineal, 1996 ; David Popenoe, *Life ithout Father: Compelling New Evidence That Fatherhood and Marriage Are Indispensable for the Good of Children and Society* New York: The Free Press, 1996 .

16   Blankenhorn and Popenoe.

parent home will never be poor during childhood. By contrast, the vast majority of children who spend time in a single-parent home will experience poverty."[1]

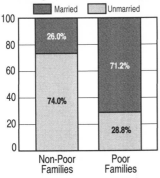

71% of Poor Families With Children are not Married
Percentage of Births Outside of Marriage

Source: Based on data from: US Bureau of the Census, American Community Servey, 2006-2008.

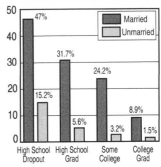

Both Marriage and Education are Highly Effective in Reducing Child Poverty In USA
Percentage of Families that are Poor

Source: Based on data from: US Bureau of the Census, American Community Servey, 2006-2008.

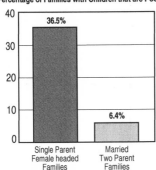

Marriage Drops the Probability of Child Poverty by 82%
Percentage of Families with Children that are Poor

Source: Based on Data from: US Bureau of the Census "American Community Servey, 2006-2008".

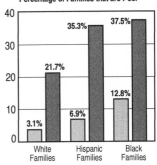

Marriage Reduces Poverty for Whites, Hispanics and Blacks
Percentage of Families that are Poor

Source: Based on Data from: US Bureau of the Census "American Community Servey, 2006-2008".

---

[1]   David T. Ellwood, *Poor Support: Poverty in the American Family* New York: Basic Books, 1998 , 46.

2. Behavioral Issues With Children: Reports of child neglect and abuse have quintupled since 1976 when data were first collected. The psychological pathology of children and youth has taken a drastic turn for the worse. Eating disorders and rates of unipolar depression have soared among adolescent girls. Teen suicide has tripled. Alcohol and drug abuse among teenagers, although leveling off in recent years, continues at a very high rate. SAT scores have declined nearly eighty points, and most of the decline cannot be accounted for by the increased academic diversity of students taking the test.[18]

3. Promiscuity: McLanahan and Sandefur conclude that children who grow up with only one of their biological parents nearly always the mother , compared to children who grow up with both parents, are three times more likely to have a child out of wedlock, 2.5 times more likely to become teen mothers, twice as likely to drop out of high school, and 1.4 times more likely to be idle out of school and out of work . These figures have increased since this research was compiled.[19]

4. Sexual Abuse: "Of all cases of child abuse in which the perpetrator is known, fully one-quarter are cohabiting 'parent substitutes,' usually boyfriends—a rate dramatically higher than the rates found among fathers, day-care providers, babysitters, or

---

18   Popenoe. pp. 61-63

19   Sara Malanahan and Gary Sandefur, *Growing Up   ith a Single Parent: hat Hurts and   hat Helps* Boston: Harvard University Press, 1997 , 39-63.

other caregivers . . . half are committed boyfriends, even though boyfriends provide only about 2 percent of all nonparental child care. About 84 percent of all cases of nonparental child abuse occurs in single-parent homes. Among the cases occurring in single-parent homes, 64 percent of the perpetrators are boyfriends. The study's conclusion: 'a young child left alone with the mother's boyfriend experiences substantially elevated risk of abuse. Girls in father-absent homes are poorly protected from sexually opportunistic males in their surrounding community.'"[20]

5. Physical Abuse: A major reason for the increase in child abuse is that unrelated men, surrogate fathers, are much more likely to abuse children than are natural fathers. And especially in single-parent and stepfamilies, such men have more access to children than ever before. Indeed, an important benefit of having a natural father in the home is precisely to protect against child abuse.[21]

6. Rape: Among girls who experience sexual intercourse by the age of 14, nearly three-quarters report that they have at times been coerced into it. And the overwhelming majority are from single-parent homes and committed by their mother's boyfriend.[22]

---

20   Blankenhorn, 41.

21   "Understanding Child Abuse and Neglect", National Research Council, Washington D.C., 1993, pdf. Available at https://www.nap.edu/download/211/.

22   Ibid.

7. Mental Health: A study by University of Texas sociologists Ronald J. Angel and Jacqueline L. Angel conclude that "father absence places children at elevated risk of impaired social development, that it hinders their school performance, and, ultimately, that it can limit their chances for optimal social mobility." They add, by way of summary, that "we can say with great confidence that father absence, at least in North America, is a mental health risk factor for children."[23]

8. Youth Violence: Regarding the rapid rise in youth violence, David Blankenhorn concludes: ". . . the single most obvious factor—the one most likely to produce the other factors is . . . fatherlessness." "There are exceptions of course, but here is the rule: Boys raised by traditionally masculine fathers generally do not commit crimes. Fatherless boys commit crimes."[24] Juvenile violent crime increased six-fold, from sixteen thousand arrests in 1960 to ninety-six thousand in 1992, a period in which the total number of juveniles in the population remained relatively stable.[25]

9. Nonparental Abuse: Leslie Margolin found that 64 percent of the nonparental abuse was committed by mothers' boyfriends—

23   Ronald J. Angel and L. Jacqueline, *Painful Inheritance: Heath and the New Generation of Fatherless Families,* Madison: University of Wisconsin Press, 1993 , 113.

24   Blankenhorn, 29-30.

25   Paul E. Tracy, *Delinquency Careers in Two Birth Cohorts* New York: Plenum Press, 1990 .

the overwhelming majority. This was especially surprising in view of the fact that these boyfriends were very infrequent caregivers; they performed only 1.75 percent of the nonparental care considered in the study. Margolin calculated that mothers' boyfriends committed 2.7 times more child abuse than their hours in child care would lead us to predict."[26]

10. Violence Against Women: Research shows that marriage is the safest place to be for women.[27] Wives are far less likely than single women to be crime victims overall. Single women are four to five times more likely to be victimized at any given time than married women. They are ten times more likely to be raped and three times more likely to be victims of aggravated assault. Research shows married women are far less likely to face domestic abuse than cohabitation women.[28]

Akerlof argues that ". . . men settle down when they get married: if they fail to get married, they fail to settle down." When men delay or avoid marriage, he goes on to say, they continue with the often antisocial and destructive behaviors of single men. And it's the role of husband—not boyfriend or father—which seems to be key. Having children by itself does not work the same transformation in men's lives.

---

26   Leslie Margolin and John L. Craft, "Child Sexual Abuse by Caretakers," *Family Relations* 38, 1989, 450-455.

27   Linda J.Waite and Maggie Gallagher, *The Case for Marriage: hy Married People are Happier, Healthier and Better Off Financially* New York: Broadway Books, 2000 , 150-160.

28   Rone Bachman, "Violence against Women," *A National Crime ictim Survey Report,* Jan., NCJ145-345, 1994.

Some key questions this information poses:

What do we do with people who didn't want a divorce? While solid lasting marriages are always the ideal, many people face divorce through no fault of their own—it was forced upon them. This can apply to both men and women. It is a hard place to find oneself in ways too many to mention. Only God's grace and mercy can heal the wounds and sense of loss that come with it. There are several good "Divorce Recovery" options that help people work through that loss. Many people have learned to make the best of a difficult situation and have thrived in spite of the obstacles against them.

What of people who want to marry but cannot? Some people who would love to get married find themselves unable, for whatever reason, to do so. Paul speaks to this in 1 Corinthians 7 and recognizes singleness might be preferred for many good reasons. The issue in society is not that people are single but that too many try to have sexual and intimate relationships without the covenant of marriage. This is where the issues come into play. Celibate singles can have productive, meaningful lives without some of the complex obligations and difficulties inherent in marriage.

Losing a Father Through Death: Research shows that the negative effects of losing a father through death are far fewer than those of losing a father through divorce or absent through nonmarital birth. It is because of the nature of the loss based on uncontrollable external factors rather than inter-relational factors.[29]

---

29   George Aerkof, "Men without Children," *The Economic Journal*, 108, 1997, 287-309.

Conclusions:

1. Abuses in marriage certainly happened throughout history and they demand a response. Our response has been to redefine marriage and value it by how well it benefits or satisfies the adults' individual emotional needs and is primarily for and about adult happiness. If happiness is the primary goal of this redefinition of marriage, then it has failed miserably. Maybe there is something the old view can teach us and maybe we should seek other solutions to the problem of abuse.

2. Trying to change the definition and nature of marriage is like trying to defy gravity. God designed marriage to be a lasting union for the benefit of the adult man and woman and the children of their union. As we have seen, efforts to improve on that design have failed.

3. While it is unrealistic to think we can change the culture, we can begin by changing the quality of individual marriages themselves. That begins by understanding the importance of the marriage covenant, each person in the covenant sacrifices on behalf of the other and learns what God says about it.

4. Because as a society we have chosen values that exalt individual autonomy at the cost of stable marriages, we face a growing crisis that is not going to go away by redefining marriage and family to the point where the terms are useless. The longer we stay on that course, the greater the crisis will become. We need to turn to God

and realize that self-sacrifice, like that modeled by Jesus Himself, must be the premise of any relationship. Two competing forces demanding their rights and wants to be met at all times will never enjoy a stable marriage.

CHAPTER 1

REVISITING GOD'S DESIGN FOR MARRIAGE: LEGO VS. PAINTER VIEWS OF MARRIAGE:

Text: *Genesis 2:18–24*
Theme: *Marriage is God's construct designed for procreation, companionship, and permanence.*

When my sons were younger, they spent hundreds of hours playing with Legos.

We bought dozens of kits, each with assembly instructions. The kits included pirate ships, castles, police and fire stations, exotic vacation places, spaceships, Star Wars themes, and more. Each kit came with all the pieces needed to build it. However, in time, the pieces all got mixed together, making assembly of the original kit difficult—you had to search through the piles with thousands of pieces to find the right ones. Eventually, the boys began to bypass the instructions altogether to make up their own creations, which no longer resembled the picture on the instructions that came with the kit.

John Wyatt uses Legos as an analogy of our contemporary view of sex and gender. If there is no God and man evolved as a cosmic accident, then there is no design whatsoever in sex, marriage or family. "We are simply a collection of constituent parts that can be changed and adapted as we like. You can try to improve or upgrade to a different model—you can reprogram the machine because that's who we are. In the words of an old Lego advertisement, "The only limitation is your own imagination."[30] The same observation could be made for marriage.[31]

This view places supreme value on the individual and his choices and encapsulates the central mantra of our time. The roots of this profound individualism go back to the period of the Enlightenment three hundred years ago, when human reason took precedence over divine revelation. French philosopher's Renee Descartes epic conclusion "cogito ergo sum" "I think therefore I am" was a quest for certainty that began with human reason and is considered the start of modernism.[32] It has since devolved into the view that truth and morality are subjective without any external authority to tell us how to behave. As Vaughan Roberts says, "It's up to us to draw our own conclusions and live our own lives." As the boys from Boyzone put it in one of their songs: *No matter what they tell you; no matter what they say; no matter what they teach you: what you believe is true.* Or, as John Stuart Mill, the founding father of Western liberalism, wrote: "Over himself, over

---

30 Vaughan Roberts, *Talking Points: Transgender* Epsom: The Good Book Company, 2016 , 36.

31 John Wyatt, *Matters of Life and Death: Human Dilemmas in the Light of the Christian Faith,* Second ed. Westmont: InterVarsity Press, 2009 , 35.

32 Stephen Toulmin, *Cosmopolis: The Hidden Agenda of Modernity* Chicago: University of Chicago Press, 1992 .

his own body and mind, the individual is sovereign. Regarding marriage, this means individual autonomy supersedes the marital union."[33]

One of the core values that come out of this is that we must be authentic—to be true to ourselves and ourselves alone. Jonathan Grant expresses it well: "Modern authenticity encourages us to create our own beliefs and morality, the only rule being that they must resonate with who we feel we really are. The worst thing we can do is to conform to some moral code that is imposed on us from outside—by society, our parents, the church, or whomever else. It is deemed to be self-evident that any such imposition would undermine our unique identity . . . The authentic self believes that personal meaning must be found within ourselves or must resonate with our one-of-a-kind personality."[34]

When applied to marriage this means that two autonomous people marry primarily for their own individual fulfillment and must be true to themselves. If the marriage fails to enhance this end, it serves no purpose and should end. Social researcher Andrew Walker summarizes the unanticipated result: "The deterioration of a marriage- and family-oriented culture has resulted in pain and suffering on a massive scale because it is a deterioration of God's plan for justice and social harmony. Abuse, poverty, lack of education, and crime are just a few of the social ills caused by

---

33   Roberts, 25-26.

34   Jonathan Grant, *Divine Sex: A Compelling ision for Christian Relationships in a Hypersexualized Age* Grand Rapids: Brazos Press, 2015 , 30.

this failure."[35] This pain and suffering couples face is this position's strongest nemesis.

Biblical Christianity lays out a very different view of sex and marriage—one that is incompatible with the Lego view. This view says that we are not a cosmic freak of nature formed through unguided, purposeless evolution. Marriage is like a wonderful painting by a loving God. It says that His beautiful masterpiece was corrupted by sin and that it is His desire to restore it to its original design. But we first must know what that original looks like and then find out what went wrong and participate in His plan to fix it. The biblical view says the two become one flesh. In this view, the social unit supersedes self-centered individual autonomy and self-fulfillment.

Let's look at what that original design looked like by considering the question, "What does Genesis tell us about why God created marriage?" We will see that marriage is a vital part of God's mandate to populate the Earth by providing loving, permanent marriage relationships that model the covenant relationship between Christ and His church.

I. God created marriage for procreation. (Gen. 1:26–28)

^{26} Then God said, "Let us make mankind in our image, in our likeness, so that they may rule over the fish in the sea

---

35   Andrew T. Walker and Eric Teetsel, *Marriage Is: How Marriage Transforms Society and Cultivates Human Flourishing* Nashville: B&H Books, 2015 . Kindle edition, 837-839. For a comprehensive study of the devastating effects of this positon, refer to the book by David Popenoe, *Life ithout Father: Compelling New Evidence That Fatherhood and Marriage Are Indispensable for the Good of Children and Society* New York: Free Press, 1996 .

and the birds in the sky, over the livestock and all the wild animals, and over all the creatures that move along the ground." [27] So God created mankind in his own image, in the image of God he created them; male and female he created them. [28] God blessed them and said to them, "Be fruitful and increase in number; fill the earth and subdue it."

A. *God is the most valuable thing in the universe and we bear His image.*

Colossians 1 tells us: Regarding, the supremacy of Christ, Paul writes,

"For in him all things were created: things in heaven and on earth, visible and invisible, whether thrones or powers or rulers or authorities; all things have been created through him and for him. [17] He is before all things, and in him all things hold together. [18] And he is the head of the body, the church; he is the beginning and the firstborn from among the dead, so that in everything he might have the supremacy."

Nothing exists that is greater or has more value than God Himself. Now, think about it, we bear the image of this great, supremely valuable God who created all things. Nothing else in creation can make this claim. We have a greater capacity to bring glory to God than any other thing in creation. So if God is sacred, then the image we bear is also sacred.

B. *Procreation is a sacred act in that it produces children who bear God's image.*

That is why Christians take such a high view of sex. It is not primarily for our pleasure and exploitation. It should not be cheapened by promiscuity or used out of the context for which God intended it. Certainly, procreation is not the only reason for marriage, but its centrality should not be diminished. Sex must be more than mutual gratification where we use others as tools to bring us pleasure. It has a divine purpose bigger than self-gratification.

Andrew Walker speaks to this saying, "In a culture that is overwhelmingly focused on the prosperity of adults, we should not be surprised that marriage has come to be understood primarily as a vehicle for the happiness of adults in which creating and raising children is an entirely separate discussion from the decision to marry. Of course, the ultimate manifestation of our new normal priorities is abortion, the elimination of a child before birth to preserve the preferred life script of adults . . ."[36] Today, whether inside the church or outside, culture has made marriage more about sexual ecstasy than viewing it as a key institution for the benefit of society.

C. *The reason that marriage is between a man and a woman is that only they can create a family with children.*

The Sexual Revolution in the '60s introduced a new paradigm where sex became more about adult satisfaction than

---

36   Andrew T. Walker and Eric Teetsel, *Marriage Is: How Marriage Transforms Society and Cultivates Human Flourishing* Nashville: B&H Books, 2015 . Kindle edition, 837-839.

about children or the needs of society. This paradigm shift has had serious implications for how we view sex and marriage today.[37] The introduction to this book gave evidence that marriage has changed dramatically over the past fifty years, and it's had devastating effects on North American society. Sociologists from all sides of the ideological spectrum recognize the negative effects of these changes which include poverty, education, and imprisonment. Yet, we seem to miss the connection between marriage and social well-being.[38]

A common argument against the view that marriage is primarily about childbearing and family is that some either do not want or cannot have children. But that does not diminish the importance of procreation as a primary motive for marriage. To make this point, author Sherif Girgis asks us to consider a sports analogy: "The kind of cooperation that makes a group into a baseball team is largely aimed at winning games. Teammates develop and share their athletic skills in the way best suited for winning—for example, with extensive practice and good sportsmanship. But such development and sharing are possible and inherently valuable for teammates even when they do not win a game. Just so, marital cooperation in both sexual and domestic life is characteristically ordered to procreation and childrearing."[39] This incapacity to bear children says nothing about the couple's character or

---

37   Ibid., 759-762.

38   Sherif Girgis, Ryan T. Anderson and Robert P. George, *What Is Marriage? Man and Woman: A Defense* New York: Encounter Books . Kindle Edition, 479.

39   Girgis, 476-478.

their value but most infertile couples see it as a regrettable loss.

We have embraced a view that marriage is primarily a romance between best friends. Romance is certainly an important part of marriage, but it is much more than that. This misunderstanding of marriage prioritizes companionship and romance above all else.[40] Think about it. If marriage is primarily about romance why should the state even be interested? No one would want the state to regulate your relationships. We would not welcome it if the state said you must have their permission if you want to start or end a relationship with a co-worker or neighbor—no matter how matter deeply you may love the person. So why do we regulate marriage? Why do we sign a covenant and have it registered by the state? The answer is simple—because only a male and female couple can bear children. That fact alone puts the marriage covenant in a unique light.

Lawyer and professor Robert George says, "We all have an interest in our neighbors' marriages that we do not have in their friendships, and marriages have a definite structure that friendships lack. We rely on families built on strong marriages to produce what they need but cannot secure: healthy, upright children who become conscientious citizens. As they mature, children benefit from the love and care of both mother and father, and from their parents committed and exclusive love for each other. Unlike friendships, which vary in kind and degree and formality, marriage has enough objective structure, apart from spouses' preferences, to be legally regulated."[41]

---

40   Walker, 729-731.

41   Girgis, 271-298.

Let us now look at the second response to our question, "What does Genesis tell us about why God created marriage?"

II. God created marriage for companionship. (Gen. 2:18–23)

The Lord God said, "It is not good for the man to be alone. I will make a helper suitable for him."[19] Now the Lord God had formed out of the ground all the wild animals and all the birds in the sky. He brought them to the man to see what he would name them; and whatever the man called each living creature, that was its name. So the man gave names to all the livestock, the birds in the sky and all the wild animals. But for Adam no suitable helper was found. So the Lord God caused the man to fall into a deep sleep; and while he was sleeping, he took one of the man's ribs and then closed up the place with flesh. Then the Lord God made a woman from the rib he had taken out of the man, and he brought her to the man.

The man said,
"This is now bone of my bones
and flesh of my flesh;
she shall be called 'woman,'
for she was taken out of man."

For the first time, God says "It is not good" in regard to man's aloneness. At each major milestone in creation, God concludes, "And it was good." Now we read, "It is not good that man should be alone." Adam did not even fully realize his aloneness until he finished naming the animals and observing that they all came in pairs—male and female. So where was his complement? There was none, and it was not good.

God creates woman out of man to be a suitable helper. To remedy the situation, God creates woman as a complement to the man. I remind you of the imagery found in our passage. God puts Adam to sleep and creates another being from him in the form of a woman and then reunites these two individual beings into a "one-flesh relationship." Here is the strange math: one becomes two becomes one again. We see this in our biological makeup. All the functions and organs of our body are designed to operate independently with one exception. The sexual organs are designed to fulfill their function only with a sexual complement. The parts are made to fit each other. Male and female are more than just two autonomous entities who exist independently for mutual self-gratification. They are designed by God to reunite the two into a one-flesh union. Sex is only part of that. Both give up their individual identities to form one. This union supersedes the individual but does not destroy the individual.

With the creation of woman and marriage, God says, "It was very good." In questioning God's plan and design for marriage, we question the very goodness of God. Modern society thinks it has a better plan. Their plan rejects God's design and lets the individual make his own creation. But if God invented marriage, then those who enter it should make every effort to understand and submit to His purposes just as we do for many other aspects of our lives.

My wife and I recently bought a high-end printer that has all kinds of great features. I spent a few hours reading the manual that came with it so I could enjoy as many of the features as I could. It does things like double-sided printing, scan to a USB or an e-mail, edge-to-edge printing, etc. I would be foolish to try many of these features without consulting the manual. The same could be said of buying a car, a boat, a Smart TV, etc. We need a manual to guide us, so we can get the full benefit of what the designer intended. The same should be true of marriage.

Plenty of people who do not acknowledge God or the Bible, yet experience happy marriages, are largely abiding by God's intentions, whether they realize it or not. But it is far better if we are conscious of those intentions. And the place to discover them is in the writings of the Scripture.

Our third response to our question, "What does Genesis tell us about why God created marriage?" is:

III. God created marriage as a permanent covenant. (Gen. 2:24)

²⁴ That is why a man leaves his father and mother and is united to his wife, and they become one flesh.

Marriage is a sacred covenant constructed and affirmed by God himself. To rephrase the popular iWorld idiom: marriage is God's construct. The well-known theologian and pastor, Dietrich Bonhoeffer writes, "Marriage is more than your love for each other . . . In your love, you see only the heaven of your own happiness, but in marriage, you are placed at a post of responsibility towards the world and mankind. Your love is your own private possession, but marriage is more than something personal—it is a status, and office. Just as it is the crown, and not merely the will to rule, that makes the king, so it is marriage, and not merely your love for each other, that joins you together in the sight of God and man."[42]

As Dietrich Bonhoeffer says, marriage is more than your love for each other. As Paul later argues, the meaning of marriage is the display of the covenant-keeping love between Christ and his people.[43]

A.   It is a permanent covenant that makes us "one flesh." This one-flesh union is the heart of what marriage is. Jesus later reminds us that this union is divinely created and is not to be torn apart. God Himself joins the two into one. John Piper says: "When a couple speaks their vows, it is not a man or a woman or a pastor or parent who is the main actor—the main doer. God is. God joins a husband and a wife into a one-flesh union. God does that. The world does not know this. Which is one of the reasons why marriage is treated so casually."[44]

B.   It is a public covenant given for the good of the individual, couple, children, and society.

Traditional, exclusively monogamous marriage brings enormous benefits of all kinds to adults and even more to children

---

42   Dietrich Bonhoeffer, *Letters and Papers from Prison*, New York: Macmillan Publishers, 1967 , 27.

43   John Piper, *This Momentary Marriage: A Parable of Permanence*, Wheaton: Crossway . Kindle edition, 135-138.

44   Ibid., 257-259.

and society at large. We can even look beyond scientific research to make that point. There has never been a culture or a century that we know of in which marriage was not central to human life. And even though the percentage of married people has decreased in Western culture, the percentage of people who hope to be married has not diminished at all— even among millennials, who are less likely to commit.

There seems to be something within us that longs for a healthy marriage. We hear it in Adam's "At last!" exuberant and spontaneous response at his first sight of Eve. It is as though God made us for marriage. So, the trouble is not within the institution of marriage itself but within ourselves.[45] Until we can discover what it is within ourselves and God's solution, we cannot enjoy what God designed for our good.

C.   It models the relationship between the church and Christ. Eph. 5:31–32

> "For this reason, a man will leave his father and mother and be united to his wife, and the two will become one flesh."[32] This is a profound mystery—but I am talking about Christ and the church."

In these verses, we get our major first glimpse of God's solution to make a marriage relationship work. The word "mystery" is

45   Timothy Keller, *The Meaning of Marriage: Facing the Complexities of Commitment with the   isdom of God* New York: Penguin Books, 2011. Kindle edition, 583.

used to refer to some wondrous, unlooked-for truth that God is revealing through his Spirit. So what is the secret of marriage? Paul immediately adds, "I am talking about Christ and the church."[46] Exploring that vision is the quest for this book.

Tim Keller says, "So, what do you need to make a marriage work? You need to know the secret, the gospel, and how it gives you both the power and pattern for your marriage. On the one hand, the experience of marriage will unveil the beauty and depths of the gospel to you. It will drive you further into reliance on it. On the other hand, a greater understanding of the gospel will help you experience deeper and deeper union with each other as the years go on."[47]

The Christian position is that we find mutual fulfillment in marriage through sacrifice—not through demanding our personal satisfaction. Jesus is our model. He made the ultimate sacrifice by dying on the cross to save us and to make us his. In response, we give up ourselves and submit to Him. We do it because we know He has taken the first step—he gave Himself up for us."[48]

In this chapter, we looked at God's original design for marriage by considering the question, "What does Genesis tell us about why God created marriage?" We saw that marriage is a vital part of God's mandate to populate the Earth by providing loving, permanent marriage relationships that model the covenant relationship between Christ and His church.

---

46   Piper, 990.

47   Keller, 6.

48   Ibid., 6.

We must choose between two conflicting views of sex and marriage. Either there is no God and marriage is like a Lego set that each individual uses to construct his own views of marriage, or there is a God who designed marriage for our good.

Let me suggest three ways you can apply these truths in your life.

1. The modern notion that autonomy and the individual's happiness and well-being are the supreme end is the primary cause for the broken state of marriage in our culture. Marriage is not about you. It is something much bigger and much better.

2. When we discover God's original plan for marriage, we can begin the process of living it out.

3. The ultimate purpose of marriage is to put the covenant relationship of Christ and his church on display. Only in understanding our own brokenness and God's sacrificial grace can we understand how to view our own marriages.

To cite Vaugh Roberts: "Art restorers respect the work and know that their job is to bring out the artist's original intention. They work at cleaning and restoring the vivid colors. They study the work and the painter so that they can carefully get it back to what it once was. They work so that people can see the original in all its glory."[49]

That is our quest for this book—to restore marriage by bringing out God's original vision so his wonderful covenant with us will be on display.

---

49   Roberts, 33.

CHAPTER 2

ACCEPTING THE GOODNESS OF GOD'S DESIGN FOR MARRIAGE

Text: *Genesis 3:1–7*
Theme: *Marriages are strengthened when we face up to our rebellious self-obsession.*

I can remember when I was still in high school, my sister was watching a romance movie where the handsome main character was telling his beautiful recently discovered true love the depth of his everlasting love.

While I was trying to hold back my natural guy gag-reflex, my sister let out a loud and deep sigh of longing. In that simple sigh, she communicated what almost every high school girl wants—the desire to be loved by someone who will sacrifice and care for her through thick and thin. We see it in romance novels and movies like *Cinderella, Snow White, Beauty and the Beast.* They are popular because of this universal appeal.

Yet, it seems the ideal and the reality seldom match up. While the girl thinks she is marrying a Prince Charming, she often finds out that what she really married was a frog. Most of us realize early on that much of this romantic idealism was never the norm—

even in the garden. But it seems that in the last few generations, a growing disillusionment has caused us to abandon the "love forever after" ideal altogether. This is no more visible than in the state of marriage in North America.

A recent Pew Research study showed that while most millennials want a loving, lasting relationship, only 26 percent—a number less than any other group in known history—are pursuing it through marriage. In the last sixty years, our culture has moved from divorce being extremely rare to now a common practice. This uncertainty of lasting marriages leads to cohabitation as the norm to "test" the relationship—like testing out a used car. Even that has changed: millennials ages 18 to 32 have abandoned both.

What happened? Why have younger people become so afraid of marriage? Certainly, the answer includes the lack of stable role models and a less-certain economy. But beyond that we all seem to instinctively know that something is broken in us. The fact that this brokenness is denied or misunderstood sets us up for failure because we misdiagnose the problem.

In the last chapter, we saw that after God created marriage He called it very good. So we know there is a God-given ideal of what was or could now be. Yet something tragic happened to make it far less than His ideal. It is a tragic event that our culture has forgotten this, and it severely impacts our relationships.

In this chapter I want us to revisit what went wrong and pose the question, "What is the root cause of destructive conflict in our marriages?" We will learn that we have rejected God's desire for us because we believe we know what is best for us better than He does. And when we act on our plan, it fails—and then our second mistake is that we think we can fix it on our own.

The first response to our question, "What is the root cause of destructive conflict in our marriages?" is:

I. We falsely believe we know what is good for us better than God does. (Gen. 3:1–4)

"Now the serpent was more crafty than any of the wild animals the lord God had made. He said to the woman, 'Did God really say, "You must not eat from any tree in the garden"?'
2 The woman said to the serpent, 'We may eat fruit from the trees in the garden, 3 but God did say, "You must not eat fruit from the tree that is in the middle of the garden, and you must not touch it, or you will die."' 4 'You will not certainly die,' the serpent said to the woman."

A. *We question the reasonableness of God's command.*

We must remember the setting of these verses. God created this wonderful world with everything we need to thrive and be happy. At the completion of the creation of woman, He oversees the first "marriage" and then gives His assessment—"It was very good." The two enjoyed a perfect relationship with each other—each with complementary roles to play in the relationship. The man was a loving leader and the woman was a nurturing "helper."

As Matthew Rueger says, "Adam, he was more complete with her than he had been without her. She was of his flesh, and he would cherish her as he did his own flesh. This intimate loving relationship established before the fall into sin was a union of two different beings with different roles within the family but of equal importance to each other and to God. The problem of sin did not change God's intent for marriage to complete man and woman in a lifelong union of love and respect."[50]

So what happened? We see the problem begin to unfold in this passage. First Satan visits the garden in the form of a serpent. The Bible often speaks of Satan as a real personal entity who is an invisible, evil force intent on turning our hearts against God.

Notice what Satan does. He asks, "Did God really say?" The intent is to get Eve to question the command of God which said, "You are free to eat from any tree in the garden; but you must not eat from the tree of the knowledge of good and evil, for when you eat from it you will certainly die." Here God has created this marvelous world for their enjoyment and fulfillment. For Him to forbid this one thing is not unreasonable. But Satan causes Eve to question God by misstating it as, "You must not eat from any tree in the garden." The strategy is very subtle. It plants a question in Eve's mind about its reasonableness.

While she caught this obvious lie of Satan, her response reveals Satan's strategy worked. In her response, she herself misstates the command by adding to it. Remember, God said, "Don't eat of the one tree," but she adds the word "touch." Now, the addition is subtle and simple, but it indicates that she is pondering the question, "What would be the harm in touching it? That seems somewhat unreasonable." The fact is, God did not say that.

---

50   Matthew W. Rueger, Sexual Morality in a Christless World St. Louis: Concordia Publishing House, 2016 . Kindle edition, 1320-1324.

B. *We question whether God really has our best interest in mind.*

Satan then outright tests God by denying the consequences for disobeying God's command. Satan says, "You will not certainly die." Eve must now ask herself the question, Is God lying to me? Is he posing a false threat to keep me from something good? Does this God who made me and the wonderful world I live in really have my best interest in mind? Maybe this serpent is right. Maybe God lied because he is not as good as we have thought.

This seems to be the very argument of atheist Michel Onfray in his book, Atheist Manifesto. He says, "Defying God's prohibition meant preferring knowledge to obedience, seeking to know rather than submitting. Or in different terms: opting for philosophy against religion. What does this ban on intelligence mean? You can do anything in this magnificent garden, except become intelligent—the Tree of Knowledge—or immortal—the Tree of Life. What a fate God has in store for men: stupidity and mortality! A God who offers such a gift to his creatures must be perverse . . . Let us then praise Eve who opted for intelligence at risk of death, whereas Adam did not realize right away what was at stake. The bliss of ignorance!"[51] Onfray's rebuttal sounds like Satan's lie.

The dilemma both Satan and Onfray present here is a false one that is based on a lie. Yet, that is the heart of the great struggle we face. As John Piper says, "I take 'the knowledge of good and

---

51   Michel Onfray, *Atheist Manifesto: The Case Against Christianity, Judaism, and Islam* New York: Skyhorse Publishing, 2011 . Kindle edition, 101/-1020.

evil' to refer to a status of independence from God in which Adam and Eve would decide for themselves apart from God what is good and what is evil. So eating from this tree would mean a declaration of independence from God." That is the issue.[52] Do we believe God or the lie? But we must be aware, because to choose poorly is to face the consequences.

C. *We question the very goodness of God.*

When we convince ourselves we are less happy or fulfilled if we obey God's plan we question the goodness of God and His design for us. But we are then left with our own design and plan which will inevitably be self-centered and its consequences tragic. The enemy of life in God is an independent and covetous will. As a result, it distorts God's image; it puts us in competition with God- a competition we cannot win.

A frequently stated hypothetical question is, "What would have happened if Adam and Eve would not have disobeyed?" This is the question C.S. Lewis addresses in one of his books of his science fiction trilogy titled, *Perelandra*.[53]

Perelandra, like the early Garden of Eden, is a world of many and varied delights. Like Eve the woman in the book is tempted only in this story does not succumb. But through avoiding the temptation and consequences she learns and grows far beyond what she would have learned by succumbing to it. In other words, we grow far more and are far better off, by obeying God. He has

---

52   John Piper, *This Momentary Marriage: A Parable of Permanence* Wheaton: Crossway, 2012 . Kindle edition, 416-444.

53   C.S. Lewis, *Perelandra* New York: Simon & Schuster, 1996 .

our best interest in mind. The God who knows us best wants our best.

The point regarding marriage is this. God designed marriage as a loving relationship between a male and a female with complementary roles to play. By acting on her own, independent of Adam, she was questioning her role in the relationship and questioning God's goodness. We do the same when we sin—we question God's goodness.

Let us now look at the second response to our question, "What is the root cause of destructive conflict in our marriages?"

II. We falsely believe we can be like God. (Gen. 3:5–7)

"For God knows that when you eat from it your eyes will be opened, and you will be like God, knowing good and evil."⁶ When the woman saw that the fruit of the tree was good for food and pleasing to the eye, and also desirable for gaining wisdom, she took some and ate it. She also gave some to her husband, who was with her, and he ate it."

A. Pride is the source of most, if not all, rebellion against God. Notice the ultimate lie. "You will be like God." This belief is the heart of what is wrong with this world. It is the root of all conflict, alienation, and pain. We foolishly believe we can be like God. Therefore, we believe we don't need Him, His plan or His will. We can make our own choices regarding what is best for us because "I am like God." But we still cannot get around the consequence of our ineptitude.[54]

What this means for marriage is that we have two people who are self-appointed "gods," who are in competition with the one true God as well as each other. Each tries to determine their own reality, their own morality, and their own importance independent of the God who created them. It is a path toward disaster because without an objective standard of fairness and morality, we are left to our own fickle judgments which are guaranteed to lead to conflict—god against god. Instead of completing each other, as God designed, they are competing with each other to have their own desires fulfilled. In contrast, you must recognize there is only one God, and you are not Him. We both must submit to Him, believing and knowing He has our best interest in mind.

Adam and Eve were naked and unashamed when God first created them. They were not self-conscious, they did not hide their nakedness, and there was a transparent, open unity that was ultimately disrupted by the fall. In this fallen world, marriage becomes a competition. In a world of false god against false god, submission has no place.

B.   When we reject God's plan, we place ourselves in opposition to Him.

The Bible often addresses us as enemies of God because we rebel against Him. The whole point of Christianity is to be

---

54   J. Grant Howard, *The Trauma of Transparency: A Biblical Approach to Inter-Personal Communication* Portland: Multnomah Press, 1979 .

reconciled to God. Notice Colossians 1:21–22: "Once you were alienated from God and were enemies in your minds because of your evil behavior. But now he has reconciled you by Christ's physical body through death to present you holy in his sight, without blemish and free from accusation." In that verse, we find our hope for stronger marriages. It begins with reconciliation to God.

C.   We can never be like God. That is the great lie that is the source of all evil.

John Piper presents the problem pride poses in this way: "By acting on this lie, Adam himself, not just his spouse, has broken covenant with God. If she is rebellious and selfish, and therefore unsafe, so am I. But the way I experience it in myself is that I feel defiled and guilty and unworthy. That's, in fact, what I am . . . So my wife might be the safest person in the world, but now my own sense of guilt and unworthiness makes me feel vulnerable. The simple, open nakedness of innocence now feels inconsistent with the guilty person that I am. I feel ashamed ... Eve is no longer reliable to cherish me; she has become selfish and I feel vulnerable to her putting me down for her own selfish ends. The other is that I already know that I am guilty myself, and the nakedness of innocence contradicts my unworthiness."[55]

Tim Keller says, "In Western culture today, you decide to get married because you feel an attraction to the other person. You think he or she is wonderful. But a year or two later—or, just as

---

55   John Piper, *This Momentary Marriage: A Parable of Permanence* Wheaton: Crossway, 2012 . Kindle edition, 416-444.

often, a month or two—three things usually happen. First, you begin to find out how selfish this wonderful person is. Second, you discover that the wonderful person has been going through a similar experience, and he or she begins to tell you how selfish you are. And third, though you acknowledge it in part, you conclude that your spouse's selfishness is more problematic than your own. This is especially true if you feel that you've had a hard life and have experienced a lot of hurt."[56]

If sin is about rejecting God's best for you and thinking you know better than Him what that might be, then the problem is complicated even more when you relate to another person. The other person will have his or her ideas. Now we have two competing views about what is best— two set of values that may conflict with each other with no objective criteria to determine how to mediate between the two. If you add to that mix the fact that both people are pursuing their own interests based on their own subjective criteria, you have the framework for destructive conflict.

Here is why marriage is in such a bad state: If you do nothing but urge people to "look out for number one," as our culture has done, you will be setting them up for future failure in any relationship, especially marriage. Our constant demands for rights creates a sense of entitlement that can never be fully met. It is better if we start by each of us seeing our own selfishness as being just as central to the problem as our spouse's, and maybe even more so. No one but you can deal with your own selfishness. Is it any wonder that Jesus reminds us that, "greater love has no one than this: to lay down one's life for one's friends" John 15:13 , and

---

56   Keller, 83/.

"Whoever wants to be my disciple must deny themselves and take up their cross daily and follow me." Luke 9:24

Our final response to our question, "What is the root cause of destructive conflict in our marriages?" is:

III. We falsely believe we can deal with the result of sin on our own. (Gen. 3:7)

7Then the eyes of both of them were opened, and they realized they were naked; so they sewed fig leaves together and made coverings for themselves.

A. We become self-centered and self-obsessed.

When the first couple ate from the tree, the covenant between them and God was broken and with it, the foundation of their own relationship collapsed. The covenant was this: God would govern them for their good, and they would enjoy him in that security and rely on him. The corruption of their own covenant love for each other was impacted by this in two ways.

1. I am self-conscious of my nakedness because I know Eve has chosen to act independent of God, and she is no longer safe. She is essentially now a selfish person who will put herself first and will judge me based on her own selfish criteria— one I am not likely to match.

2. Like Eve, I am now self-centered because of my own decision to act independently of God. I too have become unsafe, and she feels vulnerable because she knows I will

put myself first. I feel guilt because of my own sin and am vulnerable when she exposes it for what it is.[5]

B.   We become threatened and act in desperation when our sin is exposed.

When we feel desperate because our sin is exposed, and it drives us to hide. Desperation is always followed by an act that is intended to restore self-esteem. The fig leaves were Adam and Eve's failed attempt at dealing with this vulnerability by hoping others didn't see them as they really were—and it failed miserably. And so it is for all of us. Like Adam and Eve, we try to hide or cover our sin. The problem is that our act of desperation is always intended to restore our self-esteem-—not restore or address the problem that causes the rift in our relationship.

C.   Only God can address the sin issue that we try to hide. We cannot deal with the problem that has damaged our relationships by hiding. The sin is too great for us to deal with it on our own. We cannot compensate for the penalty by covering it up. We must first acknowledge our own sin and guilt before God and each other. Only then can restoration occur. That relationship is made possible through what Jesus did by dying on the cross for our sin.

In 2 Corinthians 5:15, Paul speaks to the heart of the problem, "And he died for all, that those who live should no longer live for

---

5/   Piper, 422.

themselves but for him who died for them and was raised again." There it is. There is our solution. Stop living for yourself but for him who died for you.

Marriages are strengthened when we face up to our rebellious self-obsession—not when we try to hide it.

In this chapter we revisited what went wrong to damage our relationships and posed the question, "What is the root cause of destructive conflict in our marriages?" We learned that we have rejected God's desire for us because we believe we know better. And when trying our plan, it fails, and then we think we can fix it on our own.

The sigh of romantic longing that my sister felt many years ago is a sigh we all have for something that seems elusive. What are some things we can do to put this into perspective?

1. Recognize that God created marriage for our good, and most of us long to sing the song of joy that Adam sang when God placed Eve before Him. The fact that we have the desire and the fact it is not realized shows that something is broken.

2. That broken something is us. We are self-centered creatures who have bought into a lie, and we have to stop thinking that people are going to treat us as perfectly when they will not.

3. We must acknowledge our selfishness and stop trying to "fix it" on our own. We must surrender ourselves to God first and allow His Spirit to transform our hearts.

In 2016 Elizabeth Landau, a thirty-two-year-old single person, wrote in a *Scientific American* article that a lot of people her age are, what she calls, "commitment-phobes." She writes, "I feel left behind in what *Vanity Fair* described as a 'dating apocalypse.' Of course, plenty of single men and women like me don't seek out one-night stands. But I feel like, in the dating-app era, many aren't keen on investing lots of quality time in any particular match when a better one might be a swipe away." Landau continues, "My outlook may have entered a vicious cycle: it's hard to get excited about meeting someone who won't care about you that much."[58]

As we saw earlier that millennials are the least likely group of any in history to marry. But why? More than half of the millennials surveyed by Pew characterize their own cohort as self-absorbed. "Trying to live with somebody else and putting their needs first is more difficult when you have been raised to put yourself first," says San Diego State University psychologist Jean Twenge.[59]

In this simple statement, we see the heart of the problem. The solution lies in submitting ourselves to God first and learning to submit to each other.

---

58   Elizabeth Landau, "Commitment for Millennials: Is It Okay, Cupid?" *Scientific American,* 2016 .

59   Ibid.

CHAPTER 3

BROKEN PEOPLE PRODUCE
BROKEN MARRIAGES

Text: *Genesis 3:8–19*
Theme: *e cannot fix relationships until we realize we are broken people who God wants to restore.*

I had an uncle who started to have a pain in his neck that caused him to lean his head to the left side and constantly wince in pain.

Doctors could not diagnose the problem, so he lived with the pain for years. In time his neck began to permanently lean to the side. Our family moved away but about six years later I returned and saw my uncle whose head was permanently fixed sideways from the pain. He had been diagnosed with a nerve disorder, but none of his treatments helped.

About twenty-five years later he went to a dentist to remove a bad tooth and was immediately relieved of all the pain. He suffered all those years unnecessarily due to a flawed diagnosis and treatment.

A wrong diagnosis can be costly and dangerous, yet they are not all that uncommon—I am sure doctors struggle with this concern daily.

I believe that every day we all witness a disastrous, dangerous misdiagnosis of mass proportions. Yet we continue full bore on the same path that got us into the mess that is the unraveling of marriage and the family.

The diagnosis in our culture is that man is basically good, but his self-esteem has been damaged by negative influences. Through proper education and enhancing one's self-esteem, we can address what ails us. To do that we must affirm each person's individuality—no matter how they are living or what they believe. We must teach them to be their own person, to love themselves, and to do whatever they need to do to make them happy. Don't let any outside authority dictate for you how you should live, because only you know what is best for you.

The problem with this diagnosis is that it is flat out wrong. Man is not basically good, and people who have perfectly good self-esteem are just as inclined to do evil things—I doubt Hitler or Stalin lacked self-esteem. You cannot simply educate people out of evil—it is a spiritual issue. We are self-obsessed individuals who deny the truth about who we really are, and we vie to pursue our own happiness even if it comes at a cost to others.

I want to propose a different diagnosis and solution to the problem by asking, "How does our sinful self-obsession impact our marriages?" We will look at three responses that reveal how our self-obsession causes us to hide the truth about ourselves and blame others for our flaws. This self-obsession becomes a curse that impacts our marriages in painful, destructive ways.

Our first response to our question is:

I. It causes us to try to hide the truth about ourselves. (Gen. 3:9–11)

⁹But the Lord God called to the man, "Where are you?" ¹⁰ He answered, "I heard you in the garden, and I was afraid because I was naked; so I hid."¹¹ And he said, "Who told you that you were naked? Have you eaten from the tree that I commanded you not to eat from?"

A. *We are flawed self-centered people damaged by sin.*

The problem we saw in our last chapter is that each of us questions God's good intention for our lives and we pursue our own path in defiance of His. It is grounded in the belief that we know what is best for us and that we can live and act independently of Him. The constant mantra, "I am the master of my fate" that has been indoctrinated into our culture is an echo of Eve's deception that turns her against God. If we are our own god, then others are no longer safe to us because they are out for their self-interests— nor are they focused on enhancing the one-flesh union of marriage.

When we face the truth, we know we are flawed and vulnerable creatures. Yet we do not want people to see our true selves because it is not something pretty. So, like Adam, we try to hide who we really are.[60] We hide in three major areas.

---

60   J. Grant Howard, *The Trauma of Transparency: A Biblical Approach to Inter-Personal Communication* Portland: Multnomah Press, 1979 .

I. **Fears:** David Burns identifies seven silent assumptions that produce anxiety—the vague fear that something awful is about to happen.

- Love: Some feel they will be alone and miserable if they have no one to love them. They obsess over trying to get or earn love.
- Approval: Some feel that if someone criticizes, then they have no value or worth. They obsess over getting everyone's approval.
- Omnipotence: Some feel they are responsible for everything that goes on around them. They obsess over trying to control everyone around them to absolve their fear.
- Perfectionism: Some feel that if they do not do everything perfect, they will burn in the flames of hell. They obsess over reaching an unobtainable standard of perfection.
- Achievement: Some feel that if they are not superior at something they value highly, then they are failures. They obsess over being the best.
- Entitlement: Some feel that their desires should be met by others because they deserve it. They obsess and get angry when they do not get the respect they feel they deserve.
- Autonomy: Some people feel that their fulfillment and well-being come from outside themselves. They obsess over what is happening outside their control.[61]

61   David Burns, *Feeling Good: The New Mood Therapy* New York: Avon Books, 1980 .

2. **Flaws:** We try to hide our flaws from others—and even ourselves. Here are a few examples.

   - Sexual- Every man struggles with a powerful sexual drive and is afraid that if people knew what really goes on within himself, he would be rejected and shunned. The male sex drive is something women will never understand. It can be a blessing or a curse. It can be like a monkey on every man's back that he has to learn to control.

   - Beauty- They value beauty and are always comparing themselves to others—always coming up short. They need constant affirmation from others.

   - Intelligence- Some try to act far smarter than they really are, so they hide the fact that they don't really know something, so as not to appear as stupid.

3. Failures: We do not want people to know we have failed, sometimes miserably. So we hide it in fear of rejection and lowered respect from others.

   - Sexual- When we violate a boundary from ourselves or others.

   - Substance Addictions- We hide or deny our addiction to something.

   - Unachieved expectations- We hide when we have failed at reaching a major goal.

B. *We still think we should be treated as though we are perfect.*

Like Adam, we want people to see us as though we are good and perfect—like God is. But we are not perfect, so we hide; we don't want people to see our true self. We feel naked and vulnerable to the fear that they will see us as we really are—and based on the judgementalism of some, we have legitimate cause for that fear.[62]

C. *When our imperfections are exposed, we try to evade responsibility.*

The problem with any one of these three things that we try to hide is that they always bleed out in some way. They bleed out in anger, they bleed out in avoidance, they bleed out in compulsive disorders, they bleed out in control tendencies, etc. People often see right through the things we think we are hiding, and when they expose it instead of admitting the truth, we evade our responsibility. God asked Adam a simple question, "Where are you." God asked that question not because he didn't know the answer, but because He wanted to confront Adam with the truth.

God is not deceived by our attempts to hide. The irony here is that there is a powerful freeing experience when we face the truth about ourselves. From the documentary *The Mask You Live In*, a scene shows a United States school teacher giving a group of high school boys a circular piece of paper. On one side they write what their image is, and on the other, what they are feeling. Then they scrunch up the paper and throw it to another kid. Here's how researcher Dr. Philip Zimbardo summarized the boys' messages:

---

62   Howard.

"What they said was all the same. On the outside, it said: 'Tough. Fearless. Kick your rear.' And on the inside: 'Lonely. Sad. Got no friends.' Each boy was stunned that the others felt the same way."[63]

This certainly applies to boys and men But in a sense, it applies to all of us as we try to project an outward "I-have-it-together" look while we struggle inwardly with insecurities. We need a safe place to be real about our inner world—our fears and insecurities. Our spouse should be that place.

It starts with a confession. As 1 John 1:9 says, "If we confess our sins, he is faithful and just and will forgive us our sins and purify us from all unrighteousness."

Let us look at the second response to our question, "How does our sinful self-obsession impact our marriages?"

II. It causes us to blame others for our imperfections. (Gen. 3:12–13)

> [12]The man said, "The woman you put here with me— she gave me some fruit from the tree, and I ate it." [13]Then the Lord God said to the woman, "What is this you have done?"
> The woman said, "The serpent deceived me, and I ate."

A. When exposed we evade responsibility and blame others for our wrongs. God asks Adam a very simple question, "Did

---

63   David Zahl, "Feminist Fallout? More on Underachieving Boys and Gracious G.A.W.F's." last modified May 26, 2015. http://www.mbird. com/2015/05/feministic-fallout-more-thoughts-on-underachieving-boys-and-gracious-g-a-w-f-s/.

you eat of the tree I told you not to eat?" The correct, clear, and straightforward answer is, "Yes." Yet Adam does what we all tend to do when our attempts to hide fail. Instead of accepting responsibility and facing the truth, he blames both God and Eve. He blames God by saying, ". . . the woman YOU gave me." He blames Eve by saying she gave him the fruit. Both have some truth to them, but they do not answer the fundamental question. Until we face up to the truth and deal with our culpability, we cannot restore our broken relationships. In regard to Adam, we learn in 1 Timothy 2:14 that he bears the greater responsibility because he knew what he was doing. It says, "And Adam was not the one deceived; it was the woman who was deceived and became a sinner."

B.   When blamed, others do not want to admit their imperfections. Notice God redirects his questioning to Eve and says, "What is this you have done?" Now remember, earlier in Genesis we learn that the woman's role was to be a helper to the man. Certainly, her act here was no help at all to Adam, and she also usurped her role. She too has double blame, and like Adam she evades responsibility and redirects blame.

C.   When blamed, others look for someone else to blame. That is what self-centeredness does. We want to appear as righteousness. Yet, we are not—so we blame. In this simple exchange, we see why marriages are in trouble. Our culture feeds this self-centered mantra, so we should not be surprised that North America faces historically unprecedented attacks against marriage, and the toll of such attacks is rising daily.

In their book *Mistakes ere Made (But Not By Me)*, social psychologists Carol Tavris and Elliot Aronson describe how a fixation on our own righteousness can choke the life out of love. They write: "The vast majority of couples who drift apart do so slowly, over time, in a snowballing pattern of blame and self-justification. Each partner focuses on what the other one is doing wrong while justifying his or her own preferences, attitudes, and ways of doing things . . . From our standpoint, therefore, misunderstandings, conflicts, personality differences, and even angry quarrels are not the assassins of love; self-justification is."[64]

In light of our self-centeredness, this makes sense. As author Denis de Rougemont said, "Why should neurotic, selfish, immature people suddenly become angels when they fall in love . . . ?"[65]

Good marriages are hard to achieve because there is something wrong with us. We can easily spot it in others but not so easily in ourselves. We should not be surprised that marriage takes work and for some, it means learning to accept responsibility for our own actions. Someone accredited Winston Churchill as saying, "Never ruin a good apology with an excuse."

Our final response to the question, "How does our sinful self-obsession impact our marriages?" is:

---

64   David Zahl, "500 Years After Luther, We Still Feel the Pressure to Be Justified," *Christianity Today* 2016 .

65   Denis de Rougemont, *Love in the estern orld* New York: Harper and Row, 1956 , 300.
  Diogenes Allen, *Love: Christian Romance, Marriage, Friendship* Eugene: Wipf and Stock, 2006 , 96.

III. It causes the proper God-given roles in life to be damaged. (Gen. 3:14–19)

"To the woman he said, 'I will make your pains in childbearing very severe; with painful labor you will give birth to children. Your desire will be for your husband, and he will rule over you.'

To Adam he said, 'Because you listened to your wife and ate fruit from the tree about which I commanded you, "You must not eat from it," cursed is the ground because of you; through painful toil you will eat food from it all the days of your life. It will produce thorns and thistles for you, and you will eat the plants of the field. ¹⁹ By the sweat of your brow you will eat your food until you return to the ground, since from it you were taken; for dust you are and to dust you will return.'"

A. For the man: his curse is that he will face frustration in his work. In Genesis 2:15 we learn, "... the Lord God took the man and put him in the Garden of Eden to work it and take care of it." Man was created for work but with the curse, his work is frustrated- with weeds. When you put this together with the curse for Eve you can already see an unhealthy scenario forming. The man comes home from a very frustrating day at work. He returns irritated and tired and he simply wants to crash to go into a mindless fog to avoid thinking about his fears and frustration. His frustration is expressed to the woman who wants his attention and support- so she lets her own dissatisfaction known.

B.   For the woman: her role as man's complement is impaired.

1.   She will face pain in childbearing. It appears that at creation childbearing was painless. The curse changed that. But it is the next two things that most impact marriage and lay the groundwork for the battle of the sexes.

2.   The man she is called to complement becomes insensitive and controlling.

The word translated "rule" is a rare Hebrew word that carries the idea of insensitive control. Man was created by God to be a loving attentive leader in the marriage, but his self-obsession takes his leadership role to an ugly place. It is, for this reason, our culture has an issue with the male leadership concept, instead promoting equality and gender-neutral roles as their response.

In his book *Fatherless America*, David Blankenhorn speaks to this trend by defining the Old Father versus the New Father. If you replace the word "father" with "husband," you will see how this applies. He says, "The Old Father wields power. He controls. He decides. He tells other people what to do. He has fangs. This aspect of his character generates suspicion and resentment . . . This is the heart of the matter. Many contemporary critics do not view authority—or even more accurately domination—as synonymous with male identify itself."[66]

Our culture has proposed a solution. They see our gender polarity as male and female as part of the problem, so they propose we remove the concept of gender roles altogether. To do

---

66   Blankenhorn.

so demands that we restate the words of a song in *My Fair Lady* from "Why can't a woman be more like a man?" to "Why can't a man be more like a woman?" So they propose "A New Father" who gives up his authority role and becomes more nurturing and androgynous.

The problem with the New Father model is that it denies our biology. Male testosterone makes men more aggressive. But it is also an insult to patriarchy, which has always taught that a father's role is to provide, protect, and lovingly lead his family. The problem is not male leadership and masculinity; the problem is that self-centeredness has distorted those qualities. The solution is not to remove gender distinctions but to follow the model of Jesus who sacrificed himself for his wife—the church.

3. She will become a nag trying to fix her broken husband. The word "desire" used in the phrase "your desire will be for your husband." is also a rarely used word and is used only one other time in Genesis 4:7, which states, "But if you do not do what is right, sin is crouching at your door; it desires to have you, but you must rule over it." We see here the imagery of a lion ready to pounce on its desired prey to control and consume it. That is the woman's curse—she wants her husband's love, attention, and affirmation, but his insensitive control frustrates her, causing her to try to fix and control him to get what she wants.

C. The only solution is to submit to God and submit to each other like Christ for us. This why Paul uses the covenant the church has with Jesus like that of the marriage covenant.

Philippians 2:1–12: "Do nothing out of selfish ambition or vain conceit. Rather, in humility, value others above yourselves, not looking to your own interests but each of you to the interests of the others. In your relationships with one another, have the same mindset as Christ Jesus."

Like Jesus, we do not wait for the other person to fix himself or herself before we act humbly and sacrificially to restore the relationship.

In this chapter we asked, "How does our sinful self-obsession impact our marriages?" We saw that it causes us to hide the truth about ourselves and to blame others for our problems. This self-obsession becomes a curse that impacts our marriages in painful, destructive ways.

Like my uncle who suffered from debilitating pain for twenty-five years due to a misdiagnosis, I believe our marriages and relationships suffer because we have accepted the wrong diagnosis. Our marriages are in major crisis because of it.

What are some steps we can take to reduce the impact of our selfish impulses?

1. You need to confront your own self-centeredness—don't wait for the other person to act first.

2. Accept responsibility for your sin—stop pretending to be the only victim and passing blame to others.

3. It means that before you are married and evaluating a prospective spouse, you will not find the perfect person. You need to heed the red flags but understand there will most likely be some red flags for anyone you consider. Ask yourself, *Are these issues I am ready and willing to work with and accept if they do not change?* Red flags alone are not the issue; it is your willingness to accept an imperfect person—just as they must accept you.

4. Understand that the painful vulnerability that healing a damaged relationship requires begins with self-sacrifice like that of Jesus. It is a sacrifice that may require a very high cost. But like Jesus, it is in that sacrifice that we have hope for our greatest fulfillment.

Let me illustrate this last point by citing an article in *Esquire* magazine titled, "Theater of Pain?" The article reported that during the 2011 NFL season, roughly two thousand active players suffered at least four thousand five hundred injuries, which comes out to an injury rate of 225 percent. The long list of injuries includes ". . . concussions, torn ACLs, ruptured Achilles tendons, high ankle sprains, hyperextended elbows, broken metatarsals, turf toes, stretched or compressed spines, pulled hamstrings, etc.

One NFL player who is currently playing and wants to remain anonymous relates his experiences of pain, for his children to understand when they're older. Here's a typical entry: "My left knee has been aching this entire week. I don't know why. I didn't get hit directly on it in the last game . . . When I start moving around, the muscles and tendons in my leg feel so stressed, sometimes I feel they might rupture. My lower back is so sore, painful and stiff; my right shoulder has lost some mobility for some reason. My right ankle is constantly being twisted; my left feels very weak . . . I don't sleep much, I feel super stressed, and on game day I take tons of drugs . . .

Similarly, Green Bay Packer's center Jeff Saturday says, "Right from a player's early teens, the accepted dogma is that injuries should never stop you from 'going to war' . . . The 'theater of pain' is all pervasive for today's player."

They see guys writhing in pain. They see guys crying, and they hear guys screaming. They see guys knocked out, guys go limp as a suit sliding from a hanger, guys stay horribly still, guys strapped to the board—and that's what every player fears. The board. Getting strapped to the board.

This story shows a profound dedication to sacrifice comfort in order to achieve a goal. If a man can make that kind of sacrifice for football, why can't he do the same for his wife who is far more important? What cost are we willing to pay for our marriages?[67]

---

67   Tom Junod, "Theater of Pain" *Esquire* 2013 . http://www.esquire.com/sports/a18002/nfl-injuries-0213/.

CHAPTER 4

THE EVIDENTIAL CASE FOR MARRIAGE

Text: *Proverbs 5*
Theme: *Both wisdom and evidence tell us that marriage benefits the person and society at large.*

There is an old joke, not a very good one, and one I am sure most of you have heard, but it lays the groundwork for the chapter, so I will tell it nonetheless. Feel free to roll your eyes after reading it. I won't be offended. It goes like this:

God was once approached by a scientist who says, "Listen, God, we've decided we don't need you anymore. These days we can clone people, transplant organs, and do all sorts of things that used to be considered miraculous." God replies, "Don't need me, huh? How about we put your theory to the test? Why don't we have a competition to see who can make a human being, say, a male human being?" The scientist agrees, so God declares they should do it like he did in the good old days when he created Adam. "Fine," says the scientist as he bends down to scoop up a handful of dirt. "Whoa!" says God, shaking his head in disapproval. "Not so fast. You get your own dirt."

In a very real sense, that is the situation we find ourselves in today regarding marriage and sexuality. We think we can do without God

87

and that we have a better plan for how marriage should work. But in the competition between God's design and culture's view, I want to see that God's view wins out. In the prologue we saw the older conjugal view of marriage as "a comprehensive union inherently suited for procreation and the sharing of family life. It calls for permanent and exclusive commitment. It is also a moral reality with an objective structure, which it is inherently good. In this view the state also has an interest in marriage because society needs children who become healthy adults capable of contributing to the common good and stable marriages are best suited for that."[68]

We also saw that the new view espoused by our culture says that marriage is essentially a private matter, an affair of the heart between two adults and is primarily valued by how well it satisfies the adult's individual emotional need—it is fundamentally about adult happiness. If the sense of romance is absent or one or both parties find themselves unhappy, then they have valid grounds for divorce. In other words, it is built on the emotional whims of romantic love.[69]

Too many have bought into the lie that we can change marriage's meaning and purpose without consequences. As Andrew Walker says, "Marriage has an elemental structure, like water. Just as tinkering with the number of hydrogen and oxygen atoms turns water into something else, messing with the fundamental structure of marriage means it is no longer marriage and cannot fulfill the purposes of marriage."[70] So even if we reject

---

68   Ibid.

69   Ibid.

70   Ibid.

the Bible as an authority, a convincing case can be made for the benefits of marriage simply by observing the evidence."

In this chapter I want to show that every society in history, pagan and otherwise, has recognized the intrinsic wisdom and value of conjugal marriage and its benefits to society—that is until the last fifty years. In that light, I want us to look at the question, "What can the weight of evidence, scripture, and wisdom teach us about the value of marriage?" We will look to the book of Proverbs for our answers.

Our first response is:

I. There is an ancient, universally-shared wisdom regarding marriage and sexuality. (Prov. 5:1–6)

"My son, pay attention to my wisdom, turn your ear to my words of insight, that you may maintain discretion and your lips may preserve knowledge. For the lips of the adulterous woman drip honey, and her speech is smoother than oil; but in the end she is bitter as gall, sharp as a double-edged sword. Her feet go down to death; her steps lead straight to the grave. She gives no thought to the way of life; her paths wander aimlessly, but she does not know it."

A. *The lure of an adulterous woman can be powerfully appealing.*

The first seven chapters of Proverbs are words of a father sharing wisdom with his son. From the warning in these verses, we are reminded that the powerful appeal of a sexual encounter outside the marriage covenant is not new. It has existed since the fall. Men are visually stimulated, and it is not only his wife who catches his eye. Yet, the message of this proverb is that sexual temptation is a powerful, universal attraction that works against the marriage covenant.

Notice there are several principles suggested in these verses.

1. There are sexual impulses that allure us to illicit affairs, but we have the ability to abstain from acting on them.

2. There is an objective requirement to abstain from illicit affairs. In contrast, rooted in our contemporary culture is the "playboy" philosophy, which measures manhood by his sexual prowess and promiscuity with James Bond being a typical role model.

3. We place far too much value on the sexual appeal and prowess of a person, yet sexual attraction has little to do with stable healthy relationship.

4. Manhood, in scripture, involves a willingness to restrain his sexual urges and provide for and protect his family.

B. *There are severe consequences when we succumb to her appeal.*

When this proverb was written, they did not have some of the medical advancements that reduce the impact of illicit relationships that this passage implies. But it also has allowed people to become more promiscuous, and, in that, they think they can act with impunity. What are these advances?

1. Antibiotics/Medicines- Today we have medicines and antibiotics that either eliminate or reduce the symptoms of STDs—yet they continue at epidemic rates in spite of them, and possibly even because of them, because it gives people a false sense of safety.

2. HIV- The disease continues to be contracted at extremely high proportions, especially in the gay community Google CDC MSN [1]. Contracting HIV results in a lifetime of treatments with antiviral drugs costing around eight hundred to a thousand dollars a month per person.

3. The Pill/Condoms- The availability of the pill in 1960 is one of the key catalysts for the sexual revolution. Prior to its introduction, the risk of unwanted pregnancies was a powerful deterrent for promiscuous sex. The pill and condoms reduce that risk but do not eliminate it altogether.

4. Abortion- I consider this to be the greatest tragedy of all. The most natural thing in the world is for a woman to cherish and nurture the baby in her womb. But something has happened in our culture to make this beautiful desire become distorted. We have made the god of "autonomy and self-determination" so prevalent that we use it to rationalize the killing of our unwanted offspring—that is usually the result of illicit affairs outside the marriage covenant.

---

[1] https://www.cdc.gov/std/life-stages-populations/msm.htm.

In his book *Mere Christianity*, C.S. Lewis says, "Chastity is the most unpopular of the Christian virtues. There is no getting away from it: the old Christian rule is, 'Either marriage, with complete faithfulness to your partner, or else total abstinence.' Now this is so difficult and so contrary to our instincts, that obviously either Christianity is wrong or our sexual instinct, as it now is, has gone wrong. One or the other. Of course, being a Christian, I think it is the instinct which has gone wrong . . . [Y] ou and I, for the last twenty years, have been fed all day long on good solid lies about sex. We have been told, till one is sick of hearing it, that sexual desire is in the same state as any of our other natural desires and that if only we abandon the silly old Victorian idea of hushing it up, everything in the garden will be lovely. It is not true. The moment you look at the facts, and away from the propaganda, you see that it is not. Before we can be cured, we must want to be cured. Those who really wish for help will get it, but for many modern people, even the wish is difficult. It is easy to think that we want something when we do not really want it. A famous Christian long ago told us that when he was a young man he prayed constantly for chastity; but years later he realized that while his lips had been saying, 'Oh Lord, make me chaste,' his heart had been secretly adding, 'But please don't do it just yet.'" [72]

Let us continue with our response to the question, "What can the weight of evidence, scripture, and wisdom teach us about the value of marriage?"

---

[72]   C.S. Lewis, *Mere Christianity* Los Angeles: Green Light Books, 2014 , 95ff.

II. There are consequences when we neglect to honor the marriage covenant. (Prov. 5:7–14)

Now then, my sons, listen to me; do not turn aside from what I say. Keep to a path far from her, do not go near the door of her house, lest you lose your honor to others and your dignity to one who is cruel, lest strangers feast on your wealth and your toil enrich the house of another. At the end of your life, you will groan when your flesh and body are spent. You will say, "How I hated discipline! How my heart spurned correction! I would not obey my teachers or turn my ear to my instructors. And I was soon in serious trouble in the assembly of God's people."

A. *You lose your honor and dignity with your family and friends.*

Notice that the first major consequence of an illicit relationship is not that you will get pregnant or an STD but that it impacts you as a person. It impacts your honor and dignity—something intrinsic about who we are. It unites us in an unintended one-flesh relationship. This is the point of Paul in 1 Corinthians 7:16–18: "Do you not know that he who unites himself with a prostitute is one with her in body? For it is said, 'The two will become one flesh.' But whoever is united with the Lord is one with him in spirit. Flee from sexual immorality. All other sins a person commits are outside the body, but whoever sins sexually, sins against their own body."

Most people who engage in illicit relationships are not really free as they often claim. Their passion enslaves them, so they lose the power to control it. Like the woman in Proverbs 5: ". . . but in the end she is bitter as gall, sharp as a double-edged sword. Her feet go down to death; her steps lead straight to the grave. She gives no thought to the way of life; her paths wander aimlessly, but she does not know it." We may be free to act on our desires, but we are not free to avoid the consequences.

B. ***You will eventually discover that you have been exploited for another's gratification.***

That is what is happening in our culture. We use each other for our own sexual gratification. It is not love; it is exploitation. For the woman it often goes like this: "I am lonely and feel unloved, so I will provide the sexual favors of a man in hopes it will fill my emptiness and he will love me." For the man it often goes like this: "I will appeal to a woman's desire for love to use her to satisfy my sexual urges." In both cases, they are using each other for selfish ends.

The opening prologue of this book shows the effects of this exploitation. Both adults exploited each other for their personal gratification giving no real thought to the child that results from their union. Most of these men in such relationships will never know their child and their child will never know their father. This "using" of people degrades our worth and dignity. People are not objects to be used for mutual gratification.

C. ***Your own conscience, and the public, will ultimately condemn you.***

In years past there was intense pressure on men to restrain his sexual impulses and marriage was a primary means of doing that. Our change of attitude regarding marriage has created the growth of fatherlessness. This has negative consequences not only for children and women but also for men. Men who do not father and who are not married can be a danger to themselves and to society.

The world over, young and unattached males have been a cause for social concern.

As sociologist Akerlof argues, ". . . men settle down when they get married: if they fail to get married, they fail to settle down."[3] When men delay or avoid marriage, they continue with the often antisocial and destructive behaviors of single men. When we remove that element, sexually unrestrained men become a risk to society. The prologue shows that poverty, child abuse, domestic abuse, teen pregnancies, juvenile crime and violence, abuse against women, etc., are all directly related to our diminished view of marriage and the fatherless homes it produces.

The overwhelming evidence for the connection between broken marriages, fatherlessness, and these social ailments has been known for more than fifty years. So why are we still following the same path as though we can still figure out a way to continue without its consequences? The answer is simple. We rationalize the problem away. Let us use smoking as an analogy: the association between smoking and lung cancer is well established, yet many rationalize their smoking like this analogy from David Blankenhorn:

"Research shows that not every smoker gets lung cancer. Conversely, not everyone who gets lung cancer is a smoker. Thus,

---

many factors other than smoking may contribute to lung cancer. Indeed, new regression coefficient data reveal these key findings: persistent coughing may damage lungs and is positively associated with the presence of lung cancer; healthy lifestyles, positive attitudes, and general physical fitness are positively associated with the absence of lung cancer; and some lungs are genetically more susceptible to disease, including cancer, than others. Therefore, smoking *per se* is probably misspecified as a major cause of lung cancer. Indeed, new data reveal that smoking is not a major factor in lung-related health problems of young children."[74]

The goal here is to downplay smoking as a significant cause of lung cancer—not to consider the objective data for smoking. The strategy is to disassemble smoking: to break down its different components into standalone concerns. Then the analyst can cite the causal effect of one component—such as coughing, general physical fitness, or the relative rarity of lung cancer among children who smoke—to suggest that "smoking per se" does not cause lung cancer.

This is the approach used by critics of the old view of marriage who do not want to see the crisis that the new view is creating. You see it when they try to advocate for alternative-families models. But the approach is just the same—break it down into individual components.

Let us look at our third response to our question, "What can the weight of evidence, scripture, and wisdom teach us about the value of marriage?"

---

74   Blankenhorn.

III. Marriage is far more rewarding at many levels. (Prov. 5:15–23)

"Drink water from your own cistern, running water from your own well. Should your springs overflow in the streets, your streams of water in the public squares? Let them be yours alone, never to be shared with strangers. May your fountain be blessed, and may you rejoice in the wife of your youth. A loving doe, a graceful deer — may her breasts satisfy you always, may you ever be intoxicated with her love. Why, my son, be intoxicated with another man's wife? Why embrace the bosom of a wayward woman? For your ways are in full view of the Lord, and he examines all your paths. The evil deeds of the wicked ensnare them; the cords of their sins hold them fast. For lack of discipline, they will die, led astray by their own great folly."

A. *Marriage provides a relational bond that lasts throughout your life.*

The imagery of these verses is important. Drinking from your own cistern is used in contrast to succumbing to the appeals of the scandalous woman. It simply means, "Let your own wife be the one to satisfy your desires." Both the desire and the discipline of mind should be directed to her alone.

In his study of successful men, Robert Weiss reports, "When men who have been married fifteen or twenty years are asked how marriage changed their lives, their first thought is apt to be lost freedom." 'If I weren't married, I'd probably have one h--- of a time,' is Mr. Brewer's first, immediate response. 'I'd probably spend my summers in Newport and my winters on the Caribbean.' In the next breath, Mr. Brewer offers a different vision of life without the burdens of marriage: 'Much as I wouldn't want to admit it, I'd probably be lonesome with life. Because I know quite a few guys that got divorced and what it really comes down to, a lot of them go home at night to a cold home.'"[5]

B. *Marriage promises familial and public affirmation.*

Christian sociologist Linda Waite makes this point well. She says, "Marriage is not only a private vow, it is a public act, a contract, taken in full public view, enforceable by law and in the equally powerful court of public opinion. When you marry, the public commitment you make changes the way you think about yourself and your spouse; it changes the way you act and think about the future, and it changes how other people and other institutions treat you as well."[6] Friends can dissolve their friendship by themselves, but it takes a judge to grant a divorce. Laws regulating divorce carry with them an implicit understanding of what marital obligations are.

C. *You experience deeper sexual fulfillment without guilt or remorse.*

The supposedly boring qualities of married sex have long been satirized in popular culture—taken for granted and transformed into the butt of jokes. An old joke asks, "What's the best food to curb your sexual appetite?" "Wedding cake" is the sobering answer. Over the last few generations, a new element to the old "ball-and-

---

5   Robert S. Weiss, *Staying the Course: The Emotional and Social Lives of Men Who Do Well at Work* (New York: Fawcett Columbine, 1990), 113.

6   Waite., 17.

chain" story has been added: yet that is a myth. In their excellent book, *The Case for Marriage*, Linda Waite and Maggie Gallagher confirm through evidence what the author of Proverbs realized. After looking at the best research on the subject, they conclude, "What these prominent researchers found may shock you: married people have both more and better sex than singles do."[77] In the chapter, they elaborated as to why:

Gary Smalley reminds us that marriage goes through different phases, and there is something about the marriage covenant that we need in order to get us through one of the hardest phases of all— the disillusionment phase of marriage. Most people enter marriage through the romantic experience, and at its peak it is euphoric. It is what most of our contemporary songs proclaim often and boldly. In this phase two people can become almost obsessed with each other. This phase involves the illusion that the beloved is perfect in every aspect that matters.[78]

The second phase is when the romantic experience passes, and the flaws in the other person are seen in their full light. Things that seemed inconsequential grow in significance. We begin to feel that we did not really know the person after all. It is like we wake up one day and realize the person we married is not the person we thought he or she was. And this presents us with the challenge of loving a person who, at the moment, seems like a stranger, not the person we remember marrying.[79]

---

77 Ibid., 79.

78 Gary Smalley and John Trent, *Love is a Decision* New York: Thomas Nelson, 2000 .

79 Keller.

At this phrase, we must affirm the marriage covenant to work it through. That is what marriage is. It is two flawed, self-centered people who must learn to sacrifice self for this other imperfect person, and, while it is seldom easy, it has the greatest likelihood of long-term benefit.

In this chapter we saw that there is a universally accepted view of marriage that, when ignored, has severe consequences. Individually and culturally we must renew our commitment to the marriage covenant if we are to see these consequences reversed. Like the joke at the beginning, the fact is that God's plan is still the best. I believe a crisis is looming because we foolishly believe we can do better than God's original plan. Crime, depression, and loneliness are inevitable consequences diminishing the societal importance of the marriage covenant.

I suggest three things to reflect on as you consider the content of this chapter:

1. Maybe you have succumbed to temptations outside your married covenant. God's grace may not remove the consequences, but He is a God of second chances. Renew your covenant with Him first, and begin to rebuild the trust you lost in the relationship by confessing and asking for forgiveness.

2. It seems strange that we should even feel that we need to make a case for marriage. But that is the place we find ourselves in today's culture. As a believer, we must stand apart from the culture if culture chooses to deny the benefits of covenantal marriage.

3. The first church council, as found in Acts 15, sought to resolve the question "What expectations should we place

on these new Gentile believers regarding the law?" The response from the council is surprisingly short. One of the four major things to abstain from is sexual immorality. In the Hebrew mind, what that meant is clear: sexual relations outside the covenant of a conjugal marriage is forbidden. Nothing has changed since that council wrote its dictate almost two thousand years ago.

4. Renew your commitment to God and your marriage covenant no matter what the cost—just as Jesus did for you.

An older married couple offered these words of advice to a young couple during their wedding ceremony: your love is priceless and needs to be guarded. Selfishness, pride, lack of forgiveness, and inattentiveness are but some of the many thieves capable of stealing away your love. In a sense your marriage is like a treasure chest forming a protective casing around your love, preventing your love from being stolen. Treasure chests have hard sides. The hardness protects what is on the inside . . . Many people live with the false assumption that love enables a marriage to survive. But that is not the case. Your love will not ensure your marriage will survive; it is your marriage which will ensure your love will survive. This is the very reason God ordained marriage. Marriage keeps love alive, not love keeps marriage alive.[80]

---

80   Jeff and Janet Johnson, "Marriage Protects Love; Love Does Not Protect Marriage" last modified May 7, 2012. http://www.preachingtoday.com/illustrations/2012/july/50/3012.html.

CHAPTER 5

THE DIVORCE DECISION

Text: *Matthew 19:1–12*
Theme: *The marriage covenant is to be a permanent bond that is joined by God Himself.*

There is an old nursery rhyme called "Humpty Dumpty." Of course, we all know it. We can quote it better than most Bible verses.

> Humpty Dumpty sat on a wall.
> Humpty Dumpty had a great fall.
> All the king's horses and all the king's men
> Couldn't put Humpty together again.

I would like to suggest that we are all very much like Humpty Dumpty sitting precariously on a wall, putting our shell our self-esteem at risk. Let me explain. One of the illustrations I often use in marriage counseling is that our self-esteem is like an egg. The shell is fragile and easy to crack, and if it is damaged enough, it will ooze messy yolk all over. When we start a relationship that leads to marriage, our shell is protected and strengthened by the other person. They are safe in that they affirm you, care for

103

you, and are sensitive to your well-being. We know that harsh words, even if true, will hurt the other person and damage the relationship, so we generally avoid using them—at least at that stage.

When the courting period is over, it is not uncommon for that to change. As our flaws are exposed, we do just as Adam and Eve did by evading responsibility and passing blame. That fragile shell we call self-esteem finds itself being threatened. Now, instead of the other person being a source of protection for that shell, they become a threat. Their accusations, whether they are true or false, are like darts that chip away at our fragile shell.

In time the dart throwing becomes so intense and painful that the people in the marriage believe they have only one option left—divorce. Divorce is their attempt to remove themselves from the line of fire. They fear that if they don't, their fragile shell will completely shatter, leading them to become like Humpty Dumpty—broken and irreparable with the gooey yolk of our personhood oozing all over the place. But is divorce really the best or only option? It certainly may seem so at the time when the darts are still flying. But what of the covenant? Does it become invalid?

In this chapter, we will look at the question, "What does Jesus teach us about the permanence of marriage?" We will learn that divorce is not an option, except for adultery. His position appears extreme to the modern ear, but it was radical even for His day and one that even his own disciples questioned. When challenged on his position, Jesus does not even try to soften his statement to make it more acceptable. So what do we make of His position?

I. Jesus' position on divorce and remarriage was more radical than even that of the Pharisees. (Matt. 19:1–6)

A. *Jesus was being entrapped to take a position on the two schools of thought on divorce.*

"When Jesus had finished saying these things, he left Galilee and went into the region of Judea to the other side of the Jordan. Large crowds followed him, and he healed them there. Some Pharisees came to him to test him. They asked, 'Is it lawful for a man to divorce his wife for any and every reason?' 'Haven't you read,' he replied, 'that at the beginning the Creator "made them male and female," and said, "For this reason, a man will leave his father and mother and be united to his wife, and the two will become one flesh"? So they are no longer two, but one flesh. Therefore, what God has joined together, let no one separate.'"

We are told in this passage that the Pharisees were trying to test or entrap Jesus on what was an ongoing debate in Jewish circles. I am guessing that they saw that He hobnobbed with sinners and maybe assumed He would take a soft position on divorce to accommodate his wayward followers. If so, they will be proven wrong.

To understand the trap, we need to understand the two competing schools of Jewish tradition known as the house of Hillel and the house of Shammai. These "houses" represented the two major groups of rabbis who studied the Torah. They depended on memory in transmitting the arguments. To preserve the complex arguments, a rabbi named Judah HaNasi wrote down the oral tradition in the late second century AD and became known as the Mishnah. It can safely be assumed its teachings were consistent with Jewish rabbinical teaching in the days of Jesus and St. Paul.[81]

1. Shammai- He proposes divorce is only for the case of any indecency or unchastity. His position was an interpretation of Deuteronomy 24:1 which says, "If a man marries a woman who becomes displeasing to him because he finds something indecent about her, and he writes her a certificate of divorce, gives it to her and sends her from his house." His focus was grounded in the phrase "something indecent about her"—he limited the word to sexual indecency.

2. Hillel- He proposed divorce for almost any reason if the man is dissatisfied—even if she spoiled a dish for him. R. Akiba says: Even if he found another fairer than she, for it is written, "And it shall be that if she finds no favor in his eyes." He focused on the words "no favor."

It seems Hillel won the debate between the two schools. Divorce for any reason the man determined was the practice in Israel—not that divorce was all that common. But when it happened, all a man needed to do to divorce his wife was to give her a signed and dated divorce document with the appropriate signatures of witnesses that said, "Now you are free to marry any man." Giving reasons for the divorce were not necessary;

---

81   Ruger, 838-841.

nonetheless, this was the debate that the Pharisees tried to drag Jesus into:[82]

Jesus avoids both schools of debate by avoiding the Deuteronomy passage altogether and returns to the origins of marriage. He did not fall into the trap. He knew neither one was the right, so he builds his position grounded in God's original intent. He reminds us that God joins a man and woman together permanently for their good.

This belief in the desirability, goodness, and permanence of marriage was once universal, but that is no longer true. A recent report by the University of Virginia's National Marriage Project concludes the following: "Less than a third of the [high school senior] girls and only slightly more than a third of the boys seem to believe . . . that marriage is more beneficial to individuals than the alternatives."[83]

Perhaps the main reason that young adults are wary of marriage is their perception that most couples are unhappy in their marriages. Keller illustrates this with a story, "Typical is a Yahoo! Forum in which a twenty-four-year-old male announced his decision to never marry. He reported that as he had shared his decision over the past few months to his married friends, everyone laughed and acted jealously. They all said to him that he was smart. He concluded that at least seventy percent of married people must be unhappy in their relationships. A young woman in a response

---

82   Ibid., 894ff.

83   "Teen Attitudes about Marriage and Family," *State of Our Unions* online. Last modified 2010. www.stateofourunions.org/2010/si-teen_attitudes.php.

to his post gave her own assessment: 'Everyone I know who's gotten married quickly— and failed to live together [first]— has gotten divorced.'"[84]

The problem with these beliefs and assumptions, however, is that every one of them is almost completely wrong. The evidence is overwhelming that married people live happier, more productive lives. So what changed? Legal scholar John Witte Jr. says that the earlier "ideal of marriage as a permanent contractual union designed for the sake of mutual love, procreation, and protection is slowly giving way to a new reality of marriage as a 'terminal sexual contract' designed for the gratification of the individual parties."[85] Tara Parker-Pope reminds us that marriage used to be understood to be a public institution for the common good, but is now perceived to be a private affair primarily for the benefit of the individuals in the relationship.[86]

This new view of marriage is what makes Jesus' position so hard to fathom in our culture. If sex it about me and my happiness, then terminating it is my choice alone—forget God and the fact that He is the one who joins us together. In this new view, my happiness supersedes all other commitments. It is no wonder marriage is in such a bad state of affairs.

---

84   Read Keller. Location 303.

85   John Witte Jr., *From Sacrament to Contract: Marriage, Religion, and Law in the   estern Tradition* Louisville: John Knox Press, 1997, 209.

86   Tara Parker-Pope, "The Happy Marriage is the Me Marriage," last modified December 31, 2010. www.nytimes.com/2011/01/02/weekinreview/02parkerpope.html.

The second response to our question, "What does Jesus teach us about the permanence of marriage?" is:

II. Jesus argues that what God has joined no man should separate. (Matt. 19:7–9)

"'Why then,' they asked, 'did Moses command that a man give his wife a certificate of divorce and send her away?' Jesus replied, 'Moses permitted you to divorce your wives because your hearts were hard. But it was not this way from the beginning. I tell you that anyone who divorces his wife, except for sexual immorality, and marries another woman commits adultery.'"

A. Divorce was allowed because of the hardness of our hearts. Simply put, divorce is never God's ideal. Divorce is something God hates but He knows our selfish prideful hearts are prone to harden, so He permits divorce primarily to protect the woman. This is consistent with Malachi 2: 15–16, "So be on your guard, and do not be unfaithful to the wife of your youth. "The man who hates and divorces his wife," says the Lord, the God of Israel, "does violence to the one he should protect," says the Lord Almighty."

B. Divorce is allowed in this context only for clear acts of sexual immorality. It should be noted this exemption is cited only in the Matthew passage we just read. In comparison, in Mark 10:1–12 we see Peter's account of this exchange. It does not mention the exclusion of adultery. It may be because Jesus was trying to change the focus of the issues from, "What grounds can we find to justify divorce?" to "what will it take to keep this relationship together?"

As we read this, it brings up all kinds of questions. It does not come across well to our contemporary ears. The questions that Jesus' statement poses are questions I do not have clear answers too. Questions such as: What about cases of child abuse, physical and emotional spousal abuse, selfishness to the point of not even providing adequate food and clothing, spousal abuse this includes everything from bizarre perversions to denying sex to one's spouse, etc.? All these can become destructive even life-threatening , and something has to be done. But according to Jesus, divorce does not seem to be one of the options. There are many things short of divorce a spouse can do. I don't believe that Jesus means we must have an unconditional acceptance of everything the offending spouse does—he understands the hardened selfish hearts of man. But I believe He is saying that divorce creates a huge unraveling of the marriage covenant that was affirmed by God.

Jesus clearly recognizes that when we minimize the importance of the marital bond, it causes great damage—individually and societally. He recognizes that the breakdown of the marriage is the breakdown of the home, which presents a new, more complex, and difficult set of problems. In that light, there is no such thing as a good divorce.

As David Blankenhorn says, "Yes, a few divorcing couples may be wise or lucky enough to transact a "good divorce" in which they continue to "co-parent" their children after they separate. But the vast majority of divorcing couples are not so wise or lucky.

For most divorcing couples, the marriage ends in bitterness, guilt, and pain. A small civilization has died. The children stay with the mother. The man moves out and tries to move on. When he does so, he may suffer enormously. He may have the best of intentions about not divorcing his children. But despite these feelings, most of these men lose the essence of their fatherhood. They drift away from their children almost as surely as they move away from their former homes and drift away from their former wives. This is sad. But it is the pattern."[8/]

He calls them the "Visiting Father." "He is a shadow dad, a displaced man trying not to become an ex-father. He is a father who has left the premises. He still stops by, but he does not stay. He is on the outside looking in. No longer the man of the house, he has been largely de-fathered. As a visitor, he is part father, part stranger. Physical distance, combined with estrangement from his children's mother, has radically diminished his paternity. Now a weekend and holiday dad, a treat father, a telephone father, he is frequently filled with resentment and remorse. He mourns the loss of his fatherhood much as one would mourn the loss of health. He wants to be a good father, but in ways that matter most, he cannot be. He cannot raise his children. He can only visit them."

The cultural category of Visiting Father represents a large and growing number of men. They outnumber unemployed men. They outnumbered unemployed married fathers by a ratio of nearly seven to one. They outnumber both the stay-at-home dads and the dads-with-sole-custody who have become staples of media

---

8/   Blankenhorn, 151.

discourse on family change. They dramatically affect the lives of millions of women and children. Their emergence as a mass male trend has been quite sudden.[88]

I have made this point before, but it bears repeating. In our quest to free ourselves from one set of problems we have created an even greater monster. As David Popenoe asserts, "The push for self-fulfillment, when carried to the extreme, leads not to personal freedom and happiness but to social breakdown and individual anguish."[89] And that, I believe, is where we find ourselves today. We live in a broken world with broken people, and we have to stop living with this silly naive belief that we should be happy and fulfilled at all times. I think this is the point of Jesus' position.

Our question, "What does Jesus teach us about the permanence of marriage?" has a third response.

C.   His position is so radical even his disciples were surprised. Matt. 9:10–12

"His disciples said to him, 'If this is the situation between a husband and wife, it is better not to marry.' Jesus replied, 'Not everyone can accept this word but only those to whom it has been given. For there are eunuchs who were born that way, and there are eunuchs who have been made eunuchs by others—and there are those who choose to live like eunuchs for the sake of the kingdom of heaven. The one who can accept this should accept it.'"

---

88   Ibid.

89   Popenoe, 48.

When we read these words from Jesus, I think we can all be shocked. It sounds extremely restrictive, legalistic, and insensitive when we evaluate them from our iWorld perspective. But as we read here, we are not the only ones who are shocked by Jesus' position. If it seems radical in our day, it was no less so in the day of Jesus when divorce was a greater rarity. And it was not just the Pharisees who would have responded with surprise; even His disciples couldn't quite accept it.

They argued, "If that is the case, it is better not to marry." They were, in essence, saying, "When you marry a person, you don't always know exactly what you are getting. You may find out that you unwittingly married a lemon, and if what you say is true, then you are stuck with him or her for life. That being the case, then why take the chance?"

Jesus recognizes their surprise but reaffirms his position. In His response to them, Jesus is essentially saying, "Yeah! You are right, and not everyone can accept it. In light of the risk, remaining single may be the preferred option, but with that comes the expectation of abstinence—"eunuchs by choice for the sake of the kingdom."

Obedience to this command is only possible if we put God's kingdom first.

Apart from the saving work of faith and the empowering of the Holy Spirit, marriages can become unraveled at great pain and cost to all involved. If marriage were simply about personal happiness or staying "in love" for all time, few marriages would survive.

John Piper says it this way, "Staying married, therefore, is not mainly about staying in love. It is about keeping covenant. 'Till death do us part' or 'As long as we both shall live' is a sacred covenant promise—the same kind Jesus made with his bride when he died for her. Therefore, what makes divorce and remarriage so horrific in God's eyes is not merely that it involves covenant-breaking to the spouse, but that it involves misrepresenting Christ and his covenant. Christ will never leave his wife. Ever. There may be times of painful distance and tragic backsliding on our part. But Christ keeps his covenant forever. Marriage is a display of that!" [90]

"Marriage among Christians is mainly meant to tell the truth about the gospel—that Christ died for his church who loves him and never breaks his covenant with his bride. In essence, Jesus says, 'You have heard that it was said, "You are permitted to divorce." But I say to you, I have come to conquer the hardness of your heart. I have come to die for your sins. I have come to count you as righteous. I have come to show you the drama that marriage was meant to represent in my sacrificial, covenant-keeping love for my sinful bride. I have come to give you the power to stay married, or to stay single so that either way you keep your promises and show what my covenant is like and how sacred is the covenant bond of marriage.'" [91]

In this chapter, we looked at the question, "What does Jesus teach us about the permanence of marriage?" We learned that even in His own day, Jesus' position on divorce was a radical idea that even his own disciples questioned. He does not try to soften His position to make it more acceptable but challenges us to put the kingdom of God first.

---

90   John Piper, *This Momentary Marriage: A Parable of Permanence* Wheaton: Crossway Books . Kindle edition, 299-309.

91   Ibid., 2249-2260.

Here are a few points to take away from this chapter.

1. If you make marriage simply about personal happiness, you will often find yourself disappointed. You are married to a broken, selfish person like yourself and maybe more—it is merely a matter of the degree of brokenness. Broken people produce broken relationships that can only be mended by humility and self-sacrifice.

2. The highest meaning and the most ultimate purpose of marriage is to put the covenant relationship of Christ and his church on display. That is why marriage exists. If you are married, that is why you are married. If you hope to be, that should be your dream.

3. Divorce creates a set of problems that usually exceed the complexity and difficulty of the problems you hoped to solve by divorcing. You take your problems with you because part of the problem is within yourself. Rarely is divorce the better option in spite of our feelings.[92]

We are all very much like Humpty Dumpty sitting precariously on a wall that we can fall from at any time. Our self-esteem is like a fragile shell that will break, and no one can put us back together again. Divorce does not fix that problem. We must find other ways to protect our fragile shell. Our self-esteem cannot rest on what anyone, even a loved one, thinks of us.

I do not approach this topic from a purely idealistic perspective. I have struggled with the divorce question many times

---

92   Sarah Marsh https://www.theguardian.com/commentisfree/2016/feb/11/life-after-divorce-end-marriage

as I have counseled others in painful relationships and in my own upbringing. My father died when I was seven years old and my mother moved our family of four kids from Virginia to California. She was single for four years until she met my stepfather, himself a widowed man with three kids of his own. It was not long after he proposed to my mother and they got married that they realized it was a disaster.

I now know that my stepfather was a narcissist and diagnosable schizophrenic. Then I only knew he was cruel, inconsistent, and abusive. While he never physically abused my mother's kids, I caught him several times beating his own in the garage and watching them flee in terror when I entered. He had a look of fear on his own face knowing that if I told my mother she would report it to the police, as she had already done a few times. Even though I was a good student, well behaved, and a good athlete, he would frequently demean me calling me lazy, useless, and good for nothing. At first I tried aggressively to meet his inconsistent, unobtainable standards but always came up short. It was not until one of his long, drawn-out tirades that I had an aha moment and realized the problem was not just me—and maybe not me at all. I realized that my stepfather was a narcissistic, self-centered man. I was not angry or defiant, but it was clear to me that I could not look too him for my self-esteem or let him define who I was.

In a sense, my stepfather did something for me that I needed desperately. I needed to be broken— like Humpty Dumpty. I needed to realize that my self-esteem could not come from his approval, my achievements, or my ability to control what was happening around me. My esteem has to come from the Christ who loved me and sacrificed Himself on the cross on my behalf.

I would never have come to that point had my stepfather not been a part of my life. In that sense I learned from him one of my most valuable lesson in life—Christ rebuilds broken shells. It now reminds me of an army boot-camp where they break you down before rebuilding you. The emotional intensity is all part of the process of finding where your true value comes from.

I believe that is often what God is often doing for us in marriage. He wants the emotional intensity that you are going through to break your shell and to teach that you must build your identity in someone other than your spouse or the well-being of your marriage. Jesus calls us to take up our cross, to die with Him, so that God can raise us up with Him to new life.

CHAPTER 6

GOD'S HIGH VIEW OF SUBMISSION

Text: *Galatians 3: 26–29, Ephesians 5:1–24, Philippians 2:1–11.*
Theme: *The one-flesh union of a man and woman requires mutual submission with the woman specifically called to that role.*

Tim Keller is a very successful pastor who built the largest church in New York City, an area considered difficult to reach, and he did it without gimmicks or watering down the gospel. To honor his accomplishment, Princeton Seminary made him the recipient of the Kuyper Prize which is awarded each year to a scholar or community leader who has made an outstanding religious contribution. He certainly qualified for the prize. He is both a scholar and brilliant communicator whose record reveals this acknowledgment.

When word got out that he was receiving the award, nearly immediately there was a huge outcry coming from many of the alumni and sponsors of the liberal seminary. Keller has taught and written in strong support of a biblical view of human sexuality and a complementarian view of women's roles both

119

in the church and home. Due to the outcry, he was denied the prize.[93]

One of his antagonists was Carol Howard Merritt who wrote a scathing article in the magazine, *The Christian Century*. In the article she states, *"Please understand this.* Biblical womanhood, headship, and male authority teaches women that they have no right to choose ... well ... anything. A trip the mall is up to their husband, if he decides it's his business. If he determines that she needs to stay at home and homeschool her kids instead of teaching grad school with her Ph.D., then there is no discussion. She gets no say in the matter ... I know that people are angry that Tim Keller doesn't believe in women in the pastorate. But, my friends, this goes much, much deeper than women not being able to be ordained as pastors, elders, and deacons. **Complementarianism means married women have no choice over their lives *at all*."**[94] She later argues that his view sets the stage for potential abuse.

Wow! Certainly if her claim is true, then you might wonder why anyone, especially an intellect like Tim Keller, would espouse such a view. Why would anyone support denying women any choice over their lives at all? And yet her position is reflective of

---

93   Kate Shellnut, *Princeton Seminary Reforms it views on Honoring Tim Kelller: School rescinds a major theology prize amid complaints over women's* ordination, Christianity Today, March 22, 2017. accessed May 10, 2018, http://www.christianitytoday.com/gleanings/2017/march/princeton-rescinds-tim-keller-kuyper-prize-women-ordination.html

94   Carroll Howard Merritt, *Does teaching submission encourage abuse?*, The Christian Century, March 17, 2017, accessed May 10, 2018, https://www.christiancentury.org/blog-post/does-teaching-submission-encourage-abuse

how our modern culture perceives the biblical and traditional view of marriage. Like her view, their picture of biblical marriages is one where women are inferior beings, controlled and manipulated without any say in their lives. In contrast, the same people portray modern women as free to choose their own course in life without the control of an oppressive and overbearing husband. In their view the contrast is stark—either throw off the past archaic suppressive views of women or be doomed as degraded subjects of probable abuse.

The problem is that it appears she has never read Keller's view nor his reasons for it. Her response distorts his position and misses his point completely. Simply put, she misrepresents what Keller is saying due to a simplistic misleading characterization of his view and the scriptures he bases it on.

Her rebuttal reminds me of a recent YouTube video that had gone viral. In the video British TV journalist, Cathy Newman interviews Toronto University professor and psychologist Jordan Peterson. Peterson had become known for his opposition of compelled speech laws in Toronto that mandate the use of transgendered pronouns. Peterson has been chastised in the press for his "transphobic" position and Cathy Newman set out to expose him.

Throughout the interview, there are numerous examples where Peterson makes a statement and Newman returns with the question, "So what you're saying is . . . ?" She then restates what he said and in every case, her restatement bears little resemblance to what Peterson actually said. She essentially puts words into his mouth. It soon becomes evident that she had formulated a characterization in her mind of Peterson as an insensitive, unintellectual bigot, and she was going to expose him. Instead, the opposite occurs. Peterson comes across as quite reasonable while she misses his point completely and exposes her bias instead.[95]

Similarly, no one, including myself, who holds a complementarian view of marriage would suggest that it leads to the degrading treatment of women that Carol Merritt identifies in her article. In a sense she has done what Cathy Newman did with Jordan Peterson. It is as though she is interviewing the apostle Paul and saying, "So Paul what you're really saying is that women have no rights to go to the mall, must always stay at home, and have no choice over their lives whatsoever." It completely misrepresents what Paul, or for that matter, what Keller is saying.

No one is arguing that there have not been abuses in the past due to a flawed understanding of Paul's view of marriage. But to argue that these abuses are the result of Paul's position is like arguing that the legalistic and combative Westbrook Baptist Church represents all Baptists or evangelicalism as a whole. I would argue that the abuse is not a result of Paul's or biblical teaching but the result of the fall and the resulting curse that was given to Eve that we made reference to in earlier chapters. If the curse remains in effect then the insensitive domination of women can happen whatever your view—and the evidence shows that it is happening. It is intrinsic to our sinful nature and Merritt's position will not remove that.

---

95   Cathy Newman, *Jordan Peterson debate on the gender pay gap, campus protests and postmodernism*, Chanel 4 News, Jan 16, 2018, accessed May 10, 2018, https://www.youtube.com/watch?v=aMcjxSThD54

But most of us would agree that our dominant cultural narrative weighs in favor of Merritt, so before we look closer at Paul's teaching in the next chapter, I feel it important to understand the origin and influences of this narrative and why it is so appealing. There are three primary narratives for understanding the contrasting views on men and women in both the home and in the church. So let's touch briefly on each of them first.

Egalitarian- This is the dominant position in our contemporary Western culture. It teaches that all gender distinctions in the home or society should be removed—especially regarding patriarchy. They regularly paint a picture of the past as oppressive and demeaning to women. So their answer to this oppression is to try to change society's perspectives on what is masculine and feminine so that these distinctions are removed by making male and female equal in all areas.

A recent example of this was when Pembina Hills High School in Alberta, Canada, introduced a course titled "Women's Studies" which teaches girls about hairstyles, flattering clothing, dinner party etiquette, and polite conversation-—something that as recently as ten years ago would have been a welcome course. But it produced an immediate outcry so that even David Eggen, leader of the education department for the Alberta NDP party, along with dozens of others, intervened to stop it. They felt it stereotyped females in an outdated expression of gender.[96]

---

96   Chinta Puxley, *Alberta education minister wants changes to 'women studies' course focused on hairstyling, cooking,* The Canadian Press, March 22, 2017, accessed May 10, 2018, http://edmontonjournal.com/news/local-news/alberta-education-minister-wants-changes-to-women-studies-course-focused-on-hairstyling-cooking.

Hierarchical- This view has strong historical precedence. It teaches that man has full authority over the home with the attitude that he is superior and the wife inferior. This seems to be the view that Carol Merritt, is opposed to—she simply makes no distinction between this view and the complementarian view. It could be said that this is the view that best reflects the effects of the fall in the Garden of Eden where the effects of the curse turned the male leadership role designed by God in creation into insensitive domination.

Complementary- Husband and wife are equal in that they equally bear God's image but have distinct God assigned roles in the relationship. This is the view Keller, I, and hundreds of others share. In this view both sexes have vital roles to play in the one-flesh marriage relationship where the two become one. It teaches that the relationship between the husband and wife is modeled after the relationship between Christ and his church with the husband as the head. While the woman has worth and dignity in and of herself, it is in a one-flesh relationship established by God that both sexes benefit each other in their distinct roles. In that light I believe the solution to the patriarchal abuse of the past is not to remove God's design but to redeem His design from the effects of the fall so it gives to the wife the dignity inherent in her nature. The one-flesh union of a man and woman requires mutual submission with the woman specifically called to that role. I will argue that point later in the chapter.

The equalitarian view is historically a rather recent perspective that could only have come out of a Christian worldview.[9] Its

---

9   Rodney Stark, *The Rise of Christianity: How the Obscure, Marginal Jesus Movement Became the Dominant Religious Force in the   estern   orld in a Few Centuries*, Harper: San Francisco, 1997.

position is rooted in both creation and in Galatians 3 in which Paul says, "So in Christ Jesus, you are all children of God through faith, for all of you who were baptized into Christ have clothed yourselves with Christ. There is neither Jew nor Gentile, neither slave nor free, nor is there male and female, for you are all one in Christ Jesus. If you belong to Christ, then you are Abraham's seed, and heirs according to the promise."

Out of this truth, the forefathers of the United States made a radical proposal that "all men are created equal." At the time slavery still existed and the patriarchal nuclear family was the dominant cultural institution. In time the rights of "all men" were expanded to include blacks and women where both groups were granted the right to vote. Susan B. Anthony and Elizabeth Stanton were key activists who aggressively championed the women's right to vote. Prior to that the woman's primary role in the public square was through whatever influence she bore with her husband in that they acted corporately as "one flesh."

Eventually the influence of Anthony and Stanton expanded beyond the vote and into the cultural institutions as a whole—even into the institution of marriage itself. In the 'sixties, we saw an escalation of this primarily as a result of Gloria Steinem and Betty Friedan who co-founded the National Organization for Women. Friedan's influential book titled *The Feminine Mystique*[98] opens with a chapter titled "The Problem With No Name" that defines what she sees to be the problem with traditional roles of marriage. In this chapter she describes the typical American

---

98   Betty Friedan, *The Feminine Mystique* New York: W.W. Norton and Company, Inc., 1963 .

suburban housewife as bored and unfulfilled with the menial tasks she must perform each day driven by outdated stereotypical views of gender. Friedan's solution is to cast off those oppressive bonds of housewifery by getting women out of the home where they can be free to find a meaningful role in society and to be herself—not some image of the domestic ideal imposed on her by society.

With female roles portrayed in such a light it should not surprise us that it was not long after that we began to see the rise of feminism in the church by those who shared Friedan's grievance. The problem, of course, is that historical Christianity is significantly influenced by Genesis and the apostle Paul's proscriptions in three books of the New Testament—1 Corinthians, Ephesians and 1 Timothy—all of which appear to advocate the very thing that Friedan refutes. To try to reconcile Genesis and Paul with the rising influence of feminism two books were written early on in the discussion within evangelical circles.

One book was by Paul Jewett titled *Man as Male and Female: A Study in Sexual Relationships from a Theological Point of iew.*[99] In the book he argues that the Genesis account is not one of hierarchy but of partnership. Man and woman are properly related when they accept each other as equals whose differences complement each other in all areas of life. But when he comes to the apostle Paul, Jewett gets into questionable territory by arguing that Paul simply did not always match his profound and revolutionary

99   Paul Jewett, *Man as Male and Female: A Study in Sexual Relationships from a Theological Point of iew* Grand Rapids: Wm. B. Eerdmans Publishing Company, 19/5 .

insight that he lays out in Galatians 3. In other words, he finds inconsistency in Paul's teaching on male and female roles.

Without getting bogged down in too much detail, I have several responses to Jewett's position:

1. His position begs the question, "Why is Paul's teaching authoritative in Galatians 3 but not in 1 Corinthians 11 and 14, 1 Timothy 2 and Ephesians 5?" As one who believes that all of Scripture is divinely inspired, I find Jewett's position disturbing and his explanations inadequate. Essentially he is saying that Paul is authoritative on the one teaching that Jewett favors but is misguided on the others that Jewett does not favor. How does one arbitrarily select what the authoritative passage is and what is not?

2. I find no inconsistency with Paul teaching in Galatians with that of the other proscriptive passages on husband-wife roles. In Galatians, he is arguing that it does not matter what your role in life is—we all come to salvation the same way, ". . . in Christ Jesus you are all children of God through faith . . . you are all one in Christ Jesus if you belong to Christ." In other words, your sex, ethnicity, or social status does not determine your standing before God—it is determined by faith. But that does not mean you cease to be Jew or Greek, male or female, slave or free.

Some have suggested that Galatians 3 undermines the premise for slavery that existed in his day and, if so, does it not also undermine Paul's teaching on marital roles? Regarding slavery, Paul himself suggests this idea in his letter to Philemon regarding the escaped slave Onesimus where he says, ". . . that you might have him back forever—no longer as a slave, but better than a slave, as a dear brother." Certainly, in Christ Onesimus and Philemon are equals. So while Scripture does regulate slavery, it does not mandate it and ultimately undermines it. But here is the distinction—there are explicit passages that Paul uses to argue his complementary position for male-female roles and he bases them on creation itself—not in the fallen state of man for which redemption is required or in cultural influences of his day. We find no such passages or argument for supporting slavery.[100]

3. Jewett argues Christian theologians throughout history have mostly been men and much of their chauvinist views are influenced because of it. This position has almost become a contemporary dogma which states, "European men have sought to oppress others over the years to preserve control and patriarchy." If this dogma were true then that would mean that Paul is complicit in their conspiracy. By Jewett's own admission he is saying Paul is teaching wives are to submit to the husbands but he believes Paul is simply wrong. That means Paul set all of Western Civilization on a wrong course only to be corrected by contemporary advocates of women's rights. So why appeal to Paul at all if he is so wrong? That would be okay with many contemporary advocates of women's

100   Susan Foh provides a critique of Jewett, Nancy Hardesty, Virginia Mellonkott and others who advocate evangelical feminism in her book, *omen and the ord of God: A Response to Biblical Feminism* New Jersey: Presbyterian and Reformed Publishing Company, 1979 .

rights but in doing so you also undermine the Christian foundation for women's rights as well.

A second book that influenced early evangelical feminism was by Nancy Hardesty and Letha Scanzoni titled *All   e're Meant to Be.*[101] They take a more scathing view of what they portray as the hostile male chauvinism of the past and deal in greater detail with Paul's teachings. *Christianity Today* cited their book as the twenty-third most influential book in contemporary evangelical culture so their position should not be overlooked.[102] Hardesty's book attempts to reinterpret passages long understood to promote patriarchy. They also take great effort to demonstrate the many roles that women of Scripture played—most of which I take no issue with. In contrast to Jewett, they claim to accept the authority of Paul's less favorable passages but to draw their conclusions they have to deal with words like *head* kephale , *submission* hupasatis and *for* "gar" as in, "the woman was created **for** man" that seem to clearly advocate a complementary position. But their efforts demonstrate a bias in that they begin with the presupposition that egalitarianism is an already established premise forcing them to take some interpretive liberties. If the goal of interpretation is to discern to authors one intended meaning then I believe their book fails in that quest. In that sense Jewett has the more consistent position.

---

101   Nancy Hardesty and Letha Scanzoni, *All   e're Meant to Be: A Biblical Approach to   omen's Liberation* Waco, Word Books, Waco, 1974 .

102   Letha Scanzoni, *PART 1. Coauthoring "All   e're Meant to Be" —The Beginning*, Letha's Calling: A Christian Feminist Voice, 2011, accessed May 10, 2017, https://www.lethadawsonscanzoni.com/2011/01/part-1-coauthoring-all-were-meant-to-be-the-beginning/

I cite these two books because most of what has been written in recent years uses much of the same argumentation as these authors—with some slight variations. While I have not read them all, I have read enough to conclude that most of the arguments for the debate are settled and these two books are good reflections of the egalitarian position. It does not seem likely that

some major new insight will unfold anytime soon. Enough is there to get a sense of the issue.

It has been almost sixty years since Betty Friedan wrote *The Feminine Mystique* and her influence on culture and Christianity itself cannot be understated. The pattern is the same: paint an oppressive history of patriarchy, deny or reinterpret scripture to fit our contemporary egalitarianism, and belittle those who disagree as bigoted, archaic, chauvinistic, and closeminded. So what does that leave us with? What do we teach our boys about being a husband and father? From an egalitarian position, the answer is, "The same thing we teach girls. There are no objective distinctions other than genitalia. While hormones make male boys more aggressive and girls more nurturing, they do not matter in any meaningful way." Marriage has no essential value and the primary rule is not to violate someone else's personal autonomy—married or otherwise. The admission of girls and the renaming of the Boy Scouts to Scouts USA confirms this answer. There are no substantial differences between boy and girls. The role of the male is no longer to provide, protect, and lead his home—that is a shared role with his wife and let's just hope they can get along.

But that is an answer I find unsettling because not only does it undermine what appears to be the clear biblical teaching on the subject, it also leaves us with a loss of how to teach boys and girls what it is to be a man or woman, a husband or a wife, or a father or a mother. If every idea is equal then when conflicts arise there is no way to arbitrate the better path forward—no meaningful criteria to settle the issue. Without Paul's high view of women, it is probable there would be no women's rights moment today. But being equal does not mean being "the same." Men and women are substantially different and those differences complement each other so that they both benefit. That testosterone that makes men more aggressive and the estrogen that makes women more nurturing may, in fact, be something God has given each sex and is an indicator of his design.

We can trace the devolution of marriage back to the 'sixties right about the time that Betty Friedan wrote her book. Is there a causal relationship between the two? I suggest that there is at least some and probably a close relationship. Friedan's "Problem With No Name" asserted that women were bored and unfulfilled because of their bondage to their stereotypical roles as women, as mothers, and as wives. Her answer was to get them out of the home where they could find meaning and fulfillment—something the home could not offer. Her solution has been well received but if doing so was to improve her lot in life then the reviews are mixed. While young people are finding new freedoms they are less equipped to find and form lasting relationships and Friedan's "solution" is part of the reason for that. No one knows the rules anymore.

In the rest of this chapter, I want us to look at Paul's teaching about marriage and see that while it calls specifically for submission, when understood in its context it gives honor and dignity to the woman—a dignity that is not provided in the modern alternative in which women are simply another player in the competition amongst men. To make that case Chapters 6 and 7 must be read together. In that light I want to consider three responses to the question, "How is the women's role of submission to be understood in both Scripture and culture?"

Our first response to the question is that Spirit-empowered submission is something all are called to—not just the woman. Before we look at the verses that speak to the contrasting roles of the man and a woman in a marriage relationship, we should first look at the context that we find them in.

Ephesians 5:18–21 states, "Do not get drunk on wine, which leads to debauchery. Instead, be filled with the Spirit, speaking to one another with psalms, hymns, and songs from the Spirit. Sing and make music from your heart to the Lord, always giving thanks to God the Father for everything, in the name of our Lord Jesus Christ. Submit to one another out of reverence for Christ."

The first thing to note from these verses is that we are all called to be controlled by the Spirit. One of the most powerful messages of the New Testament is that when one becomes a believer in Jesus Christ, the Holy Spirit enters into that person and begins to transform him or her from the inside out. Jesus spoke of the Spirit coming and in every Gospel and every New Testament book says something about how He empowers us to live like Jesus. But we are also told that we can resist, quench, or even grieve the Spirit of God. Paul reminds us that we need to heed that inner spiritual voice present within us and enables us to have the mind of Christ. This mind of Christ is revealed in Philippians 2:5–7 which says:

"In your relationships with one another, have the same mindset as Christ Jesus: Who, being in very nature God, did not consider equality with God something to be used to his own advantage; rather, he made himself nothing by taking the very nature of a servant, being made in human likeness. And being found in appearance as a man, he humbled himself by becoming obedient to death—even death on a cross!"

Another thing to note is that those controlled by the Spirit will manifest certain traits. Notice that Paul has told us not to be controlled or influenced by wine but, in contrast, to be controlled or influenced by the Spirit of God. Just as there are traits that one sees in a person controlled by wine there are contrasting traits in a person controlled by the Spirit. Galatians 5:23–26 identifies some of these traits:

"But the fruit of the Spirit is love, joy, peace, forbearance, kindness, goodness, faithfulness, gentleness, and self-control. Against such things, there is no law. Those who belong to Christ Jesus have crucified the flesh with its passions and desires. Since we live by the Spirit, let us keep in step with the Spirit. Let us not become conceited, provoking and envying each other."

We also learn that one of those traits is submission to one another. As Tim Keller says: "In the Greek text, verse 21 is the last clause in the long previous sentence in which Paul describes several marks of a person who is "filled with the Spirit." The last mark of Spirit fullness is in this last clause: it is a loss of pride and self-will that leads a person to humbly serve others. From this Spirit-empowered submission of verse 21, Paul moves to the duties of wives and husbands. Modern Western readers immediately focus on and often bristle at the word "submit," because for us it touches the controversial issue of gender roles. But to start arguing about that is a mistake that will be fatal to any true grasp of Paul's introductory point. He is declaring that everything he is about to say about marriage assumes that the parties are being filled with God's Spirit. Only if you have learned to serve others by the power of the Holy Spirit will you have the power to face the challenges of marriage."[103]

There is a second response to our question, "How is the women's role of submission to be understood in both Scripture and culture?" That is that the wife is specifically called to submit to her husband. Ephesians 5:22 says, "Wives, submit yourselves unto your own husbands, as unto the Lord."

The basis for this role again finds its origins in creation. In Genesis 1:28 we learned that God created male and female as His image bearers and as co-heirs as Lord of the His creation. In Chapter 2, as Lord He assigns man his first major task—the naming the animals as part of that role. When he completed the task, Adam found that he was alone, to which God said it was "not good." So God set about fixing that unfortunate state by creating woman as a suitable helper for man. It should be noted that Paul later indicates that because man was created first it matters in terms of his leadership 1 Corinthians 11:8, 1 Tim. 2:13 . It is noteworthy that Paul often makes his case for women's submission by appealing to this creation order. What this does is removes his argument as simply a cultural, rabbinical argument to one ordered in creation itself.

One of the first things Adam did at seeing his delightful new companion was to name her. Hebrew scholar, Ronald Allen, says of this, "For these reasons we take most seriously the datum that the

103   Keller, Location 656.

man named the woman whom God created after him and whom God presented to him. There are some feminists today who have attempted to evade this issue. There are also some traditionalists who have pressed this too far . . . Here is the amazing thing: when the man named the woman it was with a full consciousness that although he was formed first, and although he was exercising a role of leadership in naming her, nonetheless she was from him, she was like him, she was his equal. So the man gave her a name that means the same thing his own name means. His name for her was a happy joke; it was the feminine complement of his own name."[104]

The Spirit restores the ideal God designed at creation. In Genesis we learned that at the fall sin corrupted the relationship between husband and wife. We find there the beginning of the battle for the sexes in the curse for woman. The man will rule with loveless insensitivity while the woman will resist his leadership and try to conform him to what she desires. Both sexes are impacted and both sexes suffer as a result. The Spirit of God given to every believer works in us to become more like Christ and in a sense "undoing" the effects of the curse. We find in Christ our model for the restoration of marriage.

But we should also note that submission is not a degrading term in the Christian worldview. Remember, as we saw in the Philippians 2 passage, even Jesus submitted to God the Father even though He was equal with Him. He was not inferior because He submitted. And Jesus submitted not only to the will of the Father but in doing so He submitted himself to death itself as we saw in

104   Allen, p. 112.

Philippians 2 and also in doing so Jesus submitted Himself to us. It is in Him we find our model for submission.

In the Bible, we learn that God's kingdom is upside down. To be great in God's kingdom you must be "the servant of all." As we are reminded in Mark 9:35, "Sitting down, Jesus called the Twelve and said, 'Anyone who wants to be first must be the very last, and the **servant of all**.'" Or Matthew 20:26, "Whoever wants to become great among you must be your servant."

So to suggest that the woman is called to submit to her husband should not be the central issue in understanding the passage. The issue should be, "How do we overcome the effects of sin in marriage to enable us to restore God's original intent?" Keller again speaks to this, "Immediately after discussing the Spirit-filled life, Paul turns to the subject of marriage, showing the tight connection between marriage and the life in the Spirit. And this connection teaches us two things. First, the picture of marriage given here is not of two needy people, unsure of their own value and purpose, finding their significance and meaning in one another's arms . . . After trying all kinds of other things, Christians have learned that the worship of God with the whole heart in the assurance of his love through the work of Jesus Christ is the thing their souls were meant to "run on." That is what gets all the heart's cylinders to fire. If this is not understood, then we will not have the resources to be good spouses. If we look to our spouses to fill up our tanks in a way that only God can do, we are demanding an impossibility.[105]

The evidence also bears this out. In the rapid demise of marriage in our culture, there are some groups that have resisted

---

105   Keller, Location 602.

this trend toward broken marriages. The evidence is very clear that people whose faith is very important to them stand out in the health of their marriages. Ironically most of these are devoted believers who value God's Word and His teaching about the Holy Spirit and our roles within it. If we humble ourselves before God and are controlled by the Spirit of God it will become evident in our marriages. Let us devote ourselves to walking in the Spirit.

There is a final response to our question, "How is the women's role of submission to be understood in both Scripture and culture?" and that is that the church's relationship to Christ as the model for the wife. Notice what Ephesians 5:23–24 says, "For the husband is the head of the wife, even as Christ is the head of the church; and he is the savior of the body. Therefore as the church is subject unto Christ, so let the wives be to their own husbands in everything."

Just as Christ is the head of the church so the husband is the head of the wife. In that light, I would argue that when contrasting the two roles assigned to males and females I am convinced the male has the more difficult requirement of the two. If Jesus is our model, we have a very high bar.

In defense of Paul, we find he is not the only one who argues this point. We find a very similar statement from the apostle Peter in 1 Peter 3:1, "Wives, in the same way submit yourselves to your own husbands so that, if any of them do not believe the word, they may be won over without words by the behavior of their wives . . ."

Attempts have been made to diminish the impact of this teaching by defining the Greek word *kephale*, here translated "head" to mean "source." The basis for that position is very weak and only makes sense if you have a confirmation bias. The context is clear; Jesus' headship of the church is the model for the husband over his wife. The egalitarian view, on the other hand, invites conflict in that you cannot have two heads—in any organization, no matter how small, someone must lead. In years past we taught young men that it was important to become devoted fathers and husbands who would lead, protect, and provide for their families. In contrast, young men today are taught that they have no distinct role in marriage—often implying that their primary value, if they have one at all, is to bring home the paycheck. We have seen the results of this with the breakdown of fatherhood and marriage.

The word *submit* that both Peter and Paul use has its origin in the military, and in Greek it denoted a soldier submitting to an officer. When you join the military you lose control over your schedule, over when you can take a holiday, over when you're going to eat, and even over what you eat. To be part of a whole, to become part of a greater unity, you have to surrender your independence. You must give up the right to make decisions unilaterally. But Paul says it is to be done voluntarily, not by coercion or oppression. This ability to deny your own rights, to serve and put the good of the whole over your own, is not instinctive; indeed, it's unnatural, but it is the very foundation of marriage. This sounds oppressive, but that's just the way relationships work. Indeed, it has been argued that that is how everything works. You must be willing to give something up before it can be truly yours. Fulfillment is on the far side of sustained unselfish service, not the near side. It is one of the universal principles of life.[106]

---

106   Keller, Location 790.

A. Just as the church is to obey Christ so the woman is to obey her husband. For both sexes, there is a parallel or model found in the relationship of Jesus and His church. Just as Jesus is head of the church so the male is the head of the wife. Just as the church is to obey Jesus so the woman is to obey her husband. But remember this: Jesus is the husband's model. Like Him, he leads as a servant.

B. Absent the controlling of the Holy Spirit, both roles are subject to abuse.

The Bible says that human beings were made in God's image but sin distorted that image and only the Spirit of God can restore it. We were created to worship and live for God's glory, not our own. We were made to serve God and others. That means that if we try to put our own happiness ahead of obedience to God, we violate that image and ultimately end up miserable. Jesus restates the principle when he says, "Whoever wants to save his life shall lose it, but whoever loses his life for my sake will find it" Matt. 16:25 . He is saying, "If you seek happiness more than you seek me, you will have neither; if you seek to serve me more than serve happiness, you will have both."

C.S. Lewis puts it this way, "Even in social life, you will never make a good impression on other people until you stop thinking about what sort of impression you are making. Even in literature and art, no man who bothers about originality will ever be original: whereas if you simply try to tell the truth without caring two pence how often it has been told before , you will, nine times out of ten, become original without having noticed it. The principle runs through life from top to bottom. Give up yourself, and you will find your real self. Lose your life and you will save it . . . Nothing that you have not given away will be really yours..."[10]

In this chapter we looked at three responses to the question, "How is the women's role of submission to be understood in both Scripture and culture?" We saw that while Spirit empowered submission is something all are called to, the woman is specifically called to that role based on God's design for marriage. Sin has caused that design to be distorted, making abuse possible and something only the Spirit can renew.

There is a battle raging in our culture over what should be the relationship between a male and female in marriage. The removal of the Kuyper Prize that was granted to Tim Keller is reflective of what we are facing today. It is a cause for concern because I believe there is a direct correlation between the breakdown in marriages and rejection of biblical roles in marriage.

Here are some final things to reflect on as we consider this chapter.

1. No one is refuting the reality that patriarchy in the past has led to abuses and oppression of women. Genesis tells us it is the result of sin and the curse. The problem is self-centeredness that is intrinsic to both sexes as a result of the fall.

2. Jesus gives us the model of marriage as God's design. It only makes sense that by following this model it would

---

10/ Lewis, C.S., *Mere Christianity*, Los Angelles: Green Light e-books, 2014 , location 2656.

lead to healthier, stable marriages and evidence seems to bear this out. People who see marriage as an extension of their faith have better marriages.

3. Submission, in the Christian faith, is not demeaning or a sign of inferiority. Remember Jesus Himself submitted Himself and in doing so became the sacrifice for us all.

The decline of marriage in the last four decades is astounding, but why is that? I believe the reason is this: both men and women today see marriage not as a way of creating character and community but as a way to reach personal life goals. They are all looking for a marriage partner who will "fulfill their emotional, sexual, and spiritual desires." And that creates an extreme idealism that in turn leads to deep pessimism that you will never find the right person to marry. This is the reason so many put off marriage and look right past great prospective spouses that simply are "not good enough." This is ironic. Older views of marriage are considered to be traditional and oppressive, especially for women, while the newer view of the "I-Marriage" seems so liberating. And yet it is the newer view that has led to a steep decline in marriage and to an oppressive sense of hopelessness with regard to it. To make an I-Marriage work requires two completely well-adjusted, happy individuals, with very little in the way of emotional neediness of their own or character flaws that need a lot of work. The problem is that there is almost no one like that out there to marry! The new conception of marriage-as-self-realization has put us in a position of wanting too *much* out of marriage and yet not nearly enough—at the same time.[108]

Maybe, just maybe, Paul is on to something and we can learn about the importance of submitting to God and to each other in our relationships.

---

108   Popenoe and Whitehead., *The State of Our Unions*, accessed May 10, 2018,, www.virginia.edu/ marriageproject/ pdfs/ SOOU2004. pdf. See also: Keller, Location 437.

CHAPTER 7

A TOUGH ACT TO FOLLOW

Text: *Ephesians 5:25–33*
Theme: *The husband is to love his wife as Christ loved the church.*

A rather common but not recommended comment you might hear from a frustrated parent is, "Why can't you be more like your older brother?"

Needless to say, it is intended to motivate the child to try harder and give him or her a model of what proper behavior should look like. To the child it means that you don't match up and should change. But the universal presence of sibling rivalry suggests it probably does more to create resentment than it does to motivate the unmotivated child.

Now let's take that to the extreme. Some have asked us to imagine you are James, the younger brother of Jesus how many comedy acts are built on that scenario? . Can you imagine growing up with the perfect older brother—the one who is smarter than you, who never did anything wrong, and who is better than you in every way that really counts? Let's hope Mary never said to James, "Why can't you be like your older brother?" because she knew full well who Jesus was. The fact is no one can meet that standard; it is too high. And I can imagine that sibling rivalry did come into play. The fact that James was not a follower of Jesus until after the resurrection suggests some sibling resentment may have been present in his early years.

Sometimes I feel that's what God is saying to husbands. He says to us, "Look at my Son Jesus and emulate Him." And most of us come away thinking, "Man, there is nothing like setting the bar high." Let's face it, Jesus is the Son of God. He is perfect in every respect. So, how we can also be like Him?

In this chapter, we are going to see that the model husband we are called to emulate is revealed in Jesus and how He loved the church. Now I don't know about you, but for me that is a tough act to follow, and if my wife's role in marriage were contingent upon how well I emulated Jesus' example then I would be in a world of hurt. Frankly, I don't match up. And the evidence is pretty clear that when we look at the state of marriage in North America, I am not the only one.

But by having Jesus as our model, it gives us something to frame our understanding of how marriage should work if the ideal is lived out in our relationships. Without it we have an incomplete standard to measure things by. This morning we are going to look closer at that model and ask, "How is the husband to love his wife?" We will find that we are to love as Jesus loved the church and as we love our own bodies and to be exclusively devoted to her.

I.   As Christ loved the church. (Eph. 5:25–28)

"Husbands, love your wives, just as Christ loved the church and gave himself up for her [26] to make her holy, cleansing her by the washing with water through the word, [27] and to present her to himself as a radiant church, without stain or wrinkle or any other blemish, but holy and blameless."

A.   He sacrificed his life for her. This is the component that is missed in far too many marriages. The theme of this book is that an iWorld marriage is about me, my fulfillment, my satisfaction, having my needs and wants met as though marriage is a consumer product. None of these things promotes healthy marriages. The love that builds marriages means forsaking those values for the sake of the other if the situation calls for it. That is the nature of love. Christ modeled that kind of love when died on the cross.

B.   His first objective was to make her holy. Notice why he died: to make her holy—to make her better. The emphasis is not so much on her happiness but on the far more important issue which is her spiritual state before God. One of the great ironies is that holiness will provide happiness far more than if we try to pursue happiness apart from holiness. The pursuit of holiness should be first.

We also have this absurd notion in our culture that everything is about making everyone happy. We hear it all the time: "I am okay with it as long as it makes you happy" or "I only want to make you happy!" That is an impossible task. You cannot make a person happy. Happiness can be a fleeting emotion. Lasting happiness is a state of contentment that the individual can only attain by having certain traits that come from a proper perspective. Paul expresses that perspective in Philippians 4 where he says that he "learned to be content no matter what the circumstances." It is more accurate to say, "Because I love you I want to do the things that please you and express my love in ways that you can understand—and sometimes in ways that you might not understand. But my greatest desire is that you be holy. I will do what is best for you—not for my benefit but yours—and ultimately we both benefit in our one-flesh union."

C.   He wanted to make her shine. Jesus sought to present her to Himself as a radiant bride.

This verse helps bring into perspective how the relationship between the husband as the "head" and the wife, who is called to "submit." When we grasp what Jesus seeks to do for his bride, it helps us understand our mission within our marriages. It helps us understand what it means to be "equal but different." We see the nature of this relationship in Philippians 2:2–8. In that passage, Paul speaks of the voluntary submission and "self-emptying" of Jesus to fulfill the will of the Father. This passage is one of the primary places where the relationship between the Father and the Son becomes clear. The Son submits to his Father and the Father accepts it. We also see it in the Garden of Gethsemane where Jesus struggles hours before being taken to the cross and asks the Father to take this "cup from me." At the end of each of the three prayers he concludes, "But your will be done." The voluntary submission of Jesus to the Father does not diminish His dignity or divinity— it instead leads to greater glory for both. In response to the willful submission of Jesus, the Father exalts Jesus to the highest place—name above all names. Both the Father and the Son have the major objective to exalt the other and, in doing so, both are exalted.

Keller suggests, "Each wishes to please the other; each wishes to exalt the other. Love and honor are given, accepted, and given again . . . The Son submits to the Father's headship with free, voluntary, and joyful eagerness, not out of coercion or inferiority. The Father's headship is acknowledged in reciprocal delight, respect, and love. There is no inequality of ability or dignity. In regard to marriage, this teaches us that we are differently gendered to reflect this life within the Trinity . . . This is one of the reasons why Paul can say that the marriage 'mystery' gives us insight into the very heart of God in the work of our salvation Eph. 5:32 ."[109]

What Paul is teaching in this passage was radical in light of his culture, both Jewish and pagan, and lead to a high view of women. It is inaccurate to say that Paul was a misogynist because he does not share our contemporary feminist view of women. Sociologist Rodney Stark argues that one of the reasons why Christianity spread throughout the ancient world was due to its revolutionary new attitudes towards women. He writes:

"Recent, objective evidence leaves no doubt that early Christian women did enjoy far greater equality with men than did their pagan and Jewish counterparts. A study of Christian burials in the catacombs under Rome, based on 3,733 cases, found that Christian women were nearly as likely as Christian men to be commemorated with lengthy inscriptions. This 'near equality in the commemoration of males and females is something that is peculiar to Christians and sets them apart from the non-Christian

109   Keller, 2303.

populations of the city.' This was true not only of adults but also of children, as Christians lamented the loss of a daughter as much as that of a son, which was especially unusual compared with other religious groups in Rome."[110]

The point is this: to say males and females have different roles does not demean women any more than it is to say that Jesus' submission to the Father lessens his status in the Godhead. We need to teach men to be leaders in their home, but we must remind them that Jesus provides the model of what that kind of leadership looks like. Our iWorld has taught our young men that marriage is primarily about your own personal gratification and fulfillment. This is almost the opposite of Paul is proposing.

Let us continue with our questions, "How is the husband to love his wife?"

II.   As he loves his own body. (Eph. 5:28–30)

"In this same way, husbands ought to love their wives as their own bodies. He who loves his wife loves himself. After all, no one ever hated their own body, but they feed and care for their body, just as Christ does the church—for we are members of his body."

A.   *What he thinks of himself is reflected in his love for his wife.*

Notice that Paul is suggesting men ought to love themselves— but not at the exclusion of loving his wife. In fact he seems to be

---

110   Rodney Stark, *The Triumph of Christianity: How the Jesus Movement Became the   orld's Largest Religion* San Francisco: HarperOne, 2012 , 124-125.

implying the one enhances the other. Men who have a healthy view of themselves are not more self-centered, but rather other-centered. It is insecure men who are less able to love their wives in a healthy way because they become too self-obsessed. Their self-image is filtered through their failures and shortcomings. Secure men also are not dependent on the ups and downs of their wives for their own insecurities. They do not respond to them with hostility when they go through an emotional transition. I am convinced that arrogant, controlling men do so out of insecurity, not strength.

Women, that should also say something to you. If you degrade or disrespect your husband, putting him down will not enable him to love you more. It will feed his insecurity. That does not mean that you cannot be assertive; it simply means that you should do it with respect. I think that is why Paul adds later, "However, each one of you also must love his wife as he loves himself, and the wife must respect her husband."

B. *If he truly cares for himself, he will care for his wife.*

While men's self-centeredness is often more the result of insecurity, another issue arises even if he does truly love his wife and has a proper view of himself. And that is that men are often somewhat inept at showing love in a way that their wives understand. Many men think they are showing love by going to work, putting up with all the nonsense that happens there, and bringing home a paycheck to provide for her. Most men find pride in that—and they should. But there is another level that men, in general, are not so good at. Most men are not good at expressing love in a way that their wives understand. Christian author Gary Chapman says it this way:

"We tend to speak our primary love language, and we become confused when our spouse does not understand what we are communicating. We are expressing our love, but the message does not come through because we are speaking what, to them, is a foreign language. Therein lies the fundamental problem . . . Once we discover the five basic love languages and understand our own primary love language, as well as the primary love language of our spouse, we will then have the needed information to apply to our relationships ."[III]

In his book, Chapman identifies the five love languages as

- gift giving
- quality time
- words of affirmation
- acts of service devotion
- physical touch

It is valuable if each man learns his wife's love language.

The question, "How is the husband to love his wife?" has a third response.

III. As one exclusively devoted to her. (Eph. 5:31–33)

"For this reason, a man will leave his father and mother and be united to his wife, and the two will become one flesh."[32] This is a profound mystery—but I am talking about Christ and the church.[33] However, each one of you

---

III   Gary Chapman, *The Five Love Languages: How to Express Heartfelt Commitment to Your Mate* Chicago: Northfield Publishing , 2015.

also must love his wife as he loves himself, and the wife must respect her husband."

A.   His relationship with his wife supersedes all other relationships.

You can understand best the essence of marriage by looking at the gospel. To use apostle Paul's metaphor, Jesus is the church's "Divine Spouse." Jesus doesn't ask for anything more than what any spouse asks for. "Put me first. Have no other pseudo-gods before me." Marriage won't work unless you put your relationship and your spouse before all other earthly relationships, and you don't turn good things—like parents, children, career, and hobbies—into pseudo-spouses.

Men, it is easy to let other things dominate your attention. Work can become an obsession, along with sports, video games, technology, hunting, and now a more ominous obsession—internet porn. But once you're married, your marriage has to take priority. Your marriage has the power to influence how you move throughout life and a good marriage can help you face challenges on a better footing than if you face them alone.

Paul also has in mind that the man is exclusively devoted to his wife sexually. We will address this in a later chapter when we look at the topic of "the greener grass."

B.   Being one flesh means that we do things for mutual benefit. While we cannot always please our wives—sometimes because they have issues outside our control—we must understand that if our wives are unhappy it will impact us. We cannot simply say, "That is my wife's problem." At one level that may

151

be true, but because marriage is a "one-flesh" union, if your wife has a problem, then you have a problem. And sometimes you really are the problem. Loving as Christ loves means making the ultimate sacrifice of evaluating yourself in order to consider how to become more like Him in your relationship with your wife.

C. If he does his part, he is more likely to get respect. Notice the twofold command: men love your wives; wives respect your husbands. This simple statement is more profound than first impressions may infer. Paul is addressing the two fundamental desires of each sex. The number one desire of a woman is to be loved by her husband. When she gets anger, indifference, or neglect instead, she often loses respect for him. The number one desire for men, on the other hand, is to be respected. Lack of respect is the greatest insult you can give to a man. When he gets nagging, demeaning comments, and constant criticism from his wife, he is far less prone to show the kind of love the woman most desires. As Faramir says to Sam Gamgee in *The Lord of the Rings: The Two Towers*, "The praise of the praiseworthy is above all rewards." To be highly esteemed by someone you highly esteem is the greatest thing in the world. It goes both ways.

If I had to identify the two most important passages in Scripture pertaining to marriage, I would pick these verses. In these few words, God's whole design and intent for marriage are summarized. "For this reason, a man will leave his father and mother and be united to his wife, and the two will become one flesh. This is a profound mystery—but I am talking about Christ and the church." These verses show that marriage as a union between a man and a woman is modeled in the relationship between Christ and the church. Marriage is the closest analogy to the gospel we have.

In his book *Three iews of Marriage*, New York *Times* columnist David Brooks argues that there are three different lenses through which to think about marriage decisions—the psychological, the romantic, and the moral lens. Most popular advice books adopt a psychological lens. These books start with the premise that getting married is a daunting prospect. So psychologists urge us to pay attention to traits like agreeableness, social harmony, empathy, and niceness.

The second lens is the romantic lens. This is the dominant lens in movie and song. More than people in many other countries, Americans want to marry the person they are passionately in love with. But in their book *The Good Marriage*, Judith Wallerstein and Sandra Blakeslee conclude that only fifteen percent of couples maintain these kinds of lifelong romantic marriages.

The third lens is the moral lens. In this lens, a marriage exists to serve some higher purpose. Brooks points to Tim Keller's book *The Meaning of Marriage*, in which Keller argues that marriage introduces you to yourself; you realize you're not as noble and easy to live with as you thought when alone.[112] Brooks writes:

"In a good marriage, you identify your own selfishness and see it as the fundamental problem. You treat it more seriously

---

[112] "Our Culture's Three Views of Marriage," accessed March 7, 2018. http://www.preachingtoday.com/illustrations/2016/march/5032816.html.

than your spouse's selfishness. The everyday tasks of marriage are opportunities to cultivate a more selfless love. Every day there's a chance to inspire and encourage your partner to become his or her best self. In this lens, marriage isn't about two individuals trying to satisfy their own needs; it's a partnership of mutual self-giving for the purpose of moral growth and to make their corner of the world a little better."[113]

In this chapter, we looked at the question, "How is the husband to love his wife?" We found in today's passage that, as men, we are to love our wives as Jesus loved the church and as we love our own bodies while being exclusively devoted to her.

One can only imagine what it would have been like to have been James, the brother of Jesus, having to compare himself to the perfect older brother. Yet in a sense that is what God is saying to us men. "Why can't you be more like Jesus?"

What does that mean for us?

1. The fact is we will never fully achieve that standard because we are not God. But it gives us the ideal for what marriage should look like. Jesus provides for us something objective to measure progress by giving us a perfect model, a standard, to strive for in marriage.

2. The contrast is stark. In an "iWorld" the focus is on me and my personal gratification and fulfillment so if we both have that, great; if not, then we part ways. In God's kingdom, the focus is on loving God and our wives even

113 "Three Views of Marriage," *The New York Times* online. Last modified February 23, 2016. https://www.nytimes.com/2016/02/23/opinion/three-views-of-marriage.html.

if they are not always submissive or loveable. It may mean tremendous sacrifice on our part. It may mean we give our lives for her.

3. How that sacrifice is lived out is different for men and women, but both do it for the mutual benefit of the one-flesh covenant that God has joined together. It is no different than that of the relationship within the Godhead itself where Jesus voluntarily submits to Father who then exacts Him to a place of greater honor.

Kevin Miller has provided the following story regarding Bible scholar and pastor N.T. Wright. Wright retells the story about an archbishop who was hearing confessions of sin from three hardened teenagers in the church. All three boys were trying to make a joke out of it, so they met with the archbishop and confessed to a long list of ridiculous and grievous sins that they had not committed. It was all a joke. The archbishop, seeing through their bad practical joke, played along with the first two who ran out of the church laughing. But then he listened carefully to the third prankster, and before he got away, told the young man, "Okay, you have confessed these sins. Now I want you to do something to show your repentance. I want you to walk up to the far end of the church and I want you to look at the picture of Jesus hanging on the cross, and I want you to look at his face and say, 'You did all that for me and I don't care that much.' And I want you to do that three times."

And so the boy went up to the front, looked at the picture of Jesus and said, "You did all that for me and I don't care that much." And then he said it again. But he couldn't say it the third time because he broke down in tears. And the archbishop telling the story said, "The reason I know that story is because I was that young man."

There is something about the cross. Something about Jesus dying there for us which leaps over all the theoretical discussions, all the possibilities of how we explain it this way or that way and it grasps us. And when we are grasped by it, somehow we have a sense that what is grasping us is the love of God."[114]

Men, if we look to Jesus as our example for how we are to love our wives, this story tells it well. If we look at Jesus' love for us, it should change us and how we relate to our wives.

114   "Grasped By the Love of God," *N.T. right* online, accessed March 12, 2018. http://ntwrightonline.org/grasped-love-god/.

CHAPTER 8

FAIRY TALE MARRIAGES: THE HIDDEN DANGERS OF ROMANTIC LOVE

Text: *Song of Solomon*
Theme: *hen romance supersedes covenant as the central bond of marriage the stability of that relationship is subject to our emotional whims.*

There is a phrase that has bothered me somewhat over the years. It is one most of us have heard often and is well entrenched in our attitudes about love. It is the phrase, "I have fallen in love." Now at the surface, you might wonder why anyone could be bothered by that. I mean, who wouldn't want someone to fall in love and the euphoria that goes with it? And at one level I would agree. But at another level, my more cynical self asks, "If you can fall in love, who is to say that you cannot just as readily fall out of love?"

Let's face it, love in this sense can be a fickle thing. To make the point, how often do we also hear the phrase, "I don't love him/her anymore?" This phrase is often used to justify divorce or a breakup of a relationship. In some cases it is used when a spouse has become boring and predictable, or when someone else seems more appealing than their spouse, or sometimes the tingly feeling you once felt is gone and you have little hope of it returning. It is as though love is something we have little control over. It is like an unexpected accident like, "I was walking down the road and I stumbled over something and, oops, I fell in love."

Yet this is the dominant criteria that people today use to select a spouse. If two people love each other, then what should keep them from marrying, right? Or for that matter, why shouldn't they feel free to have sex—that is if they love it other. I mean, if two people are in love, how can it be wrong? Especially if it is "true love." Forget all the red flags that pop up along the way—love will get us through them. But when you realize the red flags were important warnings of what is to come, that tingly feeling can go away. Some of us are lucky and that love only grows deeper as time goes on, but there are no guarantees. And it may be that it grows deeper because they have a more realistic view of love. That is where love must be more an act of the will as it is the whim of an emotion and, in that, we find our problem.

In a previous chapter we discussed stages of a relationship, with romantic love often being the first stage of a relationship lasting only a few years—at best. It is an ecstatic feeling that can even be one-sided and is often grounded in an idealistic fantasy of the person but is not the real person. Our modern concept of love centers on romance. As one blog reminds us, "The word comes from medieval times and suggests love, adventure, scenic beauty, improbability, or make-believe. One ingredient of the romances of medieval times is the all-too-familiar fairytale element. *Romantic* in our current culture could be described as the opposite of logical. *Romantic*—possessing a whimsical, creative, and imaginative approach taken by that of a dreamer. While logic being a more rational, calculating, and realistic worldview."[115] This kind of love, while pleasant, does not guarantee a lasting relationship.

Like other pastors, over the years I have officiated or observed the marriage of quite a few people and with it have seen a significant change in the nature of the couple's wedding vows. In years past the focus of the vow was on the promise to love, honor, and cherish until death do us part. For the woman, it was common to even hear the words love, honor, and *obey* a word seldom heard in modern vows . More recently vows have taken a different expression. Vows now more often express their current love for each other. They tell the other of how special they are, how they make them feel, and how they want this feeling to last forever. The focus is on the love that is "now," with only the hope that it will remain throughout their lives.[116]

Now, all that is fine and moving, but does it really capture what a marriage vow is all about? The purpose of the vows is to make a binding promise of mutual love *until death do us part*. It is future-focused. What love you share now is secondary to the pledge to love throughout the relationship that ends only at death. It is a public pledge you make to everyone present and is recognized by the state. You are promising love and faithfulness even when your feelings of love are tested beyond anything you could now imagine. And most likely, they will be tested.

---

115   http://www.classichistory.net/archives/romantic.

116   See Keller, 139.

This new reality speaks volumes about this fickle basis for marriage today. In the prologue of this book on the state of marriage in North America, I showed the exponential increase in divorce, cohabitation and non-marital births, and the more contemporary and common practice of "friends with benefits"—referring to short-term sexual encounters. Since the '60s the dominant view is that marriage is essentially a private matter, an affair of the heart between two adults, in which no outsider should be allowed to interfere. Marriage is primarily for and about adult happiness. If the benefits are absent for even one party, then divorce becomes a valid option. In that most marriages today are built on a notion that romantic love, then the basis for marriage ceases to exist when that kind of love is absent.[11/]

Romantic love has always been around. An ancient book, the Song of Songs or Song of Solomon , reminds us of its universal appeal. It is kind of the Cinderella story of the Bible. But the modern Cinderella story ends where most fairytales end, which is at the wedding. We learn only that they lived happily ever after. We learn nothing of the marriage itself and the nitty-gritty stuff that makes a marriage work. It seems the fairytale ends where reality begins.

From the Song of Songs, we learn that romantic love is a wonderful gift of God, but it should lead us to something deeper and more permanent. That something is a covenantal love that goes beyond the emotional whims of romantic love to a one that is modeled in Jesus Himself—who loves us even when we are otherwise unlovable e.g., Rom. 5:10 .

11/   Ibid.

The Song of Songs is unique in the Bible. There is nothing explicitly spiritual about it and God is never mentioned in it. It does not use rich theological terms or expand on deep doctrinal insights. Neither are lots of other things you think you should find in the Bible. The order of the book is hard to follow, and the sexual content of the book is graphic, so that at certain times in history, young people were forbidden from reading the book. For these reasons, some even questioned whether the book should be included in the Bible.

The book has generally been portrayed as an allegory of God's love for Israel, or even the church's love for Christ. But it is most likely simply a collection of love songs, celebrating romantic love—something common in ancient literature and much like it is today. The title suggests that of all such songs, this is the best of songs like King of Kings or Holy of Holies.

It's more like a collection of songs centering on the wedding night and the sexual consummation of love by a bride and bridegroom. It may even be that the book had been written and performed for a wedding. In the book we find three singers—the bride, the bridegroom, and a chorus. As the book unfolds, the characters reflect upon that wedding night.[118]

As we look at this book I want us to ask, "What does the Song of Solomon teach us about love?" We learn first that:

---

118   Bryan Wilkerson, "A Sacred Romance," accessed March 7, 2018. http://www.preachingtoday.com/sermons/sermons/2006/february/ sacredromance022006a.html.

I. **Romantic love is a wonderful gift from God. (Chapters 1, 2)**

A. *It gives us pleasure.*

The book opens with the bride saying, "Let him kiss me with the kisses of his mouth—for your love is more delightful than wine." The song is telling us that one of the reasons love is so wonderful is that it is delightful, even more delightful than wine, and the kiss is an expression of that love. She eagerly wants to be kissed passionately and tenderly by the one she loves. Notice what else she says.

In verse 3 she says, "Pleasing is the fragrance of your perfumes, your name is like perfume poured out." When you pour out a vial of perfume the fragrance fills the whole room. It's the only thing you can smell. That's what happens every time she thinks of her lover—he dominates her every thought.

Verse 4 says, "Take me away with you—let us hurry! The king has brought me into his

chambers!" She fantasizes about running away with her lover and being alone with him for the night. We don't know if she is anticipating her wedding night or remembering it, but the point is she can think of nothing better than being with him.

B. *It reveals our value and potential to the one who loves us.*

In verse 6 the bride says, "Do not stare at me because I am dark because I am darkened by the sun. My mother's sons were angry with me and made me take care of the vineyards; my own vineyard I have neglected." Like many young women, the bride is self-conscious about her appearance. Her darkened skin suggests she was of humble origins accustomed to working in the fields.[119]

Like the rest of us, this woman is insecure about her desirability and attractiveness. We find she is stuck at home to work in the vineyards. She didn't have much of a life so she wants to be taken away by a lover who will allow her to become a woman, to be sexually fulfilled, to have a home and family of her own. Now, her lover, her prince says to her, "If you do not know, most beautiful of women . . ." He thinks she's desirable and wants her, and with these words her insecurities begin to fade away. He goes on in verse 9, "I liken you, my darling, to a mare, harnessed to one of the chariots of Pharaoh." You have to remember this is ancient poetry—in its day, that would be a compliment. It is not something I would advise using as a pickup line today. But it does show how he sees her and values her.

He goes on and says, "Your cheeks are beautiful with earrings, your neck with strings of jewels. We will make you earrings of gold, studded with silver." He sees both her outer and inner beauty. To him she is a princess, and he wants to show the world how beautiful she is. When you love someone and are loved in return, it brings things out of you that you didn't know were there. You're free to be your best self. That's the power, the wonder of love. It releases our beauty and potential.[120]

---

119   Ibid.

120   Ibid.

C. *It points us to an ideal that real life can never fully satisfy in a way that lasts.*

We rightfully love Cinderella stories like this. It is no wonder that romantic songs and movies dominate the media. But there is a limitation with romantic love, in that while it is a wonderful gift of God, it seldom can be maintained at its peak intensity. Life happens, distractions occur, the true person is revealed, and the flaws that we were once blinded to can soon dominate. The fantasy subsides and the real person comes out. Many become disappointed and disillusioned, feeling they were betrayed or let down.

The romance phase allows us to see each other's value and what could be. But the reason it often disappoints is that it is only a shadow of the essence of a deeper love. The world as it is now is a world of spoiled goodness—a world of decay that can only point us to something better. We live in a world of shadows that points us to a brighter world free of evil, free of pain, free of death. Romance is one of those glimpses of what that world will look like.

Paul reminds us of this in Romans 8:18–21, "I consider that our present sufferings are not worth comparing with the glory that will be revealed in us. The creation waits in eager expectation for the children of God to be revealed. For the creation was subjected to frustration, not by its own choice, but by the will of the one who subjected it, in hope that the creation itself will be liberated from its bondage to decay and brought into the glorious freedom of the children of God."

That longing in our heart is a longing that ultimately only God can fulfill. As C.S. Lewis states, "It would seem that our Lord finds our desires not too strong, but too weak. We are half-hearted creatures, fooling about with drink and sex and ambition when infinite joy is offered us, like an ignorant child who wants to go on making mud pies in a slum because he cannot imagine what is meant by the offer of a holiday at the sea. We are far too easily pleased."[121]

Our craving for romance often falls short of the ideal and can lead to some awkward or humorous moments. I am reminded of a story of a young man in a bygone era who took his favorite girl home at the end of their first date. He decided to try for that important first kiss. With an air of confidence, he leaned his hand against the wall, smiled, and said:

"How about a goodnight kiss?"

"Are you crazy?" she asked. "My parents will see us!"

"Oh, come on! Who's gonna see us at this hour?" he replied.

"No, please. Can you imagine if we get caught?"

"Come on, they're all sleeping!"

"No way. It's too risky!"

"Please, please, please. I like you so much."

"No, no, no. I like you too, but I just can't!"

"Oh yes, you can. Please?"

"No, no. I just can't."

"Pleeeeease? . . ."

Then to their surprise, the porch light went on, the door opened, and there stood the girl's sister, hair disheveled, in her

---

[121] C.S. Lewis, *The eight of Glory, and Other Addresses* New York: The Macmillan Company , 1942.

pajamas. In a sleepy voice, she said, "Dad says to go ahead and give him a kiss. Or I can do it. If need be, dad will come down himself and do it. Whatever you do, tell your date to take his hand off the intercom button."[122]

The first kiss of a romance carries with it many delightful and pleasurable emotions. But it is not always the idea we imagine and does not always prepare us for the obstacles that soon ensue.

In that light our question, "What does the Song of Solomon teach us about love?" has a second response.

II. Covenantal love is a decision to love regardless of our emotional whims. (Chapters 3-5)

A. *Romantic love has the potential to set us up for pain and disillusionment.*

In chapter 3 we find the bride sharing a recurring anxiety-inducing dream that brings her pain. She says in verse 1, "All night long on my bed I looked for the one my heart loves; I looked for him but did not find him." The search becomes intense and painful. Maybe she's afraid something might happen to him or their relationship. What if he loses interest? What if they have a falling out? What if someone or something comes between them and keeps them from getting married? Or it could be that she is remembering the anxiety she felt before she met him.[123]

---

122   Keith Todd, "The First Kiss," accessed March 7, 2018. http://www.preachingtoday.com/illustrations/2002/july/13/41.html.

123   Bryan Wilkerson, "A Holy Longing," accessed March 7, 2018. https://www.preachingtoday.com/sermons/sermons/2006/february/sacredromance022006c.html.

We know what she's going through. Every human being yearns to love and to be loved and has faced the uncertainty of romantic fickleness. We want to be held by someone who cares about us deeply. Aside from the need for food and shelter, love is the fundamental craving of the human heart. "It is not good for the man to be alone," God says. But that craving can also be the basis for intense anxiety and disappointment. Pain is a risk we take in all relationships because we have no control how the other may respond, but because romantic love is built on a fleeting emotion, it is more prone to disappoint.

B. *Romantic love focuses on the satisfaction the other person gives.*

Our culture values romantic love and the satisfaction we find from it, but it alone cannot sustain a marriage. Our contemporary conviction that romantic love is the central bond of marriage and is a "must have" to live a fulfilled is a setup. An unfulfilled craving for romantic love means you will always have a degree of insecurity in a relationship, because you are constantly looking to them to affirm you and fill your emotional void. It leads to the belief that the absence of romance means we are doomed to a hollow relationship, and that belief is incompatible with our iWorld view of marriage. Ultimately, another person cannot satisfy your emotional void—that is something that only God can provide.

C. *Covenantal love is a choice to love a person even when the emotional satisfaction may be absent.*

The irony of covenantal love is that a marriage relationship is more intimate and secure because it is permanent. It provides a richer context for romantic love to thrive. You don't have to keep questioning whether that person loves you—a vow has been made and it will not be broken because it is an act of the will. It is a choice. While romantic love can be fickle, covenantal love provides a lasting commitment that makes marriage what it should be.

The biblical perspective is radically different from the fickleness of romantic love. Is it any wonder that the once-obscure Greek word *agape* became the primary word for love in the New Testament? The central meaning of the word *agape* came to mean a sacrificial love that is an act of the will and loves an object that may be otherwise unlovable. It seeks the best for the object loved and that love is not contingent on a reciprocal relationship. It is the kind of love Christ showed when He loved us even while we were yet sinners.

For a culture that's bought into the photoshopped notion that romance equals euphoria, or blissful self-fulfillment, or nonstop infatuation, writer Heather Havrilesky offers the following advice on true romance. She says:

"After a decade of marriage . . . I'm going to tell you my most romantic story of all. I was very sick out of the blue with some form of dysentery. It hit overnight. I got up to go to the bathroom, and I fainted on the way and cracked my ribs on the side of the bathtub. My husband discovered me there, passed out, in a scene that . . . well, think about what that might look like . . . My husband was not happy about this scene. But he handled it without complaint. That is the very definition of romantic: not only not being made to feel crappy about things that are clearly out of your control but being quietly cared for by someone who can shut up and do what needs to be done under duress . . ."[124]

That story illustrates the nitty-gritty of what makes a relationship work. It is the kind of love that brings us through the daily hardships and setbacks of life and may not bring with it feelings that we generally associate with romance.

Now let us look at our final response to our question, "What does the Song of Solomon teach us about love?"

III. The search for love should ultimately lead us back to God. (Chapters 6-8)

A.   God provides the model of covenantal love.

As the Song of Songs continues to develop its theme, what we begin to see unfold is that the bridegroom's love helps the bride past her insecurities and anxieties. Their love encounters obstacles that keep them away and threaten the fiber of their relationship. But in his love, she finds security because he sees beyond her flaws and into the core of her being. It is something that is deeper than the temporary euphoric feeling of romance.[125]

It is little wonder then that for much of history this book has been read as an allegory of God's love for his people, whether it be Israel or the church. The book reveals the ideal of romantic love and how it is expressed by two lovers, but it points us to something

---

124   Heather Havrilesky, "What Romance Really Looks Like After 10 Years of Marriage," accessed March 7, 2018, https://www.thecut.com/2016/02/what-romance-means-after-10-years-of-marriage.html.

125   Allan Ross, *The Expositors Commentary: Proverbs, Ecclesiastes, Song of Songs* Chicago: Zondervan, 2008 .

richer than the fickle emotions that currently drive our relationships. We see the ideal of love fulfilled in ways that ultimately only God can express. Like the book, we see these qualities revealed in God.

1. His model shows us that His love looks past a person's flaws to love us even while we are rebellious sinners. While He craves to see us return love to Him in response, His love is not dependent on it. He is always ready to receive us back.

2. His model shows us that we are best fulfilled by sacrificially loving another. This is the lost element of love that our culture has abandoned. In God's love, the fulfillment is not in what He receives but in what He gives. He gives his life as a demonstration of His love and, in that, finds the fulfillment of His purpose.

3. His model shows us we can love a person beyond our emotional whims. Love is not driven by the ups and downs of our daily emotions or difficulties. It is grounded in the covenant, not in the feeling.

B. God loves us even we do not merit it. This is the greatest reward of them all. Like God, we do not give love because the recipient deserves it just as we do not get love because we deserve it. It is not earned. Just as there is nothing more valuable in existence than God, those who bear God's image are of immense value and worth. When we see the intrinsic value in others because they bear that image, we can love them independent of their merits.

In years passed we expected marriage and family to provide love, support, and security; for meaning in life, hope for the future, a moral compass, and self-identity, we looked to God and the afterlife. Today, however, our culture has taught us to believe that no one can be sure those things even exist. Something has to fill the gap, so we look to sex and romance to give us what we used to get from faith in God. On this matter Ernest Becker writes: "The love partner becomes the divine ideal within which to fulfill one's life. All spiritual and moral needs now become focused in one individual . . . In one word, the love object is God . . . Man reached for a "thou" when the worldview of the great religious community overseen by God died . . . After all, what is it that we want when we elevate the love partner to the position of God? We want redemption—nothing less."[126]

And so it is. We have allowed romance to replace God to find purpose and meaning and it has proved to be a fickle and failed substitute for what only God can fulfill.

In this chapter we learned that romantic love is a wonderful gift of God, but it should lead us to something deeper and permanent—a covenantal love that is modeled in Jesus Himself who loves us even when we are otherwise unlovable. When we make our vows at a wedding, they need to focus on the commitment "until death do us part." The euphoria of romantic love may be tested beyond any expectation and apart from the covenantal love of God, most marriages will not survive.

---

126 Ernest Becker, *The Denial of Death* New York: Free Press, 1973 , 160.

Some thoughts to close with:

1. "To last for the long haul and through the stresses and complexities of life, love has to be more than something we feel. It has to be something we do. We have to demonstrate it concretely in our marriage."[12/] Love must be a choice that overrides our emotions.

2. Romance is a wonderful gift of God that points us to something that ultimately only God can provide. We set ourselves up for failure and disappointment if we let it replace Him.

3. God is waiting patiently for you to say yes to Him. He longs for your love in response to His.

A sermon by Ted Danson relates the following story told at Janet Kidd's funeral. "Tedd Kidd was five years older than Janet, finished college before her, and he started to work in a city hundreds of miles away from her. They always seemed to be at different places in their lives. But they had been dating for seven years. Every Valentine's Day, Tedd proposed to her. Every Valentine's Day, Janet would say, "No, not yet."

Finally, when they were both living in Dallas, Texas, Tedd reached the end of his patience. He bought a ring, took Janet to a romantic restaurant, and was prepared to reinforce his proposal with the diamond. Another "no" would mean he had to get on with his life without her.

12/   Gary Chapman, *Love is a erb: Stories of hat Happens hen Love Comes Alive* Bloomington: Bethany House, 2010 , 12.

After the salad, entree, and dessert, it was time. Tedd summoned up his courage. Knowing that Janet had a gift for him, however, he decided to wait. "What did you bring me?" he asked. She handed him a box the size of a book. He opened the package and slowly peeled away the tissue paper. It was a cross-stitch Janet had made that simply said, "Yes." Yes: it is the word that God, in his tireless pursuit of the sinner, longs to hear."[128]

Is it any wonder that God uses marriage to illustrate his love for us? In regard to love, it is easy to get our priorities out of whack. God wants us to love Him first and foremost, and He wants us to love Him in the same way he loves us—with a sacrificial love. I believe that when we say yes to God it enables us to put other relationships into perspective where we can enjoy the delights of romantic love, but we do not depend on it to carry us through the ups and downs of life.

---

128   Shelly Rubel, "The Holy Spirit," last modified December 24, 2015. http://www.waynedaleumc.com/Dec242015Sermon.

CHAPTER 9

THE IMPOSSIBLE UNWRITTEN CONTRACTS OF MARRIAGE

Text: *Romans 7:1-8:4*
Theme: *e find greater peace in our marriages when our expectations are tempered by grace.*

There is a popular commercial series that has a character named Captain Obvious. One of the common themes of the commercials is that the internet pictures and information on the hotel you booked does not always match up with what you really get.

I can relate quite well to that. I can remember my wife, Vaunda, and I made a trip to California last year and stayed at a motel in Great Falls, Montana. Looking at the information on the website lead us to believe it was a decent, moderately priced motel. But when we got there, we discovered it was a dive. It had a bad smell, was dated and worn, and seemed to be a haven for drug addicts. We had booked the same motel for our return, but we changed it when we saw what it was.

There are many areas of life like that—where what we expect and the reality of what we get do not match up. You have probably faced this when you order something online, or when paying big bucks for a product that is defective, or you have work done on a house or car and the result is subpar.

The same can be true of marriage. We start off in the marriage with high ideals and dreams, and we begin to discover that the person we have married has weaknesses and hang-ups we did not bargain for. Sometimes you may even have seen the red flags but thought that through love and encouragement the person would change or, at least, you could overlook them. You thought you married a prince only to discover he is a frog.

Alicia Michelle says it this way, "We develop these unrealistic expectations of how our marriage should be and especially how our husbands 'should' treat us . And on days when real married-life is less than ideal, we imagine how our fantasy-spouse—let's call him *Prince Charming*—would act in that moment. Prince Charming gives the 'perfect' answer for your feelings, right? He says things like: 'Oh, honey, you're so right. Let me draw you a bath and give you a neck massage as you tell me all about it.' Prince Charming knows exactly what we need and is more than happy to give it to us giftwrapped with a lovely red bow. He is completely selfless and at our beck and call."[129]

Prince Charming has tricked many a woman about how their husbands should treat them. He is an idealized man who can slowly and inadvertently destroy the beautiful walls of your marriage. Similarly, men also have their unrealistic perspectives

129   Alicia Michelle, "Are Unrealistic Expectations Ruining Your Marriage?" accessed March 12, 2017. http://yourvibrantfamily.com/unrealistic-expectations-marriage.

of how their wives should be. In light of that, we could write a formula: unhappiness = high expectations compared to reality. The greater the gulf between the fantasy ideal and the reality, the greater the frustration and unhappiness you will find in marriage.

God understands the issue of unmet expectations. I want us to look at how to overcome our ideals and often unrealistic views of our spouses that can damage a relationship by looking at how God chooses to deal with us. We will ask, "What can the doctrine of grace teach us about dealing with the expectations we have in marriage?

I. The law is like a marriage that does not consider our weakness. (Rom. 7:1–20[130])

"Do you not know, brothers and sisters—for I am speaking to those who know the law—that the law has authority over someone only as long as that person lives? For example, by law, a married woman is bound to her husband as long as he is alive, but if her husband dies, she is released from the law that binds her to him. So then, if she has sexual relations with another man while her husband is still alive, she is called an adulteress. But if her husband dies, she is released from that law and is not an adulteress if she marries another man. So, my brothers and sisters, you also died to the law through the

---

[130]   Ray Ortlund, "Who are you married to?" last modified February 20, 2015. https://www.thegospelcoalition.org/blogs/ray-ortlund/who-are-you-married-to.

body of Christ, that you might belong to another, to him who was raised from the dead, in order that we might bear fruit for God . . . ⁷What shall we say, then? Is the law sinful? Certainly not! Nevertheless, I would not have known what sin was had it not been for the law. For I would not have known what coveting really was if the law had not said, 'You shall not covet.' . . . We know that the law is spiritual, but I am unspiritual, sold as a slave to sin. I do not understand what I do. For what I want to do I do not do, but what I hate I do. ¹⁶And if I do what I do not want to do, I agree that the law is good. As it is, it is no longer I myself who do it, but it is sin living in me."

A. *Like a marriage, the law has many demands and expectations.*

Ray Ortlund describes it this way, "We were once married to Mr. Law. He was a good man, in his way, but he did not understand our weakness. He came home every evening and asked, 'So, how was your day? Did you do what I told you to? Did you make the kids behave? Did you waste any time? Did you complete everything I put on your to-do list?' So many demands and expectations. And hard as we tried, we couldn't be perfect. We could never satisfy him . . . And the worst of it was, he was always right! But his remedy was always the same: do better tomorrow. We didn't because we couldn't."[131]

---

131   Ibid.

B. *It demands change but cannot produce the change it demands.*

That is also the problem with so many of our expectations in marriage. They may very well be good, but they are often unrealistic and cannot produce what it requires. The fact is, we are flawed and imperfect beings who cannot even live up to our own standards, much less yours or God's. Change in a person cannot be coerced, manipulated, or dictated. Change is hard in even the best of circumstances, but these often-unrealistic expectations do not make it easier. "Ought" does not mean "can." If it were true that "ought" meant "can," we would have very few alcoholics or drug addicts.

Another issue is that unlike the Old Testament law, many of these marital expectations are unwritten. They are like contracts that only one party has signed and, like the law, the penalties can be strict. Internalized anger, frustration, and disappointment will always bleed out in our relationships. At the very least, we need to state what the expectation is, so they know what criteria they are being judged by. None of us can read minds. If you cannot verbalize or clarify it, then the problem is yours to deal with.

C. *The law reveals our failings, leading to condemnation and hopelessness.*

The person who fails to meet your expectations often feels defeated and abandons hope that they can ever meet the expectation—so they give up and become emotionally distant. The constant demand that it be met only deepens the problem—even if the expectation is fair and realistic, and you believe change is possible. In our iWorld, the impact of these unwritten expectations has increased because we no longer have culturally defined roles for each partner in the relationship, and each partner is primarily concerned with their own fulfillment and satisfaction.

The problem with the Old Testament law is that we won't fulfill its demands because we can't—the standard is too high. That was the problem with the law, and that is the problem with many of our own expectations—they are unrealistic, demanding, and require great effort to change.

In a popular TED talk titled "The Secret to Desire in a Long-Term Relationship," psychotherapist Esther Perel, who has counseled hundreds of couples experiencing trouble in their marriages, notes how we tend to expect too much from our husbands and wives. Dr. Perel says, "Marriage [used to be primarily] an economic institution in which you were given a partnership for life in terms of children and social status and succession and companionship. But now we want our partner to still give us all these things but, in addition, I want you to be my best friend and my trusted confidant and my passionate lover to boot; and we live twice as long. So we come to one person, and we basically are asking them to give us what once an entire village used to provide: give me belonging, give me identity, give me continuity, but give me transcendence and mystery and awe all in one. Give me comfort, give me edge. Give me novelty, give me familiarity. Give me predictability, give me surprise."[132]

Obviously, this applies to marriage, but substitute the word *God* for the words *an entire village* and this quote also fits

132   Dr. Esther Perel, "The Secret Desire in a Long-term Relationship," quoted by David Zahl, "Infidelity, Love, and the New Shame,' *Mockingbird*, 2015.

an illustration about idolatry. So what can we do? The Serenity Prayer provides us some insight. The best-known form is: God, grant me the serenity to accept the things I cannot change, courage to change the things I can, and wisdom to know the difference.

Our second response the question, "What can the doctrine of grace teach us about dealing with the expectations we have in marriage?" is found Romans 7:21–8:4

II. Grace is like a marriage that loves in spite of our weaknesses. (Rom. 7:21–8:4)

"So I find this law at work: Although I want to do good, evil is right there with me. For in my inner being I delight in God's law; but I see another law at work in me, waging war against the law of my mind and making me a prisoner of the law of sin at work within me. What a wretched man I am! Who will rescue me from this body that is subject to death? Thanks be to God, who delivers me through Jesus Christ our Lord! So then, I myself in my mind am a slave to God's law, but in my sinful nature a slave to the law of sin. Therefore, there is now no condemnation for those who are in Christ Jesus, because through Christ Jesus the law of the Spirit who gives life has set you free from the law of sin and death. For what the law was powerless to do because it was weakened by the flesh, God did by sending his own Son in the likeness of sinful flesh to be a sin offering."

A. *Grace wants the best for us and produces it from the inside.*

God now relates to his children on the basis of grace—not law. To continue with what Ray Ortlund stated: "Mr. Law died. And we remarried, this time to Mr. Grace. Our new husband, Jesus, comes home every evening and the house is a mess, the children are being naughty, dinner is burning on the stove, and we have even had other men in the house during the day. Still, he sweeps us into his arms and says, 'I love you, I chose you, I died for you, I will never leave you nor forsake you.' And our hearts melt. We don't understand such love. We expect him to despise us and reject us and humiliate us, but he treats us so well. We are so glad to belong to him now and forever, and we long to be 'fully pleasing to him' Col. 1:10 . Being married to Mr. Law never changed us. But being married to Mr. Grace is changing us deep within, and it shows.[133]

Let us be clear. Grace is not the absence of expectations or ruling principles. God's holiness is still in effect. But it is how we are treated by Him even when the expectations of the law are not met. He treats us as He does Jesus. It changes the motive for why we try to meet His standards. It is no longer out of fear of reprisal but as one who wants to please the one who already loves us deeply and accepts us through Jesus. In other words, God does not say, "Be good and I will save you." He says, "I have saved you through faith in Jesus Christ, therefore, be good." It changes the whole motivation for pleasing God. And that becomes our model for our marriages.

B.   *Grace treats us far better than we deserve.*

More often than not we merit the judgment that we are receiving. Sometimes we do stupid things deserving of

---

133   Ortlund.

condemnation and we often wonder, "What was I thinking?" There is a story about Alice Pike who got arrested for trying to pay for her Walmart purchases with a $1 million bill. When hearing that, two questions come to mind. First, "Is there really a $1 million bill?" and, second, "What was she thinking?" The answer to the first question is no. The U.S. Treasury doesn't make a bank note with that many zeros. As far as the second question, what Alice was thinking—I don't believe she was. Alice went to the register with $1,675 worth of stuff. What is amazing is that she expected change. Was Alice really expecting that the cashier not only would, but actually could, hand over $998,325?[134]

Alice helps remind us of the irrationality of sin. Most sin doesn't make sense. We lie and expect good results. We overindulge in food or alcohol or entertainment and expect to feel better. We take what isn't ours and expect satisfaction. We refuse to resist temptation and expect peace. We act selfishly and expect stronger relationships. We ignore repentance and expect forgiveness.[135]

C. Grace gives us hope and frees us to do our best.

The marriage "contract" is like the contract we have between Christ and the church. God deals with us on the basis of grace. This "contract" is relational. It is driven by seeking the best for the person loved. In order words, Christ models for us how we are to relate to flawed, sinful people who fail to meet our expectations.

---

134 "And $998,328.45 Is Your Change," last modified March 24, 2016. http://nowiknow.com/and-998328-45-is-your-change/.

135 John Beukema, *Preaching Today.*

D. *The remedy is: die to self and take on a new life in Christ.*

John Shea puts it this way, "Whenever people expend themselves, they want results. If they lay down life, they want someone's life raised up. If they empty themselves, they want someone to be filled. They want their sufferings to bear fruit. If this doesn't happen, they're tempted to give up. The refusal of the gift quickly becomes a reason not to offer it. Instead of leaning into resistance with love, they'll back off and say, 'Well, we tried.' However, the motive for offering love is not that it be successful. Christians want a response, but they are not bound by it. They sacrifice for others because they are the recipients of sacrifice. They are the current generation of a long line of broken bodies and shed blood. This gift Christians have received, they freely give. They join the living history in enacting the dream of God, [which] is a people sustained and transformed by mutual sacrificial love."[136]

Problem: until we abandon our pride we will never be free.

Historian Daniel Boorstin suggests that Americans suffer from all-too-extravagant expectations. In his much-quoted book *The Image*, Boorstin makes this observation of Americans:

"We expect anything and everything. We expect the contradictory and the impossible. We expect compact cars which are spacious; luxurious cars which are economical. We expect to be rich and charitable, powerful and merciful, active and reflective, kind and competitive . . . We expect to eat and stay thin, to be constantly on the move and ever more neighborly, to go to a 'church

---

136   Fr. John Shea, "U.S. Catholic," *Christianity Today*, 1990, 34, no. 7.

of our choice' and yet feel its guiding power over us, to revere God and to be God. Never have people been more the masters of their environment. Yet never has a people felt more deceived and disappointed. For never has a people expected so much more than the world could offer."[13/]

The only way out of this trap is to stop expecting too much from our spouses. Define your expectations and ask, "Is this realistic to expect, and if so how do I confront and encourage him/her to address it? But marriage must first be about the sacrificial nature that Christ shared with us. Love means we relate to each other on the basis of grace, not law.

Our final response to the question, "What can the doctrine of grace teach us about dealing with the expectations we have in marriage?" is:

III. We need to deal with our marital expectations the way God deals with us.

Phillip Yancey cites an example of this in relation to sex. He says, "Marriage strips away the illusions about sex pounded into us daily by the entertainment media. Few of us live with oversexed supermodels. We live instead with ordinary people, men and women who get bad breath, body odors, and unruly hair; who menstruate and experience occasional impotence; who have bad moods and embarrass us in public; who pay more attention to our children's needs than our own. We live with people who require compassion, tolerance, understanding, and an endless supply of forgiveness. So do our partners. Such is the ironical power of sex:

13/   Barry Morrow, Yearning for More Chicago: IVP Books, 2013 , 19-20.

It lures us into a relationship that offers to teach us what we need far more—sacrificial love."[138]

Scott Larsen tells this story, "I remember being approached by a sixteen-year-old boy named Ricky after I wrapped up my first speaking session at a weekend retreat for high schoolers. 'I just hope you're not heading down a path where at the end of the weekend you're going to ask us to make some kind of commitment to follow God with our whole lives,' he said. 'Cause if you are, I want to go home right now.'

"Without pausing for breath, Ricky continues: 'I've been coming here for a long time, and I've made these promises year after year, promises I can never keep and ended up worse off than before I started, with God even more mad at me. 'Cause now, not only am I sinning, but I'm breaking another promise I made to him. And so I just want to make sure that's not where you're headed this weekend. Is it?'

"Feeling sad for Ricky and not knowing exactly how to respond to him, I took a shot in the dark and asked: 'What can you tell me about your dad, Ricky?'

"He proceeded to tell me a story from when he was in fifth grade. 'Every day when my dad came home from work, the first thing he would always ask me was, "Have you done your homework yet?" It was a pretty safe bet that I hadn't. Then one day I decided to surprise him. When he got home, I met him at the door saying, "Guess what, Dad? I did all my homework!" His response was, "Then why aren't you working on tomorrow's?"

---

138   Philip Yancey, "Holy Sex—How it Ravishes Our Souls," Christianity Today, 2003.

"Suddenly it wasn't so surprising that Ricky felt the way he did about himself and about God. He had learned that no matter how close he came, the mark of approval would always move a few notches higher. He would always come up short."[139]

We forget that we all come up short of God's holy standard and must relate to Him on the basis of His grace. If we need it in our relationship with God, then we also need it in our marriages.

In this chapter we asked, "What can the doctrine of grace teach us about dealing with the expectations we have in marriage?" We learned that the law is like a marriage that does not consider our weaknesses. We need to relate to each other as God does with us. He deals with us on the basis of grace which treats us far better than we deserve.

We have all been disappointed when what we felt was promised is not delivered. Remember, your husband cannot compete with Prince Charming who is the idealized version of a man the wife has created in her mind who always knows how to treat her.

Here are some steps for refining our expectations:

1. Write down the expectations and narrow them down to the ones that matter most to you.

2. Discuss them with your spouse to see if they agree, if it is realistic, or they are willing to act on it.

3. Make your case if needed. Eliminate the ones that are your own personal hang-ups or are too unrealistic.

---

139   Scott Larson, *A Place for Skeptics* Colorado Springs: Regal Springs , 2005.

4. Agree on a plan for change that is realistic and the accountability that may go with it—write up the contract.

5. You must start by loving the person where they are now—not where you expect them to be.

6. If they don't agree you must decide if you will remain angry, and hold it against him or her, or will let it go. But remember—anger is like taking poison and waiting for the other person to die. Sometimes, like it or not, we must learn to live with unmet expectations without letting bitterness overtake us.

In his book *Fill These Hearts*, Christopher West describes a surprising and simple discovery that changed his marriage: "Years ago [my wife] and I were out to dinner and she observed that something was different about our marriage in recent years, something good. She asked me if I had any insight into what it was. After reflecting a bit I said with a smile, 'Yeah, I think I know what it is. I think I've been realizing deep in my heart that you can't satisfy me.' She got a big smile on her face and said, 'Yeah, *that's* it. And I've been realizing the same thing: you can't satisfy me either.' I imagine anyone overhearing us in the restaurant would have thought we were about to get divorced; but to us, that realization was cause for joy and celebration. We had never felt closer and freer in our love.

"I love my wife more than words can express, and I know she loves me. But I can't possibly be her ultimate satisfaction, and she can't be mine.

He concludes, ". . . only to the degree that we are free from idolizing human beings are we also free to take our ache for perfect fulfillment to the One who alone can satisfy it." [140]

---

140   Christopher West, *Fill These Hearts* New York: Image Books, 2012 , 159-160.

CHAPTER 10

CONFLICT MANAGEMENT IN YOUR MARRIAGE

Text: *2 Samuel 14:1-15:37*
Theme: *e reduce destructive marital conflict when we identify and address the source of desperation that drives it.*

My wife had an aunt who had been married to the same man for more than forty years before he passed away long before her.

When they were both alive, my wife and I would travel south to visit with them in Monterey, California, and they were always very welcoming and enjoyable to be with. But to hear them talk to each other you would have thought they hated each other. And when he was gone at work, and the gals were talking with each other, she seldom had much good to say about him. Had she been brought up in our contemporary iWorld, she would have most likely divorced him early only on. But in years past, you stuck it out—and they both stuck it out.

Ironically when he finally passed away you would have thought her world had fallen apart—and in a real sense it did. She went into a depression and commented regularly on how much she missed him and how empty her life had become since he passed away. What appeared to us a barely tolerant co-existence was, in reality, a deeply embedded commitment that bonded them even in their adversity.

This story makes a very important point, which is: the presence of conflict in a relationship is not necessarily a sign of an unhealthy relationship. Conflict can be a normal part of a relationship and is destructive only when one feels threatened. My wife's aunt illustrates that people in past years may have understood that better than some do today.

So what is it about much of the conflict we see that can be so destructive? I want us to see that destructive marital conflict is driven by a sense of desperation that is grounded in a threat to one's self. There are numerous examples of destructive conflict in the Bible, but I want us to look at one in particular—the account of David and Absalom.

I want to ask, "What can we learn from David and Absalom about understanding destructive conflict?" We will look at three things. First, we will see that conflict operates at two levels. Second, at the emotional level destructive conflict is a feeling of desperation that leads to a drastic action. Third, we need to acquire skills and knowledge about how to deal with conflict wisely.

In order for us to understand the nature of the conflict between David and Absalom, we need to understand the setting. David, who scripture regularly identifies as, "A man after God's own heart," allows himself to succumb to the temptations of power, sex, and pride that leads him to make some destructive decisions. David sees the beautiful Bathsheba bathing on a rooftop and lusts after her. As a man of power, he uses his position to seduce her, and in the process, she conceives a child—all while her husband has been off to war. You know the story. To hide his sin David arranges to have her husband, Uriah, return from battle, hoping he would have sexual relations with her and believe the child his was own. The plan does not work. As a man of honor, Uriah refuses to enjoy the pleasures of marriage while his squadron is off suffering the hardships of war. David then does something even more hideous. He sends Uriah to the front lines knowing full well he will be killed. In a real sense David murdered Uriah—a sin that the prophet Nathan later exposes and for which David repents.

This evil decision set the course for a series of unfortunate events for David. Events that ultimately led to a devastating conflict between him and his beloved son Absalom. First, his status as a good and honest man after God's heart is now damaged. Second, his identity as a father is severely affected. His child born to Bathsheba dies, and he believes his death was a consequence of his sin. But it also impacts his other relationships as a father.

For instance, his son Amnon is impacted by his father's indiscretion by a loss of respect for David and through a damaged sense of moral discernment. In 1 Samuel 13, we are told Amnon desires his brother Absalom's daughter Tamar so much that he has her brought to his home under false pretenses, then sends his servants away and rapes her. Immediately after, he detests Tamar and sets her up to face the shame alone. It doesn't work. Word gets out to both David and Absalom. David, as the king and as a father, should punish Amnon—instead he does nothing. Probably because of his own shame.

For two years David refuses to act on behalf of Tamar, and Absalom sees David's unwillingness to act on behalf of his daughter as a betrayal. David's avoidance causes Absalom to begin a plot to destroy David and overthrow his kingdom. And in one sense, who could blame him? David had failed him.

In chapter 14 of 2 Samuel where we are told, "Two years later when Absalom's sheepshearers were at Baal Hazor, near the border of Ephraim, he invited all the king's sons to come there. Absalom went to the king David and said, 'Your servant has had shearers come. Will the king and his attendants please join me?'

"'No, my son,' the king replied. 'All of us should not go; we would only be a burden to you.' Although Absalom urged him, he still refused to go but gave him his blessing. Then Absalom said, 'If not, please let my brother Amnon come with us.' The king asked him, 'Why should he go with you?' But Absalom urged him, so he sent with him Amnon and the rest of the king's sons. Absalom ordered his men, 'Listen! When Amnon is in high spirits from drinking wine and I say to you, "Strike Amnon down," then kill him. Don't be afraid. Haven't I given you this order? Be strong and brave.' So Absalom's men did to Amnon what Absalom had ordered. Then all the king's sons got up, mounted their mules and fled.

"While they were on their way, the report came to David: 'Absalom has struck down all the king's sons; not one of them is left.' The king stood up, tore his clothes and lay down on the ground; and all his attendants stood by with their clothes torn. But Jonadab son of Shimeah, David's brother, said, 'My lord should not think that they killed all the princes; only Amnon is dead. This has been Absalom's express intention ever since the day Amnon raped his sister Tamar. My lord the king should not be concerned about the report that all the king's sons are dead. Only Amnon is dead.'"

You get the story. Absalom waits for two years, possibly hoping that David would deal with the issue of Tamar's rape. Seeing no action, Absalom sets it up so that he could kill his brother Amnon while also getting revenge on his father by causing him to believe that all his sons are dead. He wants revenge on both of them and his plan works—at least for the short term. We can observe several things.

I.   Conflict has two levels.

A.   The Problem- This involves the differences between two or more people. In this case, it was the hurt and sense of betrayal that Absalom has toward his father. The rape is a real problem that needs to be addressed, and instead of dealing with it, David avoids it. Avoidance only delays the pain you will ultimately face anyway. It is always better to face your pain up front. But the problem itself is seldom the most important component of destructive conflict.

B.   The Threat- The belief that one's self-esteem is in danger. For two years David refuses to act; all the while he should have recognized the expressed hatred and animosity that was building in Absalom. Now we find David acting under pressure to appease Absalom by allowing him to have Amnon join him in this gathering. He is being naive if the thinks that Absalom has let the matter go. In reality, Absalom used the two years to plot his revenge and David's avoidance and appeasement was not the way to deal with it. Absalom feels a threat because he believes his father does not even care enough for him or his daughter to bring justice.[141]

Like David and Absalom, in our own lives conflict also works at two levels: the problem and the threat. The problem is the simpler one to handle of the two levels. Problems can be easily negotiated and resolved. It is the threat that leads us to act out of desperation which is the hardest to deal with. That threat can be real or imagined. By imagined, it means we can live in the anxiety that comes out of our own insecurities.

The threat can be to one's status or to one's identity. For David it was both. His reputation as an honorable king and man of God and his identity pertaining to his role as a father were both intensely threated. The threat may also be invisible others who may not understand why we are afraid to face up to the problem that is clear to them.

Principle: To deal with conflict we must learn to identify the source of the threat. Like David we must face the threat to our status or identity before we can deal with situations. Face your pain up front.

C.   We should not confuse the two levels when we are trying to manage conflict.

    1.   Problem-solving attempts to solve the problem the two people are facing.

---

141   H. Newton Malony,   *hen Getting Along Seems Impossible* Grand Rapids: Fleming H. Revell , 1989.

2. Conflict-reduction seeks to reduce the threat a person feels.[142]

When we confuse the two it often makes the problem worse. Men, you know what I am talking about. Your wife says something to you about that she does not like, and you ignore her because you do not see it as a problem; or if you do, it is no big thing. But what you learn is that it is a big thing to her. In fact, she has been seething over it for days. We must learn that when she says something that is bothering her, we better listen, because if it is unaddressed, it can grow into something bigger.

It is like an old joke. A letter to a neighbor reads:

Dear Frank,

We've been neighbors for six tumultuous years. When you borrowed my tiller, you returned it in pieces. When I was sick, you blasted rap music. And when your dog went to the bathroom all over my lawn, you laughed. I could go on, but I'm certainly not one to hold grudges. So I am writing this letter to tell you that your house is on fire.

Cordially,
Bob[143]

---

142   Ibid.

143   Van Morris, "Joke About Holding Onto Grudges," accessed March 9, 2018. http://www.preachingtoday.com/illustrations/2016/may//050916.html.

Let us look at our second response to the question, "What can we learn from David and Absalom about understanding conflict?"

II. Conflict is a desperate feeling that can lead to a drastic action.

"Meanwhile, Absalom had fled. Now the man standing watch looked up and saw many people on the road west of him, coming down the side of the hill. The watchman went and told the king, 'I see men in the direction of Horonaim, on the side of the hill.' Jonadab said to the king, 'See, the king's sons have come; it has happened just as your servant said.' As he finished speaking, the king's sons came in, wailing loudly. The king, too, and all his attendants wept very bitterly. Absalom fled and went to Talmai son of Ammihud, the king of Geshur. But King David mourned many days for his son. After Absalom fled and went to Geshur, he stayed there three years. And King David longed to go to Absalom, for he was consoled concerning Amnon's death."

A. The desperate feeling is caused by the threat. If conflict were only about problems and differences, then it would be relatively easy to resolve. But it usually is more about the threat and our response than it is about the problem. The threat often leads to a sense of desperation, a sense of near panic that obsesses us. That desperation leads to a drastic action.

In the case of Absalom, the drastic action is that he fled—a common response to conflict. Because he had a perceived threat from his father, he flees to a place where he could not be found. You can almost feel the emotional intensity present in his anger at Amnon that leads him to kill him, and the anger at his father who had failed him and whom he had intended to humiliate and hurt.

Actions of this nature are driven by the desperation of the person.

B. The drastic action is always intended to restore esteem and remove the threat, not to solve the problem. Note this important point in conflict. The motive for the action is not to solve the problem but to remove the threat. That is why some of the things people do in conflict make no sense—they are often self-destructive or intended to hurt the person they feel is the threat, even if it makes things worse.[144]

C. One or both of the parties may be in conflict. The problem worsens when both parties are in a state of conflict or feeling a sense of desperation. In such a state even the simplest of problems cannot be solved. People begin attacking each other and not the problem at hand. Little problems often grow into significant divisions.

Growing up, my sons would fight quite often, usually over the most trivial of things. On one occasion they were hitting each other over a three-inch piece of blue yarn while we were driving in our blue Astro van. After a few minutes I grabbed the piece of yarn and told them to stop fighting—it was mine now. I showed them the piece of yarn and asked them, "Is this what you are fighting

---

144 H. Newton Malony, *hen Getting Along Seems Impossible* Grand Rapids: Fleming H. Revell , 1989.

over? A stupid piece of yarn?" We kept that piece of yarn in the van for years and would show it to them when they began fighting. Yes, my children fought like all other siblings.

Most destructive conflicts are not about pieces of yarn—it is about our sense of justice, our esteem, our need for love or respect, and when we do not get it, we fight. If you stop and look at the actual problem, it is often about little more than a stupid piece of yarn.

Let us look at our final response to our question, "What can we learn from David and Absalom about understanding conflict?"

III. We need wisdom to know how to deal with the conflict.

"Joab son of Zeruiah knew that the king's heart longed for Absalom. So Joab sent someone to Tekoa and had a wise woman brought from there. He said to her, 'Pretend you are in mourning. Dress in mourning clothes, and don't use any cosmetic lotions. Act like a woman who has spent many days grieving for the dead. Then go to the king and speak these words to him.' And Joab put the words in her mouth. When the woman from Tekoa went to the king, she fell with her face to the ground to pay him honor, and she said, 'Help me, Your Majesty!' The king asked her, 'What is troubling you?'

"She said, 'I am a widow; my husband is dead. I, your servant, had two sons. They got into a fight with each other in the field, and no one was there to separate them. One struck the other and killed him. Now the whole clan has risen up against your servant; they say, "Hand over the one who struck his brother down, so that we may put him to death for the life of his brother whom he killed; then we will get rid of the heir as well." They would put out the only burning coal I have left, leaving my husband neither name nor descendant on the face of the earth.'

"The king said to the woman, 'Go home, and I will issue an order in your behalf.' But the woman from Tekoa said to him, 'Let my lord the king pardon me and my family, and let the king and his throne be without guilt.' The king replied, 'If anyone says anything to you, bring them to me, and they will not bother you again.'¹¹ She said, 'Then let the king invoke the Lord his God to prevent the avenger of blood from adding to the destruction, so that my son will not be destroyed.' 'As surely as the Lord lives,' he said, 'not one hair of your son's head will fall to the ground.' Then the woman said, 'Let your servant speak a word to my lord the king.' 'Speak,' he replied. Then Joab went to Geshur and brought Absalom back to Jerusalem.²⁴ But the king said, 'He must go to his own house; he must not see my face.' So Absalom went to his own house and did not see the face of the king."

Let's stop and consider what is happening here. Joab is a faithful servant of David, and he sees David's plight. He sees David's sorrow at the death of his son Amnon and his initial response to the exaggerated claims that all of David's sons have been killed. It has to be traumatic, and he must be incapacitated in acting for multiple reasons. He is still reeling from his own indiscretion and has lost his moral authority by not acting in Tamar's defense. Now he has lost a son through the murder of another son, and for at least a brief period, thought he had lost all his sons. On the one hand, he has to be angry at Absalom; while on the other hand, he understands his actions. So when Absalom flees, David only has a few choices. One is to chase him down for punishment—something that Absalom fears and coerces him to flee. The other is to call him back to try to rebuild a broken relationship that he created the setting for. David chooses neither. He instead chooses, again, to do nothing.

In his wisdom, Joab creates a scheme to help David see his need to act. So by taking a storyline from the prophet Nathan, he creates a scenario where David would see what is needed. He recruits a wise servant to assist him. She gives a fictitious story of losing her husband and of one of her two sons killing the other son. She is being pressured to turn in the remaining son so he could be punished—leaving her with no remaining family.

The story is not true, but it does create a scenario where David's sense of justice could be fairly applied. The story really is about David and his own son Absalom. What good would it do to punish Absalom or even to have him remain in exile? He loses both sons if he does not try to reconcile. As we learn, David accepts the wisdom that is laid before him and invites Absalom back. Absalom returns, and David tries to reconcile, but unfortunately, Absalom's disdain for his father does not end here. But that is something for another story. But what we can learn from this account are three things:

A. You can learn the wisdom needed for dealing with conflict. David needed wisdom, and Joab was the person that could help him apply it. It says to us that we can learn wisdom from others about how to deal with difficult situations by people that are emotionally wrapped up in the matter.

B. We all have a natural style of dealing with conflict. We all deal with conflict in our own way, but some ways are better than others in different situations. Some avoid conflict, and even though it is often okay, there are times we must face issues head-on. Some are accommodators and seldom assert themselves even when it is important in building a relationship. Some see everything as a competition and seek to win regardless of its impact on others. Some are compromisers who can give and take on many issues but often come across as sly. Collaborations seek a solution that is a win-win for everyone but often demands too much input before accepting a decision. Knowing your natural style helps you to better understand when you need to try another style when necessary.

C.   If we find our security in Jesus alone, we can avoid destructive conflict. This is the heart of the issue. If we seek our sense of well-being primarily in our spouse, we set ourselves up for disappointment and destructive conflict. Why? Because we are married to flawed people like ourselves. He or she may at times fail you, but Jesus never will. We can learn from Him wisdom in dealing with conflict.

Harvard University initiated a new approach to learning in the Master of Business Administration program. Most programs are based on a model that if you do the required reading and pass the tests, you are granted your degree. The approach that Harvard innovated uses a case-study model. In this model students are to master more than 200 case studies of real-life situations and learn from them how to apply it to the real world. In each session they will address a case study where they read information on a problem that a real business faced, have a presenter who was part of the situation, and then discuss it and review what was done and list potential alternatives they could have used. The idea is that after so many cases, they will most likely find situations that match what they will face in the real world—not just some hypothetical information that may not pertain to what they will really face.

That is the kind of learning we need in dealing with conflict in marriage. There are no new problems in marriage. There is a limited range of problems that we will face, and we can learn from those who have already worked through them. While our situation feels unique and unsolvable to us, in reality it is not unique and usually not unsolvable.

In this chapter, we looked at the destructive conflict between David and Absalom and learned that, like them, it is grounded in desperation driven by a threat to our esteem, which we base on flawed premises. Until we find our security in Jesus we will be prone to conflict.

My wife's aunt, in our opening story, reminds us that conflict itself is not a sign of an unhealthy relationship. It becomes unhealthy when the person or the problem is perceived as a threat that must be removed.

Some things to reflect on:
1. Learn to distinguish between problem-solving and conflict-reduction. It is extremely difficult to deal with problems when you are acting out of desperation.

2. Assume others are in conflict if they act in ways that are destructive to the relationship.

3. Identify the threat that is causing you or the other person to have a sense of desperation.

4. Find your security in Christ alone. No person other than God can determine your true worth, and we know the magnitude of His love for us by looking at the cross.

In a 2011 *Leadership Journal* article, Gordon MacDonald shares the moving story about his friends Dr. Paul and Edith Rees. When the Reeses were in their nineties, MacDonald asked if they still fought after sixty-plus years of marriage.

"O, sure we do," Dr. Rees responded. "Yesterday morning was a case in point. Edith and I were in our car, and she was driving. She failed to stop at a stop sign, and it scared me half to death."

"So what did you do?" MacDonald asked.

"Well, I've loved Edith for all these years, and I have learned how to say hard things to her. But I must be careful because when Edith was a little girl, her father always spoke to her harshly. And today when she hears a manly voice speak in anger—even my voice—she is deeply, deeply hurt."

"But Paul," MacDonald said, "Edith is ninety years old. Are you telling me that she remembers a harsh voice from that many years ago?"

"She remembers that voice more than ever," Dr. Rees said.

MacDonald asked, "So how did you handle that driving situation from the other day?"

"Ah," he said, "I simply said, 'Edith, darling, after we've had our nap this afternoon, I want to discuss a thought I have for you.' And when the nap was over, I did. I was calm; she was ready to listen, and we solved our little problem."

MacDonald concluded: "These are the words of a man who has learned that conflict is necessary, can be productive, but must be managed with wisdom and grace. By the time I reach ninety, I hope to be just like him."[145]

---

145 Gordon MacDonald, "When Bad Things Happen to Good Relationships," *Leadership Journal*, 2011.

CHAPTER 11

OUR SECRET FEARS

Text: *Philippians 4:4–13, Matthew 6:25–34*
Theme: *e overcome the deepest fears that negatively impact our marriages by learning to be content in Christ alone.*

Sometimes when you hear someone like myself preach on an issue, you wonder if we can really understand what you are dealing with in your own life. Let's face it, sometimes life can be hard and the admonition to trust Jesus, or let God take control, etc., can come across as simplistic and superficial platitudes that have no bearing in real life. They may come across as the naive ponderings of a person who doesn't really grasp your reality.

I can understand the sentiment because unless you have been through a severe trial, it is hard to appreciate how it impacts the core of your being. It changes and shapes you in ways nothing else can. But unless you have been through severe trials, you cannot fully grasp the importance of having something that gives you an anchor to keep you grounded in those situations.

At a personal level, I have experienced such times over the course of my life—so I understand it when you go through it. Early in my life, it was the death of my father. Later it was my mother marrying a paranoid schizophrenic whose extreme mood swings, narcissism, and delusions created constant tension—never knowing what state of mind he would be in at any given time.

In my adult life, I had the normal stresses of life until we moved to the central coast of California. Within a month of starting the pastorate there, the central gatekeeper of the church put me on notice that he was keeping me in check—he basically stated it in those terms. I knew that if I let him have control then my ministry there was done from the start. After winning an unwelcome battle with him, his son then assumed his role. Within three years I resigned, realizing there was nothing more I could do. It was the only time I ever resigned out of duress and unhappy terms. About the same time that I resigned, the economy crashed in the States. We saw a business we invested heavily in go under, our retirement accounts dropped to less than half, and we had to withdraw from them at a low point just to get by. The house that we had invested three hundred thousand dollars in dropped three hundred thousand dollars in less than a year, causing us to lose it all. In all, we lost around five hundred thousand dollars that we had carefully saved and invested. Needless to say, it was a very stressful time.

I know what it is like when your world crumbles around you. I also know what it is like to realize that when we cannot control what is happening, then we must trust God even more. But just as difficult is when we live our lives in fear of the potential for these worst-case scenarios. In other words, even when things seem to be going well, we still live in the constant fear that danger is looming just around the corner. We call it anxiety—fear in the absence of real danger—the belief that if what I am imagining actually happened it would be unbearably awful. And because of this undefined fear, we miss out on the peace and contentment we should otherwise enjoy.[146]

In marriages, as in life, we will have times when everything seems to be crumbling around us. In a typical marriage there will be at least one time in the relationship where one or both parties will be severely tested. Those events shape your relationship in ways nothing else can.

In this chapter I want us to consider what we can do to help us get through such times. I want us to ask, "How can you endure the hardships that negatively impact your marriage?" We will learn that God is with us in even our worst marital situations, and giving Him control provides the peace that passes understanding, enabling us to endure all things.

I. God is with you in even your worst marital situation. (Phil. 4, 5)

"Rejoice in the Lord always. I will say it again: Rejoice! ⁵ Let your gentleness be evident to all. The Lord is near. "

We cannot fully appreciate what this passage is telling us until we understand the setting of these words. Paul is not speaking out of ignorance or naiveté. He is writing this from a Philippian prison and was put there unjustly by the Jews, who were persecuting him for preaching the gospel of Jesus. Already he had suffered beatings and humiliation at their hands and this was one of many of his imprisonments. We can read about the setting for this passage

---

146   Burns, 269 ff

in Acts 16:22–31: "The crowd joined in the attack against Paul and Silas, and the magistrates ordered them to be stripped and beaten with rods. ²³ After they had been severely flogged, they were thrown into prison, and the jailer was commanded to guard them carefully. ²⁴ When he received these orders, he put them in the inner cell and fastened their feet in the stocks. ²⁵ About midnight Paul and Silas were praying and singing hymns to God, and the other prisoners were listening to them. ²⁶ Suddenly there was such a violent earthquake that the foundations of the prison were shaken. At once all the prison doors flew open, and everyone's chains came loose. ²⁷ The jailer woke up, and when he saw the prison doors open, he drew his sword and was about to kill himself because he thought the prisoners had escaped. ²⁸ But Paul shouted, 'Don't harm yourself! We are all here!' ²⁹ The jailer called for lights, rushed in and fell trembling before Paul and Silas. ³⁰ He then brought them out and asked, 'Sirs, what must I do to be saved?' ³¹ They replied, 'Believe in the Lord Jesus, and you will be saved—you and your household.'"

Notice in our Philippians passage we learn that Paul is practicing what he is preaching. He is praising God and singing hymns even as he is in prison. You can only imagine what Silas, the jailer, is thinking. Paul's example, along with his life being saved after the earthquake, attracts him to the gospel, and he wants what they have, causing him to ask, "What must I do to be saved?" If God was with Paul even in a detestable Roman prison is He not also with you in your marriage when things are not going well? Just like Paul, we can rejoice in even the worst of circumstances.

One of the greatest anxiety-producing fears that people face is loneliness. The fear that those they love the most will abandon them cripples many couples and creates tremendous insecurity. Inside and outside of marriage, the thought of being alone motivates people to compromise their most basic values in the hopes that others will love and accept them. The fear of being alone drives much of what they do and think, and yet the irony is that because of that fear, it drives people away-—they come across as too needy or manipulative.

They even have a name for it—the "Princess Syndrome"— which affects millions worldwide. These are females that try too much to be like others read: insecure and tend toward extreme jealousy. They seem to feel the need to stir up drama to make their lives more exciting. They want the best things in life but can seldom afford them and spend beyond their means. Their whole identity is measured by what people think of them in the hopes they will be loved and admired. Instead, they are perceived as needy and demanding.[14]

Another irony is this—people are most secure when they have Christ as the center of their lives. This is Paul's point. He understood that the Lord was always near, and that is all that really mattered. This is one of the great assurances of the Christian faith.

Dallas Willard tells the story of a little boy whose mom had died. He was especially sad and lonely at night. He would come into his father's room and ask if he could sleep with him. Even then, he could not rest until he knew that not only was he with his father, but that his father's face was turned toward him. "Father, is your face turned toward me now?" "Yes," his father would say. "You

---

14/   https://www.psychologytoday.com/us/blog/princess-recovery/201203/combating-princess-syndrome.

are not alone. I'm with you. My face is turned toward you." When at last the boy was assured of this, he could rest. Dallas Willard concludes, "How lonely life is! Oh, we can get by in life with a God who does not speak. Many at least think they do so. But it is not much of a life, and it is certainly not the life God intends for us or the abundance of life Jesus came to make available."[148]

Our question, "How can you endure the hardships that negatively impact your marriage?" has a second response.

II. Giving God control provides peace that surpasses understanding. (Matt. 6, 7)

"Do not be anxious about anything, but in every situation, by prayer and petition, with thanksgiving, present your requests to God. [7] And the peace of God, which transcends all understanding, will guard your hearts and your minds in Christ Jesus."

This could be translated, "Stop worrying about anything." It brings to mind what Jesus says in Matthew 6:25–34, "Therefore I tell you, do not worry about your life, what you will eat or drink; or about your body, what you will wear. Is not life more than food, and the body more than clothes? [26] Look at the birds of the air; they do not sow or reap or store away in barns, and yet your heavenly Father feeds them. Are you not much more valuable than they? [27] Can any one of you by worrying add a single hour to your life? [28] And why

148   John Ortberg, *God is Closer Than You Think* Grand Rapids: Zondervan, 2005 , 10.

do you worry about clothes? See how the flowers of the field grow. They do not labor or spin. [29] Yet I tell you that not even Solomon in all his splendor was dressed like one of these. [30] If that is how God clothes the grass of the field, which is here today, and tomorrow is thrown into the fire, will he not much more clothe you—you of little faith? [31] So do not worry, saying, 'What shall we eat?' or 'What shall we drink?' or 'What shall we wear?' [32] For the pagans run after all these things, and your heavenly Father knows that you need them. [33] But seek first his kingdom and his righteousness, and all these things will be given to you as well. 34 Therefore do not worry about tomorrow, for tomorrow will worry about itself. Each day has enough trouble of its own."

Clearly Jesus and Paul both understand our propensity toward worry and anxiety. Anxiety is caused when we imagine different scenarios in our mind and each one of them has an awful ending. It is as if the thing I imagine will be awful, horrible, terrible. We can live constantly with this undefined fear that something awful is just around the corner, overestimating the probability of danger, and exaggerating its degree of terribleness.

One of the things I often do in counseling is to ask a person, "If the awful thing you are imagining really happened, what would it mean?"

An example may look something like this:

Person: My boyfriend didn't call me this weekend as he promised.

Me: Why does that upset you?

Person: That means he's neglecting me. He doesn't really love me.

Me: Suppose that were true. What would that mean?

Person: That would mean there's something wrong with me. Otherwise, he would be more attentive.

Me: Suppose that were true. What would that mean?

Person: That would mean I was unlovable and I would always be rejected.

Me: Why does that upset you?

Person: It would mean I would end up alone and miserable.[149]

Do you see what she has done? She is anxious because of her fear of being alone and miserable, and she obsesses over a simple missed phone call. The reality is that he probably got distracted and did not see the importance of it, which has nothing to do with his interest in her. But that is how anxiety works.

Paul gives us the alternative to obsessing over such things. His alternative is prayer and thanksgiving. Prayer is asking God to provide you with what you really need not necessarily what you want or think you need . Thanksgiving is thanking God for who He is and what He has done and will do. We can learn to stop destructive, unproductive worry by learning to discipline our minds and hearts to obsess over praiseworthy things.

Our final response to our question, "How can you endure the hardships that negatively impact your marriage?" is this:

III. Jesus will enable you to endure all things. (Phil. 8-13)

> [8] Finally, brothers and sisters, whatever is true, whatever is noble, whatever is right, whatever is pure, whatever is

---

149   Adapted from a method by David Burns, *Feeling Good: The New Mood Therapy* New York: William Morrow and Company, 1980 pp. 269-270.

lovely, whatever is admirable—if anything is excellent
or praiseworthy—think about such things. [9] Whatever
you have learned or received or heard from me, or seen
in me—put it into practice. And the God of peace will
be with you. [10] I rejoiced greatly in the Lord that at last,
you renewed your concern for me. Indeed, you were
concerned, but you had no opportunity to show it.[11] I am
not saying this because I am in need, for I have learned to
be content whatever the circumstances. [12] I know what
it is to be in need, and I know what it is to have plenty. I
have learned the secret of being content in any and every
situation, whether well-fed or hungry, whether living in
plenty or in want. [13] I can do all this through him who
gives me strength.

A. Focus your thoughts on praiseworthy things. In this verse
we find the alternative to anxiety. If anxiety is an obsession
of our thoughts of an imagined danger, then the answer
is to change how we think. The implication of this passage
is that we can control how we think, especially if we have
the Holy Spirit residing within us. Instead of focusing on
how bad things could get if the awful thing we imagine
happened, we need to focus on things that are true, noble,
right, pure, lovely, and admirable. Think on things that are
praiseworthy. That is what prayer enables you to do, and
that is why it is so important to your life. If our emotions are
created by our thoughts and beliefs, then if we change our
thoughts to the things Paul lists, our emotions, including
anxiety, are more productive. While normal stress can be

productive and healthy, nothing good ever comes out of anxiety.

B.   We need very little to experience peace. Rich people are seldom happier people. Always getting what we want is not the path to contentment. Sometimes it is in the sacrifice or the absence of what we want that we begin to realize what is really important. People who suffer and are deprived of something they value can learn that they can still be fully content when it is not there.

I am always pleased when I travel to third-world countries to see how even in their poverty many have learned contentment. I saw it years ago when I traveled to Belarus and saw the joy in the faculty and students of the Bible college at which I taught. The average wage per person was thirty dollars a month, yet so many were upbeat and excited about their faith. I also saw it in Mexico at orphanages I visited. Those who are poor by our standards are often rich in faith.

C.   Contentment is not based on circumstances. This is a key point. Paul learned to be content no matter what his circumstances or what he possessed. Money, food, and even health did not determine the nature of his contentment. He learned to be content no matter what the circumstances because of his relationship and standing with Jesus.

Paul was a man who was in prison, had been beaten and left for dead, and suffered health issues even as he writes these words of encouragement. But he learned to be content and to rejoice. His thoughts, beliefs, and attitude determined the nature of his joy. He was thankful in even the worst of settings. The importance of thankfulness has been confirmed over and over again, even by people outside of our faith.

For instance, two psychologists, Dr. Robert A. Emmons of the University of California, Davis, and Dr. Michael E. McCullough of the University of Miami, have done much research on gratitude. In one study, they asked all participants to write a few sentences each week, focusing on particular topics.[150]

One group wrote about things they were grateful for that had occurred during the week. A second group wrote about daily irritations or things that had displeased them, and the third wrote about events that had affected them with no emphasis on them being positive or negative . After ten weeks, those who wrote about gratitude were more optimistic and felt better about their lives. Surprisingly they also exercised more and had fewer visits to physicians than those who focused on sources of aggravation.

Another leading researcher in this field, Dr. Martin E. P. Seligman, a psychologist at the University of Pennsylvania, tested the impact of various positive psychology interventions on 411 people, each compared with a control assignment of writing about early memories. When their week's assignment was to write and personally deliver a letter of gratitude to someone who had

---

150   Lauren Dunn, "Be Thankful: Science Says Gratitude Is Good for Your Health," last modified May 12, 2017. https://www.today.com/health/be-thankful-science-says-gratitude-good-your-health-t58256.

never been properly thanked for his or her kindness, participants immediately exhibited a huge increase in happiness scores. This impact was greater than that from any other intervention, with benefits lasting for a month.[151]

Of course studies such as this one cannot prove cause and effect. But most of the studies published on this topic support an association between gratitude and an individual's well-being. And how much truer is this, then, for the believer who has the hope that God will be with us now and for eternity?

This also applies to marriage where other studies have looked at how gratitude can improve relationships. For example, a study of couples found that individuals who took the time to express gratitude for their partner not only felt more positive toward the other person but also felt more comfortable expressing concerns about their relationship.

In this chapter we asked, "How can you endure the hardship that negatively impacts your marriage?" We learned that God is with you in even your worst marital situation, and giving Him control provides the peace that surpasses understanding, enabling you to endure all things.

Sometimes when you hear someone like myself speak on an issue you wonder if we can really understand what you are dealing with in your own life—our principles often seem idealistic with little bearing on reality. But like Paul, who wrote powerful words of encouragement from prison, we can learn the true source of contentment in life and in our marriages from a man who saw the worst.

---

151   Harvey Simon, M.D., https://www.health.harvard.edu/healthbeat/givging-thanks-can-make-you-happier.

What are some things that you can learn from all this?

1. Your marriage will have times when things are hard—guaranteed. Work through those times; usually they pass, and your marriage is renewed. If we cut it short, we may miss out on something better.

2. Watch that you don't let those hard times create anxiety for when things are not going well. Sometimes we can demonize a person beyond their real selfishness because we are seeing through the lens of the worst-case scenario. There are some things about your spouse that you do not like that you must learn to live with.

3. Understand that your spouse cannot replace God. The more we can be content in our relationship with Jesus, the less dependent we are on our spouse for our sense of well-being.

A customs officer observes a truck pulling up at the border. Suspicious, he orders the driver out and searches the vehicle. He pulls off the panels, bumpers, and wheel cases but finds not a single scrap of contraband, whereupon, still suspicious but at a loss to know where else to search, he waves the driver through. The next week, the same driver arrives. Again the official searches, and again finds nothing illicit. Over the years the official tries full-body searches, X-rays, and sonar, anything he can think of. And each week the same man drives up, but no mysterious cargo ever appears, and each time, reluctantly, the customs man waves the driver on.

Finally, after many years, the officer is about to retire. The driver pulls up. "I know you're a smuggler," the customs officer says. "Don't bother denying it. But [darned] if I can figure out what you've been smuggling all these years. I'm leaving now. I swear to you I can do you no harm. Won't you please tell me what you've been smuggling?"

"Trucks," the driver says.[152]

In regard to the importance of marriage, at times it's easy to miss the most important, obvious thing: that only God can provide the peace and contentment that helps you through hard times. Remember, your spouse is going through those times as well.

---

[152]   The smuggler and the truck. www.reddit.com

CHAPTER 12

HOW TO HANDLE BETRAYAL AND REJECTION IN MARRIAGE

Text: *Matthew 18:21–35*

Theme: *Anger at betrayal can be resolved by restorative confrontation.*

The husband of a young woman at the church I pastored years ago had horrible spending habits. He was a man who seldom worked and always had an excuse for why—none of them was very convincing. He was healthy, capable, and jobs were available but none suited his interests. His wife had a good job and supported them both. But she discovered that he was applying for credit cards without her knowledge, drawing from their bank account, and buying things they could not afford.

After several years of heated confrontations over the topic issue, things came to a head. She forced him out of the house and told him not to come back until he got a job and dealt with his spending problems. A few months after he left, she received a legal notice that a lien was being held against her house and she would lose it unless a massive debt she did not even know about was paid off. In time other unknown bills were coming to her. While he was gone he was creating debt and she was liable for it because she was still married to him. She rightfully felt betrayed. The person that was supposed to provide for her, or at the very least help her, had instead ruined her credit and put her in a very difficult situation.

That feeling of betrayal is something I have seen often over the years. I have seen it in someone who discovers their spouse is having an affair. I have seen it in spouses who have been deceived. I have seen it in people whose spouses committed a criminal felony, wreaking havoc on their family. There are also people who are just evil and many of them are married. We can think of drug dealers, or Bernie Madoff and other embezzlers who have cheated people out of their money, all the while married to unknowing spouses.

What is a person to do in such cases? Maybe some of them could have been discovered before the marriage but you don't want to do background checks on the person you love, and we know that some people hide some of their evil traits. Others become disillusioned with life and change during the marriage, so you could not predict their betrayal anyway. For some, it may be that their bad action is the result of a short-term lapse of judgment, but the hurt is still deep.

Over my lifetime I have seen numerous occasions of betrayal in marriages, so I know the problem is real and divorce seems to be the standard contemporary response. So I want to focus on the question, "What can we learn from God about how to handle betrayal in marriage?" We will look at three responses.

I. God clearly understands the reality of betrayal and rejection.

A. Hosea's marriage to Gomer symbolizes Israel's betrayal.

One of the minor prophets of the Old Testament is Hosea. The book opens saying, "When the Lord began to speak through Hosea, the Lord said to him, 'Go, marry a promiscuous woman and have children with her, for like an adulterous wife, this land is guilty of unfaithfulness to the Lord.' ³ So he married Gomer daughter of Diblaim, and she conceived and bore him a son."

God gives an astounding command to Hosea to go and marry a prostitute. The reason, we later learn, is that Hosea's marriage will illustrate how Gods people, Israel, has betrayed Him and prostituted themselves with other Gods. He wants us to have a clear picture of what Israel and we are doing to Him. He wants us to have a sense of what He feels, and the book elaborates on this betrayal in poetic detail. The very people He loved, protected, and provided for have turned away from Him to false Gods who give them nothing. He is offended, and He wants them to grasp what is at stake. He knows what it is to be betrayed.

B. We see the same thing with Judas Iscariot. Judas shows that greed and disillusionment lead to betrayal. We are told in Luke 22, ". . . the chief priests and the teachers of the law were looking for some way to get rid of Jesus, for they were afraid of the people. ³ Then Satan entered Judas, called Iscariot, one of the Twelve.⁴ And Judas went to the chief priests and the officers of the temple guard and discussed with them how he might betray Jesus. [5] They were delighted and agreed to give him money. [6] He consented and watched for an opportunity to hand Jesus over to them when no crowd was present."

Here was the man that Jesus trusted implicitly and who knew Jesus as few knew Him. But as things began to heat up, Judas became disillusioned. When he realized that was not going to set Himself up as king, as he thought, he figured he could at least get something out of it, so he began plotting on how to betray Him and did so for a few pieces of silver. We know the rest of the story. Judas has gone down throughout history as the epitome of betrayal.

C. Peter's rejection shows that even the most devoted can fail us. Peter was Jesus' most trusted disciple and often promised deep loyalty. Even when Jesus told Peter he would betray Him, Peter denied it. And yet when the heat was on, and just as Jesus predicted, Peter betrayed Him and abandoned Him at His hour of greatest need.

Principle: We live in a fallen world where the most beloved can betray us.

Kevin Miller tells a personal story that illustrates this point. He tells the story that right after he finished sixth grade, his family moved to a new town in the fall just as he started junior high. He suddenly found himself in a school he didn't know, in a town he didn't know, with people he didn't know. He felt very alone.

Every day he would walk home alone, wondering, *Is there a friend here for me?* Then one day a kid named Earl invited him to his house and Miller jumped at the offer. Earl was kind of like the other kids, but, unlike them, he wasn't particularly concerned about personal hygiene. Earl knew how to sneak into a parking lot near his house where the electric company parked its trucks and heavy equipment. There they would clamber all over the big rigs and the augers and had a lot of fun. Earl and I began to build a friendship.

Miller eventually realized that the kids who seemed to be the most popular were not Earl and had little to do with him. They were two guys, Mike and Eddie. As Miller continues,

"So when Mike and Eddie finally invited me over to their house, I was exhilarated. This was my ticket to the big time. But I had one problem. Wherever Mike and Eddie were, Earl was not; and wherever Earl was, Mike and Eddie were not. And if I was going to hang out with Mike and Eddie, I could not be seen with Earl. I knew it.

"So I made a decision. I went over to Mike and Eddie's houses, and I struck up a friendship with them, and I was *in* with those popular kids. When Earl called me, I kept putting him off by saying, 'I'm, uh, kind of busy.'

"All those years since that time, there's still a shame around that betrayal, because the truth is, I betrayed Earl. I handed him another rejection in his life when he'd probably had so many. But I wanted something: I wanted that *in*, I wanted that popularity. If I had to hurt him, I would do it."[153]

---

153   Kevin Miller, "7th Grade Boy Achieves Popularity by Betraying Friend," accessed March 9. 2018. http://www.preachingtoday.com/illustrations/2012/april/4041612.html.

That is the essence of betrayal: It says, "I am willing to hurt you to get something for myself." And in that self-centeredness, we find a lot of pain and disappointment. It is what some of us face at times in our lives, but it is what God faces every day. He has loved us and has created this marvelous world for us, and every day he hears people say it is all a cosmic accident caused by time and chance. They won't even acknowledge that the very laws of nature are His design.

There is a second response to our question, "What can we learn from God about how to handle betrayal in marriage?"

II. There are two primary responses to betrayal. (Heb. 13:4–6, Matt. 18:21–35)

A. Retributive Justice: This is the most common response to betrayal. It intends to punish the offender. "An eye for an eye and a tooth for a tooth." Certainly since morality is based on the holiness of God, this also requires Him to punish wrongdoing—including betrayal. In fact, in Hosea, we find that this is His initial response to Israel's adultery as expressed through the story of Gomer. He says,

"Rebuke your mother, rebuke her, for she is not my wife,
and I am not her husband.
Let her remove the adulterous look from her face and the unfaithfulness from between her breasts. Otherwise, I will strip her naked and make her as bare as on the day she was born;
I will make her like a desert, turn her into a parched land, and slay her with thirst.

I will not show my love to her children because they are the children of adultery.

Their mother has been unfaithful and has conceived them in disgrace.

She said, 'I will go after my lovers, who give me my food and my water, my wool and my linen, my olive oil and my drink.'

"Therefore I will block her path with thorn bushes; I will wall her in so that she cannot find her way. She will chase after her lovers but not catch them; she will look for them but not find them. Then she will say, 'I will go back to my husband as at first for then I was better off than now.' She has not acknowledged that I was the one who gave her the grain, the new wine and oil, who lavished on her the silver and gold—which they used for Baal.

"Therefore I will take away my grain when it ripens, and my new wine when it is ready.

I will take back my wool and my linen, intended to cover her naked body. I will punish her for the days she burned incense to the Baals; she decked herself with rings and jewelry, and went after her lovers, but me she forgot, declares the Lord."

We can certainly appreciate the tone in God's response to Israel like that of Hosea to Gomer's adultery. When we are wronged we want justice, and rightfully so. Even God demands justice. But there must be something better and that is where the next point comes in.

B. Restoration Justice: To forgive the offender in order to restore the relationship. This response places a primary emphasis on rehabilitating the offender to restore the relationship.

Our response to betrayal should not be either/or. Both retributive and restorative justice have a place. There must be some negative detriment to bad behavior, especially for that of the unrepentant, who will keep repeating destructive behaviors. Evil must be identified and confronted. It cannot be hidden away, but once exposed, we must offer something more than just retribution as our response. The objective should always be toward rehabilitation and restoration. There are dangers that go with it. Some people will abuse it—like controlling people who often go into repentant mode but return back to old controlling patterns when the pressure is off. There is also the danger of enabling people, like drug addicts or alcoholics, where we support the bad behavior in the name of love. Tough love that holds such a person to account is motivated by our love, not by our hurt.

C. Forgiveness is to be given regardless of the merit.

This is the point that Jesus makes in Matthew 18, "Then Peter came to Jesus and asked, 'Lord, how many times shall I forgive my brother or sister who sins against me? Up to seven times?' [22] Jesus answered, 'I tell you, not seven times, but seventy-seven times.'

Jesus then tells a parable of a man who was forgiven much but that same man refused to forgive one whose debt was small. The passage makes two key points.

I. God has granted you forgiveness far beyond what you merit; and in return, God asks you to forgive to an extreme, and that is possible only if you fully grasp the magnitude of His forgiveness toward you.

II. You should forgive others in the same way God forgives you. You can be angry at someone whose offense is far less than yours.

Principle: Restorative justice should always be our primary objective.

My mother understood the difference between the two responses to betrayal or rejection. I remember my stepfather beating his youngest daughter excessively out of anger, and my mother stepped in to stop Him and called the cops on him when he refused to stop. It worked; the only times I know that he ever did it again was when I caught him in the garage, and he stopped as soon as he saw me, knowing that if I told my mom, she would call the police. Yet she did not threaten divorce as a means to control and in part to protect his kids. She modeled for me something important about responding to betrayal—some of which I will point out at the application at the end. Note: there are certainly times when a person must remove themselves from a violent situation to protect themselves and their kids.

Let us look now at the final response to our question, "What can we learn from God about how to handle betrayal in marriage?"

III. Jesus models for us the essence of restorative justice. (Luke 24:45–49)

A. He calls us to repentance when we have been the betrayer. After his resurrection, Jesus never held His disciples' betrayal against them. I am sure they felt it. I am sure that when Jesus asked Peter three times "Do you love me?" Peter felt guilty because it was only weeks before that that he rejected Jesus up to six times. He could see their repentance in their joy.

B. He forgives people when they act out of their ignorance and/or repent. It is also noteworthy that even as Jesus is on the cross being mocked and despised while he was dying that he prayed, "Father, forgive them because they don't know what they are doing."

C. He welcomes us back and no longer holds the offense against us. Forgiveness means to "let go of the debt that is held against you." It is not just for them—it is for you. Resentment and anger that results from betrayal can eat at your soul.

Principle: God is the only one we know who will not betray our trust.

In his book *Delighting in the Trinity*, Michael Reeves compares two ways to look at God. First, there is the common view that God is the Supreme Ruler of the Universe. Reeves contends that if God is the Ruler, and the problem is that I have broken the rules, the only salvation he can offer is to forgive me and treat me as if I had kept the rules. Then he gives the following analogy:

"But if that is how God is if he is primarily the Ruler , my relationship with him can be little better than my relationship with any traffic cop. Let me put it like this: if, as never happens, some fine cop were to catch me speeding and so breaking the rules, I would be punished; if, as never happens, he failed to spot me or I managed to shake him off after an exciting car chase, I would be relieved. But in neither case would I love him. And even if, like God, he chose to let me off the hook for my law-breaking, I still would not love him. I might feel grateful, and that gratitude might be deep, but that is not at all the same thing as love. And so it is with the divine policeman: if salvation simply means him letting me off and counting me as a law-abiding citizen, then gratitude not love is all I have. In other words, I can never really love the God who is essentially just the Ruler. And that, ironically, means I can never keep the greatest command: to love the Lord my God."

But then Reeves offers another way, the biblical way, to think about God—consider Jesus Christ, the Son of God, and the beauty of the Triune God. Reeves writes again: "It is a lane that ends happily in a very different place, with a very different sort of God. How? Well, just the fact that Jesus is 'the Son' really says it all. Being a Son means he has a Father. The God he reveals is, first and foremost, a Father. 'I am the way and the truth and the life,' he says. 'No one comes to the Father except through me' John 14:6 .

That is who God has revealed himself to be: not first and foremost Creator or Ruler, but Father."[154]

We cannot treat the ones we love as police would treat a lawbreaker. Our response must be different. Your anger at your spouse may be justified, but it is not the end of the story no more than it is for God in how He treats us.

In this chapter we learned that God understands betrayal because He has been betrayed—and we have been His betrayers. But he provides for our restoration.

How does this apply to my opening story of the young lady whose husband created a debt she became liable for. Here was my advice to her:

1. In our world we seem to have only one response to betrayal, and it can be stated in three simple words: divorce the jerk. While we can understand, it cannot be our first response.

2. There are options short of divorce that are seldom considered and where restoration is the goal. Here are some possible steps:

    a. Confront the person head-on. Don't avoid or ignore the issue just because it is painful.

    b. Very clearly express your anger and your issues.

    c. Be aware of false repentance. I have seen many offenders feel bad for what they did, but they return back to bad behaviors when the heat is off.

---

154   Michael Reeves, *Delighting in the Trinity: An Introduction to the Christian Faith* (heaton: IVP Academic, 2012 , 20-21.

d. Leave if threatened, or better yet, have the offender leave.

e. Leave the door open for reconciliation, but write up the list of conditions before reconciling and agree on ways they will be enforced. Often a third party is needed but understand that when lawyers get involved, they almost always recommend divorce.

f. If you must protect yourself, then consider legal separation—it is not the same as divorce and protects you from potential abuse but makes reconciliation easier.

Tennessee Williams tells the story of Jacob Brodsky, a shy Russian Jew who runs his father's bookshop. Jacob's dream seemed complete when he married his childhood sweetheart, Lila, a beautiful, exuberant French girl. The life of a bookshop proprietor suited him fine, but it did not suit his adventurous young bride. An agent for a vaudeville touring company heard Lila sing and talked her into touring Europe with their show.

In the process of explaining to Jacob that she had to seize this opportunity and leave, she also cleft a chasm-sized hole in his heart. But before she left, he gave her a key to the bookshop and said, "You had better keep this because you will want it someday. Your love is not so much less than mine that you can get away from it. You will come back sometime, and I will be waiting."

Lila went on the road, and Jacob went to the back of his bookshop. To deaden the pain, he turned to his books as someone else might turn to drugs or alcohol. Weeks turned into years and when fifteen of them had passed, the bell above the bookshop's front door signaled the arrival of a customer. It was Lila. The bookshop's owner rose to greet her. But to her astonishment, her abandoned husband didn't recognize her and simply spoke like he would to any other customer. "Do you want a book?" Stunned and trying to maintain her composure, she raised a gloved hand to her throat and stammered, "No—that is—I wanted a book, but I've forgotten the name of it." Regaining some poise, she continued, "Let me tell you the story—perhaps you have read it and can give me the name of it."

She then told him of a boy and a girl who had been constant companions since childhood. As teenagers they fell in love, eventually married, and lived over a bookshop. She told him their whole story—the vaudeville company's offer, the husband's brokenhearted gift of the key, the return of the wife who was never able to part with the key. How, after fifteen years, she finally came to her senses and returned home to him.

Then with a desperate plea, she said, "You remember it—you must remember it—the story of Lila and Jacob?" With a vacant, faraway look, he merely said, "There is something familiar about the story. I think I have read it somewhere. It seems to me that it is something by Tolstoy." Only the heartbreaking, metallic echo of the key dropping to the hard floor interrupted her horrified silence. Lila, having let go of the key as well as her hope, fled the bookshop in tears.

And Jacob returned to his books.[155]

---

155   Matt Heard, *Life with a Capital L: Embracing Your God-Given Humanity* Portland: Multnomah Books, 2014 , 39-40.

This sad story shows us how disappointing or tragic life-events can crush our hopes and dreams. But the gospel can restore our hope in Christ's ultimate victory and enable us to forgive in ways beyond our own abilities apart from Christ.

CHAPTER 13

THE ANATOMY OF ADULTERY

Text: *2 Samuel 11*
Theme: *Being committed to God and our spouse protects you from inappropriate relationships.*

Something that stirred up controversy some time ago was when U.S. Vice President Mike Pence stated to *The Hill* that he practiced the "Billy Graham rule." That meant that he never eats alone with a woman other than his wife, and that he won't attend events featuring alcohol without her by his side, either. This was one of the four things developed by the evangelist and his to team avoid any hint of sexual indiscretion.

When Pence's position became public, the rule was immediately criticized for restricting opportunities for women to network with male colleagues. Ministry leader Tracey Bianchi said, "Women are marginalized and cut out of opportunities to network, share their ideas, and advance in the organization."[156] Laura Turner tweeted, "What the Billy Graham rule does is reduce women to sexual temptations, objects, things to be avoided. It is

---

156 "The Billy Graham Rule," accessed March 12, 2018. https://en.wikipedia.org/wiki/Billy_Graham_rule.

dehumanizing, anti-gospel" and "It treats temptation to stray from one's marriage as unavoidable, and present in every encounter with a woman, locating sin in her, not you."

While the rule may have the potential for abuse, I empathize with its intent. It was intended to avoid the scandals that have plagued evangelists and ministers over the years. A lot of adulterous affairs have begun with simple innocent encounters of members of the opposite sex. I have also seen some good men whose image was destroyed because of a woman scorned or falsely accused of inappropriate advances.

Allen Petersen, citing his own experience says, "I had just arrived in a Michigan town to begin a series of meetings in the church on Sunday. It was a small, colorless community, common people, no sophistication. At this Saturday night get-acquainted reception, a church woman sat down beside me . . . For a moment we exchanged pleasantries. Then in a matter-of-fact way she handed me a piece of paper with her address and phone number. 'I thought you might get lonely while you're here. If you'd like to drop over some afternoon, give me a call. My husband is gone all week working in Detroit. The last speaker we had at the church came over several times; I think you might enjoy it. I thought you might get lonely while you're here.'"[15]

The Bible gives us the perfect account of how simple, innocent encounters can lead to something more. In that light I want to ask, "What does David's affair with Bathsheba teach us about adultery?

---

[15] J. Allen Petersen, *The Myth of the Greener Grass* Wheaton: Tyndale House Publishers, 1983 , 25-26.

I. Most affairs start with an innocent momentary temptation. (Chapters 1-3)

In the spring at the time when kings go off to war, David sends Joab out with the king's men and the whole Israelite army. They destroy the Ammonites and besiege Rabbah. But David remains in Jerusalem. ² One evening David gets up from his bed and walks around on the roof of the palace. From the roof, he sees a woman bathing. The woman is very beautiful, ³ and David sends someone to find out about her. The man says, "She is Bathsheba, the daughter of Eliam and the wife of Uriah the Hittite."

A. *Temptation can come in the course of a normal day with things going well.*

As with David, most affairs start from innocent encounters. As Florence Littauer says, "No man or woman gets up in the morning and looks out the window and says, 'My, this is a lovely day! I guess I'll go out and commit adultery.' Yet many do it anyway.¹⁵⁸ Most men are stimulated visually and have numerous episodes on any given day where brief glimpses of attraction quickly fade. But that is where his choices begin. Either a man will govern his passions and find peace, or he lets himself be dominated by them and becomes unhappy.

B. *Temptation can come when you are unprepared, relaxed, and confident.*

It was a normal day, and everything was going fine. The nation was victorious in war and expanding its boundaries.

---

158   Peterson, 24.

Nothing would indicate the string of events that would soon be set in motion to destroy David's reputation. As E. Allen Petersen states, "I believe this affair came as something of a surprise to both David and Bathsheba. Neither one had planned for this an hour before it happened. It was not the result of flirtation or lecherous conniving. David was a man after God's own heart, and Bathsheba was a faithful wife to her courageous and patriotic husband. David was just coming off a season of prosperity and fame."[159]

C. *Temptation convinces you that the thing you desire is good for you. (James 1:13–15)*

Temptation never considers the consequences—it only considers the immediate gratification. James describes it this way: ". . . each person is tempted when they are dragged away by their own evil desire and enticed. [15] Then, after desire has conceived, it gives birth to sin; and sin, when it is full-grown, gives birth to death."

The lie of temptation is that acting on the object of desire is good for us when, in fact, it is not. James 1 warns us, "Don't be deceived, my dear brothers and sisters. [17] Every good and perfect gift is from above, coming down from the Father of the heavenly lights, who does not change like shifting shadows." Things that are truly good are consistent with the will of God. It brings us back to the Garden where Eve questioned the goodness of God.

It is in these earliest stages of temptation where must practice self-control. Most of our daily actions are automated. We do them with little thought or energy. Think of driving your car to work:

---

159   Petersen, 26.

you back out of the driveway, and before you know it, you are there. Likewise, we "automatically" comb our hair, climb stairs, and do the dishes.

But we also engage in controlled behaviors. These behaviors require conscious thought and effort. Think of driving in a foreign country where cars are on the "wrong" side of the road. Or assembling a piece of furniture with confusing instructions. Or using a software program for the first time. Both automated and controlled behaviors are needed in life. If we had only automated behaviors, we would be like simple robots, mindlessly repeating the same actions every time. But if we had only controlled behaviors, we'd have to intentionally plan and execute every single thing that we do. But we can train the automated impulses.

Plato described self-control as an elephant with a rider on its back, but he uses the analogy differently that of John Haidt who was quoted in the introduction I wonder if Haidt was not aware of Plato's analogy in forming his own . The elephant is a strong animal, weighing six tons. It's also prone to wander off in search of food or whatever else catches its eye. The rider is smart—he knows what needs to be done and is good at planning. The rider is also weak compared to the elephant. For a short time, the rider can control the elephant using muscle, but this never lasts long. The rider soon tires and the elephant can do what it wants. But the rider can train the elephant so that it does what it should do with little effort from the rider. The elephant in Plato's analogy is automated behavior—strong, powerful, but not good at planning and prone to stray. The rider is controlled behavior, who knows what needs to be done but struggles to control the elephant. Willpower or self-control is the strength of the rider.[160]

The Bible speaks of self-control as a good thing. Self-control is a fruit of the Spirit Gal. 5:23 . A person who lacks it is like a city without walls Prov. 25:28 . It's something that church elders should have Titus 1:8 . The practice of Christianity requires self-control. David, when he saw Bathsheba, needed self-control but he failed to apply it at the time he needed it most.

There is a second response to our question, "What does David's affair with Bathsheba teach us about adultery?"

II. The decisions that follow the temptation determine the outcome.

"Then David sent messengers to get her. She came to him, and he slept with her. Now she was purifying herself from her monthly uncleanness. Then she went back home. [5] The woman conceived and sent word to David, saying, 'I am pregnant.'

[6] "So David sent this word to Joab: 'Send me Uriah the Hittite.' And Joab sent him to David. [7] When Uriah came to him, David asked him how Joab was, how the soldiers were and how the war was going. [8] Then David said to Uriah, 'Go down to your house and wash your feet.' So Uriah left the palace, and a gift from the king was sent

___

160   Bradley Wright, "Can You Control Yourself?" *Christianity Today*, May 2017.

after him. ⁹But Uriah slept at the entrance to the palace with all his master's servants and did not go down to his house.

¹⁰David was told, 'Uriah did not go home.' So he asked Uriah, 'Haven't you just come from a military campaign? Why didn't you go home?'

¹¹"Uriah said to David, 'The ark and Israel and Judah are staying in tents,[a] and my commander Joab and my lord's men are camped in the open country. How could I go to my house to eat and drink and make love to my wife? As surely as you live, I will not do such a thing!'

¹²"Then David said to him, 'Stay here one more day, and tomorrow I will send you back.' So Uriah remained in Jerusalem that day and the next.¹³ At David's invitation, he ate and drank with him, and David made him drunk. But in the evening Uriah went out to sleep on his mat among his master's servants; he did not go home."

Let's look at a few observations regarding these verses.

A. Adultery, pregnancy, deception, murder, family tragedy and divine judgment all started with one look. While most men's eyes are typically drawn to attractive women, it seldom goes past the initial impulse—as it should. If David had simply looked away and gone on with his day, in a short time he would have thought little of it. But he allows himself to let it his eyes linger too long, and it stimulates him to indulge in his baser instincts.

B.   Temptation affects decisions regarding your fantasies, your flesh, your faith and your future.[161] David's first decision is to "check up" on this beautiful woman to indulge his fantasy but then takes it a step further and has her brought to his palace flesh . He uses his position as king to put her in a difficult situation. It also affects his faith—the choice to disobey God in an act he knows to be wrong. And as we will see, it impacts his future. It becomes the cause of great pain in his life that would never be the same again.

C.   Things don't just happen; there are usually underlying reasons why people cheat.

No one accidentally finds themselves alone in a room together with someone they are attracted to. Small incremental decisions lead to that context. It sometimes starts with something emotional that is lacking in a marriage relationship and is often a sign of a need for help, an attempt to compensate for deficiencies in the relationship due to situational stress, a warning that someone is suffering.[162] But we must remember circumstances don't make a man, they reveal him. The way to deal with the marital deficiency is not to violate the marriage covenant, yet we are always looking for shortcuts, and superficial lust is an attractive route to consider but leads to a dead end.

C.S. Lewis offers this illustration of lust: "Supposing you are taking a dog on a leash through a turnstile or past a post. You know

---

161   Peterson, 23.

162   Ibid.

what happens apart from his usual ceremonies in passing a post! . He tries to go to the wrong side and gets his head looped round the post. You see that he can't undo it, and therefore pull him back. You pull him back because you want to enable him to go forward. He wants exactly the same thing—namely to go forward; for that very reason he resists your pull back, or, if he is an obedient dog, yields to it reluctantly as a matter of duty, which seems to him to be quite in opposition to his own will; though in fact it is only by yielding to you that he will ever succeed in getting where he wants. The dog believes the lie that the only way forward, the only way to get what it wants, is to push ahead. Lewis, the dog-owner, affirms the longing of the dog to go forward, but he must pull the dog back in order for it to actually make any progress."

So what should you do when you fall into sin? Ask for forgiveness *and* redirection. Lewis continues, "You may go the wrong way again, and again [God] may forgive you: as the dog's master may extricate the dog after he has tied the whole leash round the lamp-post. But there is no hope *in the end* of getting where you want to go except by going God's way."[163]

Let us now look at our third response to our question, "What does David's affair with Bathsheba teach us about adultery?"

III. Covering up the affair is the typical and predictable response. (Chapters 14-27)

"In the morning David wrote a letter to Joab and sent it with Uriah.[15] In it, he wrote, 'Put Uriah out in front

---

163   Trevin Wax, "C.S. Lewis Talks to a Dog About Lust," *The Gospel Coalition Blog, February 2017.*

where the fighting is fiercest. Then withdraw from him so he will be struck down and die.'[16] So while Joab had the city under siege, he put Uriah at a place where he knew the strongest defenders were. [17] When the men of the city came out and fought against Joab, some of the men in David's army fell; moreover, Uriah the Hittite died.[18] Joab sent David a full account of the battle. [19] He instructed the messenger: 'When you have finished giving the king this account of the battle, [20] the king's anger may flare up, and he may ask you, "Why did you get so close to the city to fight? Didn't you know they would shoot arrows from the wall? [21] Who killed Abimelech son of Jerub-Besheth[b]? Didn't a woman drop an upper millstone on him from the wall, so that he died in Thebez? Why did you get so close to the wall?" If he asks you this, then say to him, "Moreover, your servant Uriah the Hittite is dead."'

[22] "The messenger set out, and when he arrived he told David everything Joab had sent him to say. [23] The messenger said to David, 'The men overpowered us and came out against us in the open, but we drove them back to the entrance of the city gate. [24] Then the archers shot arrows at your servants from the wall, and some of the king's men died. Moreover, your servant Uriah the Hittite is dead.'

[25] "David told the messenger, 'Say this to Joab: "Don't let this upset you; the sword devours one as well as another. Press the attack against the city and destroy it. Say this to encourage Joab."

[26] When Uriah's wife heard that her husband was dead, she mourned for him. [27] After the time of mourning was over, David had her brought to his house, and she became his wife and bore him a son. But the thing David had done displeased the Lord."

Note some observations from this passage:

A. Living a lie for one night requires many lies to cover it up.

David, a man after God's own heart becomes cunning, treacherous, ruthless, and unconscionable. In one masterstroke of evil design, David moved quickly and decisively to do all three at once. Bring Uriah home from the war, let him sleep with Bathsheba a night or two, and send him off to war to be killed. All done in the attempt to cover up his adulterous act.[164]

B. The strategy is always the same: protect yourself, blame others, deny the affair, and eliminate the evidence.

Since Adam's time, all men instinctively want to cover their tracks, "because their deeds are evil."[165] What was intended to be a clandestine and passing pleasure now requires a detailed strategy of deception. Living a lie one night, if not confessed completely, requires many lies to cover it. Living a lie makes it easy to start telling lies, in fact, necessitates it. It inevitably hurts marriages.

---

164 Petersen, 26.

165 John 3:19.

C.   Three ways in which infidelity hurts marriages:
   - It causes pain to the offended party. It breaks faith and
     their self-esteem and value to their partner. They begin
     comparing and asking, "What's wrong with me?"
   - It masks the real problem; it avoids dealing with the
     real issues of the intimacy of a relationship—issues that
     are most likely your own and not your spouse's.
   - It destroys character. He wants to restore his trust and
     intimacy with his wife but lies to hide the affair. It is a
     double bind; he loses either way. Instead of bringing
     her closer, it sends her further away. Galatians 6:7 says,
     "Do not be deceived: God cannot be mocked. A man
     reaps what he sows. [8] Whoever sows to please their
     flesh, from the flesh will reap destruction; whoever
     sows to please the Spirit, from the Spirit will reap
     eternal life."

If you read, watch, or listen to the news at all, you would
have heard about a story of a certain United Airlines flight where
a passenger was forcibly removed from an overbooked flight; he
screamed and fought as a security officer wrestled him out of his
seat and dragged him down the aisle by his arms.

Needless the say the video went viral as people roundly
criticized the way the issue was handled and presented a public
relations nightmare for the airline. The Twitterverse offered up
a list of alternative mottos for United: "Would you like a neck
pillow? Or a neck brace?" "We overbooked, but you pay the
price." "We have red-eye and black-eye flights available!" "We put
the hospital in hospitality." "You can run, but you can't fly." As

the *Huffington Post* comments, however, "It's unlikely United will take them up anytime soon." [166]

Sometimes the mistakes we make can feel like our own personal "PR nightmare." Thankfully 1 John 1:9 tells us what do: "If we confess our sins, he is faithful and just and will forgive us our sins and purify us from all unrighteousness."

In this chapter we learned that David's night of pleasure became a nightmare of pain. We learned that his baby died. His beautiful daughter, Tamar, was raped by her half-brother Amnon. Amnon was killed by older brother Absalom. Absalom was separated from David for three years and came back to form a conspiracy against him. When Absalom was finally killed in an ambush, David broke into tears and sobbed, "Oh, Absalom, my son, my son!"

What changes a man chosen by God so that he becomes wily, sinister, and a destroyer of all he and others hold dear? The lessons from David are obvious and apply to all of us. The "Billy Graham rule" was formulated because it acknowledges the damage adultery causes and is an attempt to reduce its likelihood of happening.

What can we do to avoid finding ourselves in a compromising situation?

Remember:

1. No one, however chosen, blessed, and used by God, is immune to an extramarital affair.

2. Anyone, regardless of how many victories he has won, can fall disastrously.

---

166 Lee Moran, "You Carry On, We Carry Off: The Savage New Spoof United Airlines Slogans," last modified April 11, 2017. https://mashable.com/2017/04/11/united-airlines-new-mottos-twitter-hashtag/#hUrBKXohDmq7/.

3. The act of infidelity is the result of uncontrolled desires, thoughts, and fantasies.

4. Your body is your servant, or it becomes your master.

5. A Christian who falls will excuse, rationalize, and conceal, the same as anyone else.

6. Sin can be enjoyable, but it can never be successfully covered.

7. One night of passion can spark years of family pain.

8. Failure is neither fatal nor final.[16]

Men and women alike need to learn that self-control can be both automatic and intentional. N. T. Wright describes this process as virtue: "Virtue is what happens when someone has made a thousand small choices requiring effort and concentration to do something which is good and right, but which doesn't come naturally. And then, on the thousand and first time, when it really matters, they find that they do what's required automatically. Virtue is what happens when wise and courageous choices become second nature." Intentional habit formation is central to the New Testament's call to holiness and sanctification. Citation N.T. Wright, "*After You Believe: hy Christian Character Mattes.*"

16/   Peterson, 32.

CHAPTER 14

COHABITATION: BUILDING A RELATIONSHIP ON A SHAKY FOUNDATION

Text: *1 Thessalonians 4:1–12*

Theme: *Building a healthy, lasting relationship requires both parties to commit to a permanent covenant relationship with God and others.*

Back in my UPS days while attending seminary, one of the workers who worked across the belt from me as we loaded package cars was a guy named Gary. Somehow we got on the topic of marriage, and he told us that he saw no need for marriage—or at least the publically recognized covenant we call marriage. He argued, "I don't need a piece of paper to love one someone. That's all it is, a piece of paper. All it does is complicate things."

In those few words, Gary summarized the common contemporary view of marriage. In this view marriage is simply about two individuals who love each other—so why do you need a piece of paper to prove it. And if this is all that marriage is, then who can argue with him? All the frills, responsibilities, and expectations are not necessary.

But we might ask, "What is the difference between the marriage contract and the cohabitation deal, and why does it really matter?" Linda Waite points out that the prime difference between marriage and cohabitation in contemporary North American culture has to do with time horizons and commitment. What makes marriage unique among emotional and financial relationships is the public vow of permanence. With marriage, partners publicly promise each other that neither one will be alone any longer. Cohabitation, by contrast, is seen by partners and society as a temporary arrangement. They want to leave the back door open should they decide to leave. For that reason, the majority of cohabiters either break up or marry within two years.[168]

And no wonder. The idea of permanence has been replaced with personal autonomy. For many cohabiters, the idea of a relatively easy exit with no well-defined responsibilities constitutes cohabitation's biggest attraction. They view marriage as a bigger commitment than living together, and they do not feel ready at this time to take on the larger responsibilities of another person that marriage represents. Cohabiters, in other words, have a shorter time horizon than spouses do.[169]

Both biblical and empirical evidence shows that we can only form lasting, healthy relationships if both parties begin the relationship with the idea of permanence and as a commitment made before God and others. I want to look at the question, "Why should we value and protect the sacred covenant of marriage between a man and a woman?" and look at three responses.

---

168   Waite., 38.

169   Ibid., 39.

I. Evidence demonstrates that marriage is superior to cohabitation for the good of both the individual and society. (1 Thess. 4:1–8)

The Bible never uses the word, "cohabitation" but that does not mean the practice is not recognized. Biblical sexuality can be summarized in six words, "Abstinence until marriage, fidelity within it." Anything outside of that context is regarded as sexual immorality- that includes cohabitation. Notice what Paul says about this topic.

"As for other matters, brothers and sisters, we instructed you how to live in order to please God, as in fact, you are living. Now we ask you and urge you in the Lord Jesus to do this more and more. [2] For you know what instructions we gave you by the authority of the Lord Jesus.
[3] It is God's will that you should be sanctified: that you should avoid sexual immorality; [4] that each of you should learn to control your own body in a way that is holy and honorable, [5] not in passionate lust like the pagans, who do not know God; [6] and that in this matter no one should wrong or take advantage of a brother or sister. The Lord will punish all those who commit such sins, as we told you and warned you before. [7] For God did not call us to be impure but to live a holy life. [8] Therefore, anyone who rejects this instruction does not reject a human being but God, the very God who gives you his Holy Spirit." The point of this passage is that there are consequences for

abandoning this principle and the evidence seems to bear this out.

A.   Married people live happier lives than cohabiting couples.

The negative stereotype of marriage in our culture is misleading and has led to a dramatic rise in cohabitation rates over the last five decades.[170] As recently as the 1980s, only 13 percent of the children of moderately-educated mothers were born outside of marriage. By the late 2000s, this figure rose to a striking 44 percent.[171] In 1960, 72 percent of American adults were married but only 50 percent were in the year 2008 with only 33 percent among millennials.[172] Young adults who see this have become wary of marriage and believe their chances of having a good marriage are not great—or may even lead to boredom God forbid . As comedian Chris Rock asks, "Do you want to be single and lonely or married and bored?"[173]

This prevailing negative perspective on marriage has led many young adults to see cohabitation as an option between two unpleasant options—marriage or mere sexual encounters. As

---

170   Wilcox, Bradford, "The State of Our Unions Marriage in America," accessed March 9, 2018. www.stateofourunions.org and http://americanvalues.org.

171   Ibid., See also, "The Decline of Marriage and the Rise of New Families," accessed March 9, 2018. http://pewsocialtrends.org/2010/11/18/the-decline-of-marriage-and-rise-of-new-families/2/.

172   Ibid., See also www.hamptonu.edu/ncaamp.
Timothy Keller, *The Meaning of Marriage: Facing the Complexities of Commitment with the   isdom of God* London: Penguin Publishing Group . Kindle edition, 5.

173   Keller, 283.

a result, over half of all people now live together before getting married; whereas, in 1960 virtually no one did—at least it was very rare.[1/4] One-quarter of all unmarried women between the ages of twenty-five and thirty-nine are currently living with a partner, and by their late thirties, more than 60 percent will have done so.[1/5] The overwhelming number of people want to be married, but they avoid it out of fear, based on the information they have. But this drive toward cohabitation is built on faulty information about marriage. The reality is that virtually every study done confirms that married people are happier, healthier, wealthier, and more productive than people who cohabit.

Waite and Gallagher's *The Case For Marriage* concludes: "Most social scientists who have studied the data believe that marriage itself accounts for a great deal of the difference in average well-being between married and unmarried persons. Indeed, loneliness is probably the negative feeling most likely to be alleviated simply by being married." The latest research shows the skeptics are wrong: In real life, the public legal commitment represented by that "piece of paper" makes a big difference. The married really are emotionally healthier than their single counterparts because they've chosen to live in this particular type of committed relationship. The commitment married people make to each other is reinforced and supported not only

---

1/4   Wilcox, 84.

1/5   Mindy E. Scott, et al., "Young Adult Attitudes about Relationships and Marriage: Times May Have Changed, but Expectations Remain High," *Child Trends*, July 2009, www.childtrends.org/Files/Child_Trends-2009_07_08_RB_YoungAdultAttitudes.pdf.

by their own private efforts and emotions but by the wider community . . ."[16]

B.   Children flourish in homes with two married parents. We have long known the negative impact that divorce has on children. So if that is true of divorce, then it only makes sense that they suffer even more in the instability of cohabitation where couples part at much higher rates. In cohabitation, the male partner is often not the father and often cannot relate to them as such. As Waite says, "On average, children lucky enough to have married parents lead emotionally and physically healthier, wealthier, longer, better educated, and more financially successful lives as a result."[17]

C.   There are less psychological and social ailments. Much could be said about this, but let me cite one point. If the great theme of marriage is union, the counter of cohabitation is individualism. Cohabitation is attractive as an alternative to marriage, not only because it is nonbinding and nonlegal but also because it accommodates a very different style of life. But the price of this freedom can be high. By consciously withholding permanent commitment, cohabiters do not reap the advantages of a deeper partnership. Because they do not feel responsible for each other's well-being, cohabiters do not seem to regulate each other's behaviors in the same way spouses do and generally do not reap the profound physical health benefits married couples get. Because the future of their

16   Ibid., 77.
17   Ibid., 140.

partnership is so uncertain, cohabiters cannot risk becoming interdependent as married couples do.[18]

We can think of cohabitation much like we do of buying a car. When I buy a car, I take it for a test drive. I am comparing it to dozens of other options and trying to decide if this is the one for me. And even if I buy it and don't like it, I can sell it and get another one later. Similarly, one of the main reasons that people cohabit is that they have bought into a negative view about the risks of marriage and have decided they want to find out if this potential partner they are involved with is compatible as a permanent mate. So they decide they will give it a test drive by moving in together. It seldom works out.

The problem is that people are not like cars. You cannot test drive them and dispose of them or trade them in for another model without severe emotional damage to at least one of them. It permanently shapes how we view future relationships and destroys the idea of trust. People need to know you are with them through thick or thin.

The second response to our question, "Why should we value and protect the sacred covenant of marriage between a man and a woman?" is:

II. Marriage models God's sacred covenant with us. (Eph. 5:32)

This is something cohabitation cannot do. We return back to our theme verse for this book: "For this reason, a man will leave

---

18   Waite., 44.

his father and mother and be united to his wife, and the two will become one flesh. [32] This is a profound mystery—but I am talking about Christ and the church."

A.   Marriage in Scripture is a publicly recognized covenant. Even in today's secular world we still seem to think this public commitment benefits society. How much more so if we know that it is God who also recognizes it and binds it?

B.   The marriage covenant is more conducive to stable relationships because it is built on commitment and trust.

Cohabitation builds relationships on the idea of a back door. In other words, "If I find this relationship is not working, I always have a backdoor exit." Now think for a moment what that means. It says, "I do not trust you enough, and you do not trust myself enough to commit to a lifelong relationship, so we will live together instead, and we can leave at any time one of us chooses to." Think about what this means: the foundation of your relationship is built on distrust and with it comes the potential that either one of you can choose the timing on the way out. You can't build a steady relationship on that. If you started your relationship with distrust, then you have to go back and rebuild the foundation—one based on trust. Why? Because distrust as the foundation itself is shaky.

C.   Deciding is better than sliding when forming a relationship.

Many slide into a relationship. They start dating and spending time together and enjoy being together but are not ready for the commitment of marriage. So they decide just to move in together. No real commitment, just superficial agreements over financial arrangements, no long-term discussions about children or careers or how responsibilities are to be shared. There is no covenant, no vow, and no public recognition. Just a relationship that feels good at the time but ignores the rough and tumble that goes with commitments that make a relationship work.

What a covenant does is set the terms of the relationship—the most fundamental of which is, "this is permanent." Cohabitation is built solely on individuals' changing moods and as a result, leads to relational instability.

Countries with individualistic traditions have some of the highest rates of instability in the West. Scott Stanley at the University of Denver[179] demonstrates that couples who cohabit prior to a public engagement are far more likely to flounder in their marriages. As one author states, "We think that's because they are more likely to experience sliding into marriage rather than deciding to be together and then getting married. In some ways, cohabitation is sort of like being at McDonald's compared to having a nice meal at one's home. Cohabitation is quick, it's convenient, and it can taste good. But it doesn't leave the same feeling in your stomach as a good home-prepared meal does, and it's not as healthy and as enriching for you." Cohabiters have more individual freedom to do exactly what they like, but they have more difficulty reaping the kinds of benefits that come from jointly planning for the long

179 Center for Marital and Family Studies. Accessed March 7, 2018. https://www.du.edu/ahss/psychology/marriage.

haul.[180] Should that surprise us? If God gives us His standards for our good, it only makes sense that we disregard them at our own risk.

Now let us look at our final response to our question, "Why should we value and protect the sacred covenant of marriage between a man and a woman?"

III. Marriage brings into check the radical individualism that drives cohabitation. (1 Thess. 4:9–12)

> "Now about your love for one another we do not need to write to you, for you yourselves have been taught by God to love each other. And in fact, you do love all of God's family throughout Macedonia. Yet we urge you, brothers and sisters, to do so more and more, and to make it your ambition to lead a quiet life: You should mind your own business and work with your hands, just as we told you, so that your daily life may win the respect of outsiders and so that you will not be dependent on anybody."

This passage is telling us to love one another. Love means that we seek the best for the object loved and Jesus is our model for that. It includes three things:

A. The marriage union balances individual autonomy with the common good. When a culture stresses individual rights over

---

180   Waite, 45-46.

the common good we should not be surprised that people act accordingly—even in marriage. Most cohabiters give little serious thought to how their marriage, or lack of it, affects those around them. This includes children, family, schools, culture, etc. It is about "me."

B.   Self-sacrifice is foundational to the marriage covenant. And this is what many cohabiters do not want. Marriage will change us; we have to give up something. Many men say they do not want to marry because they do not want to change. They do not want their freedoms taken away. And yet this is what marriage is, and it is what most men need. They need marriage to bring their passions in check and to live for something other than themselves.

C.   God's grace can enable us to flourish in spite of our failures in marriage, but we may still face consequences.

One of the challenges, when I speak on marriage, is that I know many that I am speaking to are not married. For some it is not a choice. Either they never married, or a spouse left them. They are not in sin and should heed Paul's words of encouragement to singles in 1 Corinthians 7:25–35. But in today's society, I know there will always be those in the room who have lived together and possibly still are living together. God's grace and forgiveness are available, but as the Scripture reminds, we must confess it as sin and put it behind us. God is always ready and willing to accept us, but we must not remain in that state—even if it has become comfortable to us.

A small article in *The   eek*, a secular source for world and American news, made the following statement: "Want to help America's economy and yourself at the same time? Then get married." The advantages of raising kids in a stable household are well documented: "Children of married parents are more likely to graduate high school, less likely to go to jail, and more likely to delay sexual activity." . . . [Kids from single-parent homes] are "five times as likely to live in poverty." Men who marry, research has shown, are more productive at work, are paid better, and are more likely to be employed than their unmarried counterparts. Economist Stephen Moore has pointed out that marriage is a "far better social program than food stamps,

Medicaid, public housing, or even all of them combined."[181]

Yet despite the advantages of connubial life, "single-parent families have exploded." Today, more than 43 percent of American children are born out of wedlock. To restore the vigorous economic growth that built America's middle class, we first need to restore the "pro-growth" institution of marriage.[182]

In this chapter we saw that both biblical and empirical evidence show that we can only form healthy, lasting relationships if both parties begin the relationship with the idea of permanence and as a commitment made before God and others.

Since my days at UPS, I have heard many people like Gary tell me that marriage is only a piece of paper that just complicates things. But we ignore the moral aspects of being obedient to God

---

181   Stephen Moore, "Marriages Strengthen Our Country and Ourselves,"
The   eek, November 2014.

182   Wilcox.

and its great benefits to both the individual and society with such a view.

Here are some things to ponder as you reflect on this chapter:

1. A person is not like a car. You cannot test drive and throw a person away if things do not work. That is why "seeing if this person is compatible" will assure you they are not. No two people are compatible. Marriage is about putting two incompatible people together and learning to make it work.

2. The nature of the marriage relationship versus cohabitation is fundamentally different. If cohabitation is about keeping the back door open in case it is needed, then marriage is about closing the back door—thus, the high divorce rate of cohabiters who eventually marry. Closing the back door changes the relationship.

3. The ongoing emphasis on autonomy and individualism will assure us that unstable relationships will continue to be the norm. Until we understand that marriage is about sacrifice, as modeled by that of Jesus, we will always have high divorce rates and high cohabitation.

Time magazine recently featured an article that asked, "Is monogamy over?" The article offered various opinions, including "monogamy is a charade" that leads to "institutionalizing dishonesty," and "[monogamy] is just an option, not the default," and "There's no right, there's no wrong." *Time* also featured Pastor Andy Stanley who offered this biblical view: Monogamy is more like an endangered species. Rare. Valuable. Something to be fed and protected. Perhaps an armed guard should be assigned to every monogamous couple to ward off poachers. Perhaps not.[183]

The value a culture places on monogamy determines the welfare of its women and children. Women and children do not fare well in societies that embrace polygamy or promiscuity. In the majority of cases, sexual freedom undermines the financial freedom of women. Sexual freedom eventually undermines the financial and emotional security of children.

If we are only biology, none of the above really matters . . . If we are only biology, monogamy was probably a flawed concept from the start. But very few of us live as if we are only biology. As a pastor, I've officiated my share of weddings and I've done my share of premarital counseling. I always ask couples why they are getting married. Survival of the species never makes the list.

The *I* and *you* that inhabit our bodies desire more than another body. We desire intimacy—to know and to be fully known without fear. Intimacy is fragile. Intimacy is powerful. Intimacy is fueled by exclusivity. So, no, monogamy is not obsolete. It's endangered.[184]

---

183   David Barash, "Monogamy Is Not Natural But It's Nice," *Time*, September 2015. http://time.com/collection-post/4028151/david-barash-is-monogamy-over.

184   Ibid.

‖ CHAPTER 15 ‖

I THINK I MARRIED
THE WRONG PERSON

Text: *Hosea*
Theme: *The bond of marriage is grounded in the covenant—not in the ideal person.*

Some years ago there was a popular movie whose message was that somewhere in the world is a perfect soulmate made just for you in heaven—you just have to find him or her. The movie, called *Made in Heaven*, tells the story of two people who had a few chance encounters on Earth and had an immediate sense of some deep connection. It is clear that they were made for each other before they were ever born, and until they connect with each other, they will never feel complete or fulfilled. The plot is that that these encounters did not bring them together due to interference and heaven must intervene.

This popular notion of a soulmate, which suggests that God has a person out there for you to simply discover has no basis in reality. Yet many single people are looking for their perfect soulmate who will complete and satisfy their most basic longings—and many married people fear they missed connecting with them.

The belief originated with Plato, an ancient Greek philosopher, who taught that men and women were made in one body but separated by the gods as a curse. Each man and woman scours the Earth for that undiscovered spouse so the two can again become one.[185] The problem is that this view makes us half-persons. If each woman constantly searches for the man who will "complete" her, she can never be complete. It also means she will be searching for this nonexistent perfect person who will fulfill her in a way the non-soulmate never could. Even worse, she cannot live for Christ. I believe this misplaced search for a soulmate is counterproductive to the real work of building healthy, lasting marriages. Why? Because it leads to disillusionment when we find that marriage, by nature, is two self-absorbed people who are bound primarily by a covenant. In that light it is better to seek out someone with a common faith, character, and values—and even then there can be tension. When you discover you are left with an unsatisfactory partner, then that is when the real work of building a relationship begins.

I want us to see that the bond of marriage is grounded in the covenant we made, not in discovering the ideal soulmate. In that light, let's ask the question, "What do you do if you think you have married the wrong person?"

To answer this question, I want us to return to the book of Hosea—a book we looked at a few chapters ago when we looked at how to handle betrayal in marriage. If you recall from that chapter, we learned that the book opens saying, "When

---

185   Plato, "Symposium," Translated by Benjamen Jolett, *Gutenberg*. Accessed March 7, 2018. http://www.gutenberg.org/ebooks/1600.

the Lord began to speak through Hosea, the Lord said to him, 'Go, marry a promiscuous woman and have children with her, for like an adulterous wife, this land is guilty of unfaithfulness to the Lord.' ³ So he married Gomer, daughter of Diblaim, and she conceived and bore him a son."

In these verses, God gives an astounding command to Hosea to go and marry a prostitute—not a person we would consider ideal marriage material. And if there was ever a wrong person to marry, this would be it. We later learn that Hosea's marriage illustrates how Gods people, Israel, has betrayed Him and prostituted themselves with other gods. God wants us to have a clear picture of what Israel is doing to Him, and what better way than to use the covenant of marriage. The book can be broken down into two main sections: Hosea's wayward wife and God's wayward people. So let's again ask the question: "What do you do if you think you have married the wrong person?"

I. Understand that the ideal marriage is not about the person but the covenant. (Hosea 1-3)

This notion that there is an ideal person out there for you has led to more disillusionment among couples than just about anything else. This book should help dispel that notion. The first three chapters of the book tell about how Hosea handled his wayward wife. At the same time that she enjoyed Hosea's love and generosity, she was running from man to man, causing disgrace to him. She abandoned her children and scorned her faithful husband. The book is not flattering to her in any way. In these chapters we notice three things:

A. Hosea was commanded by God to marry a prostitute. It assures that Hosea will face disappointment, betrayal, and unfaithfulness. But this does not diminish the permanence of the marriage covenant. We are reminded again, just as we have been throughout this book, that marriage is to be modeled after the covenant that Jesus has with His church, or, as in this case, God and Israel. The book reveals several things.

- The hero in this book is God. He is faithful even though Israel prostituted herself by worshipping false gods. Still Yahweh God shows unfailing in His love for her. He honored the covenant He had made with her even when she did not.
- It was to call them to repentance. Sometimes we need word pictures to help us understand something clearly, and this book is an example. If Israel could see for themselves that they are like Gomer, Hosea's wife, then they could understand why God is angry and why they need to reconcile with Him.
- It was to reveal God's willingness to forgive. God wants Israel to abandon the false gods they have cherished and to return to Him. We find He is willing to forgive them of their unfaithfulness, but they must repent.

B. Throughout most of history, a person did not choose his or her spouse. Marrying a prostitute was not Hosea's choosing. Similarly, historically, most cultures had someone other than the couple themselves, choose their mate. It was usually the father. We find an example when we learn that Abraham chose Isaac's wife for him. We find it in Hindu cultures where a child's mate is determined while he or she is very young.

I read a book recently on Crazy Horse, the chief of the Sioux tribe who confronted General Custer at the famous Battle of the Big Horn. In the book, Stephen Ambrose writes how Native Americans selected their spouse. He says, "In legal theory, the girls had no say in the choice of a husband, but in practice, most Sioux fathers would bend with the wishes of their daughters. In the usual case, the father of the prospective bride would put the matter to her. If she was willing to marry the suitor, she put the matter back into his hands, meekly submitting to her father's will. If she disapproved she let her feelings be known; when that happened, the father would refuse the ponies and other gifts offered by the suitor. But the father might insist, in which case the duty of the girl to submit to his wishes was clear. The girls had little basis for making a choice because courtship among the Sioux was terribly restricted."[186]

Frankly, I like the idea that I was able to choose my own spouse. I understand our modern aversion to having someone choose for us. But remember, we bear greater responsibility when we choose our own spouse. In our culture we pride ourselves on the fact that we get to make our own choices in regard to who we marry. But let's not forget that approach is historically novel. It also means we bear full responsibility when we choose. If you choose poorly you

186   Stephen Ambrose, *Crazy Horse and Custer: The Parallel Lives of Two American Warriors* New York: Open Road Integrated Media . Kindle edition, 136-137.

have no one but yourself to blame. We must also keep in mind that:

- Just because we choose our own partners does not mean we are less responsible to honor the covenant. God does not lessen the nature of the covenant because we choose badly.
- Just because divorce is now easier and more available does not mean the covenant before God is less binding. Our cultural laxness toward the marital bond is not shared by God.
- Just because divorce is more acceptable in society does not mean God's views on it have changed.

C. We need more than passion and romance to drive our decision. I am convinced that so many of the values that we look for in a mate are superficial and not ideally suited for strong marriages. We value things like good looks, sex appeal, charm, humor, etc.; whereas, we should be looking more at things like integrity, character, responsibility, faithfulness, etc.—things that are not so romantic or sexy. But we must also realize that:

- Even if we think we have married our soulmate, we can be disappointed. There are no guarantees that your Prince Charming will always sweep you off your feet. In fact, I would suggest you will find he is as flawed a person as you are.
- If we can realize the truth that there is no such thing as a soulmate, it is easier to get to the root of what makes a marriage work.

Debra Fileta puts it this way, "I think this philosophy of a 'soulmate' has done far more harm than good in our society . . . Beyond the fact that the term is founded completely in a fairytale, it's also entirely unbiblical. It is a title that promotes 'feeling' and 'energy' that attracts one person to another. It's a dangerous concept because it fools you into believing that love and marriage hinge on emotional ecstasy. And even more detrimental is that it gets you to believe that you are incomplete until you come face-to-face with the love of your life."[187] The fact is that feelings come and go. Those who build their relationships on the foundation of "feeling" will find that when the rain comes—their love quickly crumbles.

Fileta continues, "Don't freak out if the feelings aren't magical or mystical because frankly, they were never intended to be. Look for qualities, traits, and characteristics that are attractive based on the things you know you need and want in a relationship. Find a relationship that emits healthiness, wholeness, and respect. Take it one step at a time, and be assured that in a right relationship, feelings will always be present, but they can never be the foundation of a healthy relationship. True love is based on a healthy combination of facts and feelings and a whole lot of good choices. May God give you the wisdom to choose well."[188]

---

187   Debra Fileta, "Why There's no Such Thing as a Soul Mate," last modified October 11, 2016. http://truelovedates.com/why-theres-no-such-thing-as-a-soul-mate.

188   Ibid.

II. Look to God's model of what unfailing love looks like when a flawed partner strays. (Chapters 4-13)

The next eleven chapters of Hosea give a vivid description of God's interactions with His wayward people. We see three major themes in these chapters:

A. God's standard for us is high because He is Holy Hosea 4-7 . Hosea provides a scathing assessment of Israel. Her idolatry permeated every area of her life and character including the priesthood, and God deemed her incurable. God's holiness was violated, and her acts were found intolerable. Her lists of offenses are long and intense.

God could easily have asked, "Did I figuratively marry the wrong person?" Israel's rebellion, like that of Gomer, could have easily have led to outright abandonment. We would not be surprised if God had simply said, "Enough is enough! I am leaving you and letting you deal with your own demise." Yet we find that He hung in there with them.

B. God holds us to account for our actions because He is just Hosea 8-10 . These chapters outline the discipline that God gave Israel. It was severe, but it properly matched the nature of their offense. These verses dispel the notion that harsh discipline is inconsistent with love.

Hebrews 12:5–12 remind us of the relationship between God's love and His discipline: "My son, do not make light of the Lord's discipline, and do not lose heart when he rebukes you, because the Lord disciplines the one he loves, and he chastens everyone he accepts as his son. Endure hardship as discipline; God is treating you as his children. For what children are not disciplined by their father? If you are not disciplined—and everyone undergoes discipline—then you are not legitimate, not true sons and daughters at all. Moreover, we have all had human fathers who disciplined us, and we respected them for it. How much more should we submit to the Father of spirits and live! They disciplined us for a little while as they thought best; but God disciplines us for our good, in order that we may share in his holiness. No discipline seems pleasant at the time, but painful. Later on, however, it produces a harvest of righteousness and peace for those who have been trained by it."

Applied to marriage, this suggests that it is loving and appropriate to confront sinful behavior and demand correction of a wayward spouse. The goal of love is not to condemn or affirm bad behavior but to produce change that removes the rift in the relationship.

C. God is unwavering in his patience and forgiveness because He is love Hosea 11-13 . In spite of all that Israel had done, God did not abandon them and was willing to forgive them. That is the message of Hosea. That is the nature of a covenant marriage. It does not ignore and minimize the offense, but it also does not give up on the person.

God was never disillusioned with us in this sense; he never says, "I choose the wrong people." Why? Because He did not start with a flawed assumption about our true nature; he knows we are sinners. But He models for us how we are to be with our own spouses who share our flaws—much like that of Hosea thankfully few of us are in such a relationship . Once we have married the person, the matter of who we married becomes moot—the person we choose to marry is the person we are called to love.

Every marriage should begin with three assumptions:

1. The person I am marrying is imperfect.

2. I may not be able to change certain traits of that person.

3. I must somehow love the imperfect person I am married to.

Kyle Benson puts it this way, "Lacey married Andrew, who tends to be loud at parties. Lacey, who is shy, hates that. But if Andrew had married Molly, he and Molly would have gotten into a fight before they even got to the party. That's because Andrew is always late, and Molly hates to be kept waiting. If someone is late, Molly feels taken for granted; something in her childhood made her sensitive about that. If Molly were to confront Andrew on being late, Andrew would have believed that her complaining was an attempt to dominate him. That's something he gets upset over rather quickly.

"If Andrew had married Leah, they wouldn't have even made it to the party, because they would be fighting about Andrew's lack of help with the housework. This makes Leah feel abandoned, something that makes her stomach queasy. And Andrew would have seen Leah's complaining as an attempt to dominate him."

Since we are never perfect, and our soulmates are never perfect, our imperfections are bound to cause two types of problems: solvable problems and unsolvable problems. Solvable conflicts can be as simple as setting up a relationship ritual such as a five-minute coffee chat to feel more emotionally connected. Solvable conflicts reach a resolution and rarely get brought up again.[189]

Regarding unresolvable problems, we must learn that the idea that we can solve all of our relational problems is a fairytale; get used to it.

III. Restoration should always be our driving motive. (Hosea 14)

A. Marriage is about the painful task of changing us to think beyond ourselves. Our contemporary obsession with personal fulfillment promotes the idea that marriage is about the happiness of both parties. This suggests that we must accept each other just as we are and should not demand the other partner change. Yet this flies in the face of reality. Any healthy marriage requires we give up something of value for the benefit of the marriage.

B. The errant partner bears the responsibility for his unfaithfulness. Love may require us to confront inappropriate behavior. Silence or avoidance is seldom the best response to conflict reduction. The expectation that the other person changes inappropriate behavior is not out of place. You will face pain either way, whether you deal with it now or later.

---

189   Kyle Benson, "Choosing a Lover is Choosing to Love a Set of Problems," last modified February 29, 2016. http://kylebenson.net/soulmate-problem.

The difference is you have more control if you address it before you have fully demonized the other person.

C. In our unfailing love, we must call them to repentance. Remember, the goal is restoring the relationship. If their behavior is creating a rift, calling them on it has a place.

D. Ultimately it is the covenant that must sustain any marriage. It may be years before a person changes, but hanging in there is better than quick abandonment. In fact, God often uses these hard times to change us as well. It is these painful periods of life that God uses to produce something far greater.

Ravi Zacharias quotes a powerful poem that can be applied to how the difficulties and disillusionment of marriage can be used by God to shape us. It is called, "When God Wants To Drill A Man." It goes like this:

When God wants to drill a man,
And thrill a man,
And skill a man
When God wants to mold a man
To play the noblest part;

When He yearns with all His heart
To create so great and bold a man
That all the world shall be amazed,
Watch His methods, watch His ways!

How He ruthlessly perfects
Whom He royally elects!

How He hammers him and hurts him,
And with mighty blows converts him
Into trial shapes of clay which
Only God understands;
While his tortured heart is crying
And he lifts beseeching hands!

How He bends but never breaks
When his good He undertakes;
How He uses whom He chooses,
And which every purpose fuses him;
By every act induces him
To try His splendor out-
God knows what He's about.

– *Anonymous*

God can use the torturous moments of marriage to mold us into something that makes us better. Each blow of the hammer shapes us into someone useful for His glory. Let us not stifle the work of God by cutting it short by giving up on that person.

In this chapter we found that the bond of marriage is grounded in the covenant we made, not in discovering the ideal soulmate waiting for us out in the world. We asked the question, "What do you do if you think you have married the wrong person?" and we learned that the ideal marriage is not about the ideal person but about the covenant we have made with God and our spouse.

The fact is that there are no soulmates made for us in heaven that we must scour the world trying to locate. We must instead seek out someone that shares our commitment to Christ and supports our desire to be like Him. Ironically, we may find out that in doing so we will match up quite well with that person.

Let me finish with some ways to apply the lessons of this chapter.

1. People who are unhappy in their marriage sometimes claim that they did not marry their soulmate and therefore should divorce and begin the search for their true soulmate. This is nothing more than an excuse—an unbiblical excuse.

2. A marriage may not be as unified and joyous as a couple wishes it to be. A husband and wife may not have the physical, emotional, and spiritual unity that they desire. But even in this instance, the husband and wife need to work on developing true intimacy by obeying what the Bible teaches about marriage.

3. If we give ourselves to God and seek His guidance, He promises to direct us: "Trust in the LORD with all your heart and lean not on your own understanding; in all your ways acknowledge him and he will make your paths straight."

4. Even if a marriage was not God's desire, it is still within His sovereign will and plan. God hates divorce and "marrying the wrong person" is never presented in the Bible as grounds for divorce.

5. Ultimately, God is our completer.[190] As Jerry Root

---

190   Eric Metaxas, "How 'soul mate' nonsense is destroying Christian Marriages," last modified September 28, 2015. https://www.lifesitenews.com/opinion/how-soul-mate-nonsense-is-destroying-christian-marriages.

and Stan Guthrie point out, putting others in God's place—expecting them to give us what only He can—is a naked form of idolatry and will only lead to deep disappointment.

6. The soulmate idea suggests that marriage is all about *me*, that I need to find someone who understands *me* perfectly, who makes *me* happy. Marriage should be about finding someone *you* can make happy.

Ronald Reagan once quipped that the trouble with his political opponents "is not that they are ignorant. It's just that they know so much that isn't so."[191] That describes our modern problem with our soulmate view of marriage. It just isn't so. As J.R.R. Tolkien once wrote to his son, "No man, however truly he loved his betrothed and bride as a young man has lived faithful to her as a wife in mind and body without deliberate conscious exercise of the will, without self-denial."[192]

---

191 "Ronald Reagan Quotes," accessed March 6, 2018 , https://www.brainyquote.com/quotes/ronald_reagan_440/32.

192 "To Michael Tolkien," accessed March 6, 2018 , http://glim.ru/personal/jrr_tolkien_42-45.html.

CHAPTER 16

MARRIED TO A FOOL

Text: *1 Samuel 25*

Theme: *Being married to a fool requires great wisdom and maturity.*

His name was Mike. Mike was wealthy and very generous. He could be likable and charming, and I am sure his wife saw those attributes when she married him. But there was another side to Mike; he could be very opinionated and controlling, leading him at times to be verbally abusive to his wife. He would demean her in public in ways that left her speechless and humiliated.

A few years into my pastorate at that church he came to me angry and emotional. He told me his wife was behaving badly—possibly even having an affair. Knowing Mike and his controlling tendencies, it did not take me long to figure out what was going on. All the things his wife was doing fit the pattern of a distraught wife. But because controlling people also tend to be highly jealous, I questioned his assessment of his wife's unfaithfulness in light of her character.

I told him the problem, as I saw it, in how he was treating his wife and why I was questioning his evaluation of what was going on. Like others in the past, he got mad and left. Shortly after, I did find out his wife was inappropriately attentive to another man, validating Mike's suspicions.

A few months later Mike returned to my office to thank me for our earlier meeting. I was surprised since that seldom happens. He told me that when he left my office earlier he was furious with me, but it caused him to question, *hat if it is true*? So he found a ministry called "Life Skills," which helps abusive husbands change. He took a profile test and learned that he showed all the traits of an abuser and he then went to sessions to deal with the issue. It was after completing his first stage that he came to thank me. It began to change his life, and he now leads sessions for the ministry.

There are far too many stories like Mike's, but most do not recognize their abusiveness or allow themselves to change; as a result they keep hitting the same brick wall. In many marriages like Mike's, there is one person who is dysfunctional and everyone else has to learn how to work around them. In fact, there is a field of study called "Conjoint Family Therapy" built around the idea that dealing with behavioral issues in children requires you to also consider the key person that is creating a dysfunctional dynamic in the family.[193] We have learned that a high level of maturity and wisdom is required to handle abusive people.

In this chapter I want us to look at an example of such a person in the Bible and see how his wife handled a crisis that he created because of his foolish actions and behavior. We will look at

---

193   Virgina Satir, *Conjoint Family Therapy* East York: Hushion House, 1993 ; *Peoplemaking,* Palo Alto: Science and Behavior Books, 1988 .

a woman named Abigail and ask, "What can we learn from Abigail about how to handle being married to a fool?"

I. Your spouse's foolish acts may sometimes require your skillful intervention. (1 Sam. 25:1–13)

There are three characters in our story. With two of them, we see different responses in how they dealt with the dysfunctional character in the story. The name of the dysfunctional character is Nabal.

A. Nabal's foolishness becomes apparent as the story unfolds.

"Now Samuel died, and all Israel assembled and mourned for him, and they buried him at his home in Ramah. Then David moved down into the Desert of Paran. ² A certain man in Maon, who had property there at Carmel, was very wealthy. He had a thousand goats and three thousand sheep, which he was shearing in Carmel. ³ His name was Nabal and his wife's name was Abigail. She was an intelligent and beautiful woman, but her husband was surly and mean in his dealings—he was a Calebite.

⁴ "While David was in the wilderness, he heard that Nabal was shearing sheep. ⁵ So he sent ten young men and said to them, 'Go up to Nabal at Carmel and greet him in my name. ⁶ Say to him: 'Long life to you! Good health to you and your household! And good health to all that is yours! ⁷ Now I hear that it is sheep-shearing time. When your shepherds were with us, we did not mistreat them, and

the whole time they were at Carmel nothing of theirs was missing. [8] Ask your own servants and they will tell you. Therefore, be favorable toward my men, since we come at a festive time. Please give your servants and your son David whatever you can find for them.'

[9] "When David's men arrived, they gave Nabal this message in David's name. Then they waited.

[10] Nabal answered David's servants, 'Who is this David? Who is this son of Jesse? Many servants are breaking away from their masters these days. [11] Why should I take my bread and water, and the meat I have slaughtered for my shearers, and give it to men coming from who knows where?' [12] David's men turned around and went back. When they arrived, they reported every word. [13] David said to his men, 'Each of you strap on your sword!' So they did, and David strapped his on as well. About four hundred men went up with David, while two hundred stayed with the supplies."

Notice two things in the story's plot.

1. David protected Nabal's people and sheep when they were grazing in his territory. He did it as an act of kindness and generosity. We learn later that Nabal's servants saw it and appreciated it.

2. David needs some food for his men and politely asks Nabal for a return favor. It was an ancient cultural expectation that when someone asks for some food, you provide it for them. David's request is fair, especially in light of what he had done.

B. Nabal rudely and ignorantly rejects David and his request. Nabal doesn't just reject the request, he does it in an offensive way. He does not consult with his servants and he does not check to find out who David is. He simply jumps to the conclusion that David and his men are just riff-raff trying to scourge a free meal.

C. David responds to Nabal's foolish offense by preparing for a fight. Needless to say, it is certainly not the best response in that the servants who he is going to wipe out are not to blame. Like many scenarios, an angry response seldom matches the nature of the offense.

Nabal's arrogant foolishness reminds us of people we know who are so self-obsessed that they create misery for themselves and others. I always wonder, why can't they see in themselves what seems so obvious to others? Don't they see how foolish and abusive they are? The answer is "no"—at least until they face the consequences of it.

My most difficult role in counseling is to get people to see themselves as they really are. You can't change something if you can't see the problem, and even then it may seem too overwhelming to deal with. I have used the Johari window to help people understand how we all have blind spots. Four quadrants: 1. Known to self; 2. Known others; 3. Unknown to self; 4. Unknown to others.[194]

---

194   Kenneth Blanchard and Paul Hersey, *Management of Organization Behavior* Englewood Cliffs: Prentice Hall, 1988 , 2/8.

The Johari Window

$\longrightarrow$ Feedback $\longrightarrow$

	Known to Self	Known to Others
Known to Others	I Public Area	II Blind Area
Unknown to Others	III Hidden Area	IV Unknown Area

Disclosure (↓)

The bigger our window, the better equipped we are to deal with issues because we see ourselves as we appear to others. For that reason I give profile and personality tests to help people see themselves because unless they do, they will continue to behave as they always have. Don't be afraid of seeing yourself as you really are. It may not be pretty but until you do you cannot change. Don't wait until the pain to stay the same exceeds the pain to change. But be assured, there will be pain either way.

There is another response to our question, "What can we learn from Abigail about how to handle being married to a fool?"

II. Your skillful intervention may require wisdom, risk, and subtlety. (1 Sam. 25:14–32)

"One of the servants told Abigail, Nabal's wife, 'David sent messengers from the wilderness to give our master his greetings, but he hurled insults at them. Yet these men were very good to us. They did not mistreat us, and the whole time we were out in the fields near them nothing was missing. Night and day they were a wall around us the whole time we were herding our sheep near them. Now think it over and see what you can do, because disaster is hanging over our master and his whole household. He is such a wicked man that no one can talk to him.'

"Abigail acted quickly. She took two hundred loaves of bread, two skins of wine, five dressed sheep, five seahs of roasted grain, a hundred cakes of raisins and two hundred cakes of pressed figs and loaded them on donkeys. Then she told her servants, 'Go on ahead; I'll follow you.' But she did not tell her husband Nabal.

"As she came riding her donkey into a mountain ravine, there were David and his men descending toward her, and she met them. David had just said, 'It's been useless—all my watching over this fellow's property in the wilderness so that nothing of his was missing. He has paid me back evil for good. May God deal with David, be it ever so severely if by morning I leave alive one male of all who belong to him!'

"When Abigail saw David, she quickly got off her donkey and bowed down before David with her face to the ground. 24 She fell at his feet and said: 'Pardon your servant, my lord, and let me speak to you; hear what your servant has to say. Please pay no attention, my lord, to that wicked man Nabal. He is just like his name—his name means Fool, and folly goes with him. And as for me, your servant, I did not see the men my lord sent. And now, my lord, as surely as the Lord your God lives and as you live, since the Lord has kept you from bloodshed and from avenging yourself with your own hands, may your enemies and all who are intent on harming my lord be like Nabal. And let this gift, which your servant has brought to my lord, be given to the men who follow you.

'Please forgive your servant's presumption. The Lord your God will certainly make a lasting dynasty for my lord, because you fight the Lord's battles, and no wrongdoing will be found in you as long as you live. Even though someone is pursuing you to take your life, the life of my lord will be bound securely in the bundle of the living by the Lord your God, but the lives of your enemies he will hurl away as from the pocket of a sling. When the Lord has fulfilled for my lord every good thing he promised concerning him and has appointed him ruler over Israel, my lord will not have on his conscience the staggering burden of needless bloodshed or of having avenged himself. And when the Lord your God has brought my lord success, remember your servant.'"

The story we just read is Hebrew wordplay:

- Nabal means fool- Foolishness, and wickedness are often associated in scripture. We learn he is an arrogant, mean fool who is clueless about who he has offended.
- Abigail means wisdom. Wisdom and righteousness are often associated in scripture. I am sure that in being married to a guy like Nabal she has had to learn wisdom. In today's world a woman could divorce, but in her world, it is not an option. Even so, I am not convinced divorce is generally the right response even though it is more accepted in our culture. I respect people who stick in there in these contexts. It means they understand the nature of the marriage covenant.

B.   Abigail has to intervene between two proud men bent on destruction. We see:
- Nabal- who fails to appreciate David's authority and kindness and is oblivious to the threat that he created. He naively goes about life unaware that his life could soon end.
- David- she intervenes on behalf of David for acting on his anger to potentially kill a person for his foolishness. David has not yet become king, which happens in 2 Samuel, but he has established his reputation and stature for anyone remotely aware of what's going on. Certainly Abigail was aware, and she knew the real risk they were facing.

C.   She skillfully defuses the situation by her wisdom and carefully chosen words. What can we learn from her response?

- Abigail accurately understands the situation. She carefully listens to the warning from her servants. One of the first steps in gaining wisdom is to listen and try to get a realistic, accurate assessment of what is happening.
- Act quickly. Her quick and wise response prompts her to appease David's anger. She has to quickly figure out what to do and get everything together on a moment's notice.
- Focus attention and energy on the best approach—not on your powerlessness.
- See it from the perspective of the other. In her appeal to David, we find she has no delusions regarding the situation or the wicked nature of her husband. She essentially says, "Nabal is his name and folly is his game." She has probably seen and lived with his foolishness and meanness for some time. She is saying, "We both know he is a moron, but is it fair to let everyone suffer for his stupidity?"
- She provides for David the things he requested. That part of the issue is settled by her offering, but it is the offense that is the greater issue and she knows she must address it. Now David's ego must be appeased—the very type of thing she is experienced in.
- She praises his good nature and sense of fairness. There is a lot of praise, humility, and brownnosing in her appeasement.
- She asks for his compassion and restraint. Her main objective is to save everyone's life, including that of her

husband. It required great restraint and humility to do so.

Abigail's response provides an incredible guide for dealing with hotheads—in this case, two. Wisdom is the fine art of maneuvering between what is good and what will work. We can be idealistic with no sense of reality, or realists with no sense of could or should be. She could see the right path between the two extremes.

Unfortunately in life we lose the idealism and become a cynical realist. In his newest book, *Poke the Box,* Seth Godin shares this thought: "Sooner or later, many idealists transform themselves into disheartened realists who believe that giving up is the same thing as being realistic."[195]

We need both, idealism and realism, but even more so we need the wisdom to know the difference. We are reminded again of "The Serenity Prayer" which says it well: "God, grant me the serenity to accept the things I cannot change, Courage to change the things I can, and wisdom to know the difference." Abigail models that very well.

Let us return to our question, "What can we learn from Abigail about how to handle being married to a fool?"

III. Wisdom is often rewarded beyond our expectations. (1 Sam. 25:3–44)

"David said to Abigail, 'Praise be to the Lord, the God of Israel, who has sent you today to meet me. May you be

---

195   Seth Godin, "Poke the Box," *The Domino Project,* 2011.

blessed for your good judgment and for keeping me from bloodshed this day and from avenging myself with my own hands. Otherwise, as surely as the Lord, the God of Israel, lives, who has kept me from harming you, if you had not come quickly to meet me, not one male belonging to Nabal would have been left alive by daybreak.'

"Then David accepted from her hand what she had brought him and said, 'Go home in peace. I have heard your words and granted your request.' When Abigail went to Nabal, he was in the house holding a banquet like that of a king. He was in high spirits and very drunk. So she told him nothing at all until daybreak. Then in the morning, when Nabal was sober, his wife told him all these things, and his heart failed him, and he became like a stone. About ten days later, the Lord struck Nabal and he died.

"When David heard that Nabal was dead, he said, 'Praise be to the Lord, who has upheld my cause against Nabal for treating me with contempt. He has kept his servant from doing wrong and has brought Nabal's wrongdoing down on his own head.

"Then David sent word to Abigail, asking her to become his wife. His servants went to Carmel and said to Abigail, 'David has sent us to you to take you to become his wife.' She bowed down with her face to the ground and said, 'I am your servant and am ready to serve you and wash the feet of my lord's servants.' Abigail quickly got on a donkey and, attended by her five female servants, went with David's messengers and became his wife."

Let us note some observations for these verses. We learn

A. David ends his plan to annihilate Nabal and his servants. The strategy works. He honors her request, and in the meantime, Abigail leaves a good and lasting impression with David. Had she not intervened, the story could have a very different ending.

B. Nabal dies after stressing out over the news of what happened. I am sure that when Abigail told him what she did, he stressed out over realizing the crisis she averted through her wisdom. He would have been killed. He offended a very important man with the potential to wipe him out and take his life. He dies of a heart attack from the stress this reality puts him under. David does not even have to deal with the issue.

C. Abigail_accepts David's request to become his wife. After Nabal dies, Abigail is free to marry. Remember, with Nabal gone, in her culture she could find herself destitute—property and wealth would not go to her. David's offer must have been pretty appealing in a culture like hers.

This story gives me hope. David is remembered in scripture as a man after God's own heart and when you read the Psalms you see why. Yet this account, which is before his affair with Bathsheba, reveals a very flawed man. He was willing to kill a man for his foolish arrogance and he marries multiple women, something God did not favor.

The reason David gives me hope is twofold. The first is that David, with all his sinful blunders, was still loved by God. That means that maybe I have some hope as well. But better yet, with the New Covenant that we are now under God deals with us on the basis of grace. This means I am motivated to serve God not because I can earn his favor but because He has already granted me favor through faith in Jesus Christ. Just as God has extended me grace, I am now called to model him to extend grace, even to the likes of my counselee Mike from the opening story , prior to his transformation.

In this chapter we looked at how Abigail handled a crisis that her husband Nabal created because of his foolishness and asked, "What can we learn from Abigail about how to handle being married to a fool?"

When we look at Mike's control and jealousy, we learn nothing has changed in human temperament since the days of David and Abigail. People still try to maneuver around angry dysfunctional people and figure out how to make the best of the crises they create. It is encouraging when we see men like Mike face up to their worst traits and take action to deal with them. There are three things this lesson teaches us:

1. I wish there we more people like Mike who are willing to take a deep look at themselves and see why they are controlling and how it impacts those around them. You might be that person; if so, you need to take a personal assessment and seek change.

2. Abagail provides for us a model for the steps we can take in dealing with a fool.

3. Far too many are oblivious to the dangers that lie ahead due to their foolish blindness. If you have a dysfunctional person in your life, realize that every marriage needs at

least one person with the wisdom to pilot the direction of the relationship. Maybe you are the one God has called to be wise.

I imagine you're familiar with the phrase "ship of fools." It was a common medieval motif used in literature and art, especially religious satire. One such satire is Hieronymus Bosch's famous oil painting by the same name, which now hangs in the Louvre in Paris. This marvelous work, which is filled with symbolism, shows ten people aboard a small vessel and two overboard swimming around it. It is a ship without a pilot captain , and everyone onboard is too busy drinking, feasting, flirting, and singing to know where on earth the waves are pushing them.

They are fools because they are enjoying all the sensual pleasures of this world without knowing where it all leads. Atop the mast hangs a bunch of dangling carrots and a man is climbing up to reach them. Yet above the carrots, we find a small but significant detail: a human skull. This is the thirteenth head in the painting, unlucky in every imaginable way. The idea is that these twelve fools, who think all is perfect, are sailing right to their demise. The only pilot on board, the only figure leading the way, is death.[196]

The Bible speaks often of foolishness and its destructive affects. In contrast, Abagail was characterized by her wisdom. She navigated the rough waters of a looming storm with great skill. While we need more Mikes who recognize their abuse, we need even more Abagails who can help make us aware of the dangers we could face if we stay the course.

---

196   Douglas Sean O'Donnell, The Beginning and End of Wisdom Wheaton: Crossway, 2011 , 41-42.

CHAPTER 17

LIFE CRISES THAT IMPACT MARRIAGES

Text: *Psalm 51, 1 Samuel 12:13–23*
Theme: *hen dealing with a major life crisis, let God handle what you and your spouse cannot.*

Not long before Vaunda and I moved to Canada we the got news about Christian musician Steven Curtis Chapman tragically losing his daughter. Stephen and most of his family were at home, and the younger kids were playing outside. The family included three biological children and three adopted children—two from China. Their older son, Will, was returning home from an errand and one of the young adopted girls, Maria, ran up to the SUV he was driving, but he did not see her. In the process he hit her, and she soon died.

I can remember another story from my childhood regarding friends a few houses down from ours in Virginia. Nine-year-old Karen ran into her parent's bedroom to answer the phone. In her rush, she knocked over her father's loaded gun and it discharged when it hit the floor, killing her instantly.

Life is filled with stories like this. They are examples of a major crisis that dramatically changes our lives and how we relate to each other. Times like this can put a huge strain on marital relationships. Things like miscarriages, job losses, and financial collapse add an emotional stress that limits our capacity to support and encourage each other because we are all dealing with the same pain. It is hard to give comfort when you are needing it yourself. Pain can be all consuming and it is hard for others to lean on us when we can barely hold ourselves up.

This problem is exacerbated when you, or your spouse, bears some of the fault for the crisis.

In fact, we have learned that times such as this put a huge strain on marriage. The spouse that we hope will give us support cannot offer it because they too are obsessed with their pain. And if they share some of the guilt, they can become the focus of our anger so at the same time they feel the oppression of guilt. For this reason it seems that many otherwise stable marriages become unraveled when tragedy strikes. We know divorce rates go up for people under marital and emotional stress.

In this chapter I want us to look at an example of a tragedy that was caused by the guilt of the key party—David. In that light we will ask the question, "How should you deal with a crisis in which you bear some responsibility?"

I. You should accept full responsibility for your guilt. (Pss. 51:1–5)

Psalm 51 shows us the two extremes brought together by Gods unfailing love. It reveals David's extreme guilt and God's extreme mercy. We learn God can make us righteous, whiter than snow, in spite of our extreme guilt. We learn a lot about God, sin, forgiveness, and salvation.[19]

> [1] "Have mercy on me, O God, according to your unfailing love; according to your great compassion blot out my transgressions.
> [2] Wash away all my iniquity and cleanse me from my sin.
> [3] For I know my transgressions, and my sin is always before me.
> [4] Against you, you only, have I sinned and done what is evil in your sight; so you are right in your verdict and justified when you judge.
> [5] Surely I was sinful at birth, sinful from the time my mother conceived me."

The context of this Psalm is found in 2 Samuel 12:14–19

This psalm is written right after David's affair with Bathsheba and the murdering of her husband. Nathan the prophet is confronting him and warns him of the following:

> "Nathan replies, 'The Lord has taken away your sin. You are not going to die. [14] But because by doing this you have shown utter contempt for the Lord, the son born to you will die.'
> [15] After Nathan had gone home, the Lord struck the child that Uriah's wife had borne to David, and he became ill. [16] David pleaded with God for the child. He fasted and

---

[19]   Derek Kidner, *Psalm 1-72* Chicago: InterVarsity Press, 1975 , 189.

spent the nights lying in sackcloth on the ground. ¹⁷ The elders of his household stood beside him to get him up from the ground, but he refused, and he would not eat any food with them.

¹⁸ "On the seventh day, the child died. David's attendants were afraid to tell him that the child was dead, for they thought, 'While the child was still living, he wouldn't listen to us when we spoke to him. How can we now tell him the child is dead? He may do something desperate.'

¹⁹ "David noticed that his attendants were whispering among themselves, and he realized the child was dead. 'Is the child dead?' he asked. 'Yes,' they replied, 'he is dead.'"

David pleads with God for mercy. Verses 1, 2 The power of God's Word to transform a person is no more apparent than in David's response to Nathan's warning. David pleads to God for mercy, not for justice, in that he knows any punishment he receives is well deserved. Yet for all his unworthiness, David knows he still belongs to God. In these words David makes an audacious request—he asks God to wash away all of his iniquity—like the washing of dirty clothes or blotting out something. David recognizes he is not fit for God's presence of his people.¹⁹⁸

David recognizes the magnitude of his sin and confesses it. Verses 3–5 While others have been hurt by David's sin, he recognizes that, at heart, all sin is against God. While our confession should include those who have been hurt, it must start with God. David fully acknowledges that any verdict that God brings against

---

198   Ibid., 190.

him is well deserved and that this sin was a reflection of his overall character, not just a one-time event. To summarize these verses, he is saying, "My sins are my own, they are inexcusable, and they are a reflection of my true character."

Today, as always, we tend to confess "halfway." We accept partial responsibility and blame the rest on others or our circumstances. We have a propensity to try to justify ourselves.

In their book, *Mistakes were Made (But Not by Me)*, social psychologists Carol Tavris and Elliot Aronson describe how a fixation on our own righteousness can choke the life out of love. They write: "The vast majority of couples who drift apart do so slowly, over time, in a snowballing pattern of blame and self-justification. Each partner focuses on what the other one is doing wrong while justifying his or her own preferences, attitudes, and ways of doing things . . . From our standpoint, therefore, misunderstandings, conflicts, personality differences, and even angry quarrels are not the assassins of love; self-justification is."[199]

A recent study titled "I Cheated but Only a Little" is based on a series of studies involving more than 4,000 people, and the researchers found that people who only partially confessed a transgression felt worse than those who do not confess at all. The lead author, Dr. Eyal Pe'er, has an interestingly biblical angle on the results. He says, "Confessing to only part of the guilt of one's transgression is attractive to a lot of people because they expect the confession to be more believable and guilt-relieving than not confessing. But our findings show the exact

199   David Zahl, "500 Years After Luther, We Still Feel the Pressure to Be Justified," *Christianity Today* 2016 .

opposite... People seeking redemption by partially admitting their big lies feel guiltier because they do not take complete responsibility for their behaviors." The *Harvard Business Review* summarized the research this way: "Confession is a powerful way to relieve guilt, but it works only if you tell the whole truth."[200]

In this Psalm, we see no attempt by David to diffuse and redirect blame. The first step in genuine restoration is to take full responsibility for your guilt and appeal to God for mercy.

II. Let go of what happened and move on. (Pss. 51:6–13)

"Yet you desired faithfulness even in the womb; you taught me wisdom in that secret place.
Cleanse me with hyssop, and I will be clean; wash me, and I will be whiter than snow.
Let me hear joy and gladness; let the bones you have crushed rejoice.
Hide your face from my sins and blot out all my iniquity.
Create in me a pure heart, O God, and renew a steadfast spirit within me.
Do not cast me from your presence or take your Holy Spirit from me.
Restore to me the joy of your salvation and grant me a willing spirit, to sustain me.

---

200   Andrew O'Connell, "A Partial Confession Makes You Feel Worse," *HBR Blog Network/The Daily Stat* (2014 ; "Telling the Whole Truth May Ease Feelings of Guilt," *American Psychological Association* 2014 .

Then I will teach transgressors your ways, so that sinners will turn back to you."

David accepted the consequences of his sin in 1 Samuel 12:20–23. Let's read what he did.

"Then David got up from the ground. After he had washed, put on lotions and changed his clothes, he went into the house of the Lord and worshipped. Then he went to his own house, and at his request, they served him food, and he ate.
His attendants asked him, 'Why are you acting this way? While the child was alive, you fasted and wept, but now that the child is dead, you get up and eat!'"
"He answered, 'While the child was still alive, I fasted and wept. I thought, "Who knows? The Lord may be gracious to me and let the child live." But now that he is dead, why should I go on fasting? Can I bring him back again? I will go to him, but he will not return to me.'"

Forgiveness and mercy do not always mean we won't face the consequences of our sin. David recognizes that. In this intensely emotional appeal to God, he does not question or begrudge whatever punishment God saw fit to impose. That is a key part of repentance: we accept what we deserve. And the consequences do not end with the death of the baby either. It affects his whole family, something we looked at a few chapters ago. We learned that one of his sons raped another of his son's daughters. The offended son, Absalom, killed his brother and attempted a coup against his father, only to be killed in his attempts. While painful, it appears David accepts this as part of God's judgment.

His relationship with God is restored—whiter than snow Verses 6–9 . In verse 7 he refers to the hyssop that was used in the cleansing of lepers, but it is in the words, "Wash me, and I shall be whiter than the snow" that we find his trust in God's ability to cleanse us fully. As Derek Kidner says, "With God there are no half measures" when it comes to the cleansing of sin.[201] Think about that. God supernaturally makes a darkened sinner whiter than snow.

He is miraculously renewed in his spirit. Verses 10–13 David takes it even a step further. He asks for more than just being cleansed. He then asks God to take his selfish reprobate heart that led to his sin and create within him a new and clean heart and give to him the right spirit. He is asking for a miracle. It's something that only God does and is instantaneous, but it is also sustained over time. It is a prayer for holiness. It is a plea to God to help him avoid further offenses against Him.

In this prayer, he is probably reminded of Saul who preceded him as king. David saw how the Spirit of the Lord left him Saul in 1 Samuel 16:14. Once that happened Saul hardened his heart against God and never repented. In a sense, this psalm shows us a stark contrast with the repentant David versus the unrepentant Saul. In fact, in his plea, David asks that God use His forgiveness and unfailing love to be a model that he can use to teach others in the future.

Letting go is often even harder than a confession in that we feel that we must keep punishing ourselves. Steve Brown tells a

---

201   Ibid., 191.

story that illustrates this: Early in his ministry he counseled a woman who had been unfaithful to her husband some twenty years earlier. For years that sin haunted her, and Steve was the first person she had ever told about it. After we talked and prayed for a long time, he recommended that she tell her husband. That, by the way, isn't always the advice. In this case he knew the woman's husband and knew that her revelation would probably strengthen their marriage after he dealt with the initial shock. Brown goes on to say, "It wasn't easy for her, but she promised she would tell him. 'Pastor,' she said, 'I trust you enough to do what you ask, but if my marriage falls apart as a result, I want you to know I'm going to blame you.' She didn't smile when she said that, either.

"That's when I commenced to pray with a high degree of seriousness. I pray best when I'm scared. 'Father,' I prayed, 'if I gave her dumb advice, forgive me and clean up my mess.' I saw her the next day, and she looked fifteen years younger. 'What happened?' I asked. 'When I told him,' she exclaimed, 'he replied that he had known about the incident for twenty years and was just waiting for me to tell him so he could tell me how much he loved me!' And then she started to laugh. 'He forgave me twenty years ago, and I've been needlessly carrying all this guilt for all these years!'"[202]

Perhaps you are like this woman: You've already been forgiven years ago but you can't let it go, and you've been haunted by a load of guilt for years. Like David, we need to let it go.

---

202   Steve Brown,   *hen Being Good Isn't Enough* (Magnolia: Lucid Books, 2014 , 10-11.

III. Praise God for His forgiveness and unfailing love. (Pss. 51:14–19)

"Deliver me from the guilt of bloodshed, O God, you who are God my Savior, and my tongue will sing of your righteousness.

Open my lips, Lord, and my mouth will declare your praise.

You do not delight in sacrifice, or I would bring it; you do not take pleasure in burnt offerings.

My sacrifice, O God, is a broken spirit; a broken and contrite heart you, God, will not despise.

May it please you to prosper Zion, to build up the walls of Jerusalem.

Then you will delight in the sacrifices of the righteous, in burnt offerings offered whole; then bulls will be offered on your altar."

A. Because he can take a sinner and make him righteous. Verses 14-17 The horror of David's sin continues to plague him. It is not the consequences of sin that he is concerned about—it is the guilt. He praises God for His righteousness but greater yet is His willingness and ability to make a sinner righteous. David has been shamed into silence due to his sin and he longs to worship again freely, and he believes that he will because of God's unfailing love. God values a contrite heart over our sacrifices and offerings.

B. David's restoration becomes a model for all of us. Verses 18-19 It is most likely that the last two verses were added later, sometime between the captivity of Israel and the rebuilding of the temple. They are an interpretation of verse 16, and they become the words of the nation who was in exile due to their failures. These verses express their own repentance and restoration. They essentially fulfill David's request to use his experience of forgiveness as a lesson for others.[203]

If we can't let go of our past and our failures, we cannot fully worship God. It questions God's ability to fully forgive. It is no wonder that Satan is called the accuser. He tries to magnify the degree of our guilt to demoralize us and hinder our ability to worship God.

We can learn a lot about some of Satan's strategies in spiritual warfare by studying the military strategies of some of the warriors of old. In his book *Head Game*, author Tim Downs writes:

"Psy-ops stands for Psychological Operations, a form of warfare as old as the art of war itself. An early example of this can be found in the battle strategies of Alexander the Great. On one occasion when his army was in full retreat from a larger army, he gave orders to his armorers to construct oversized breastplates and helmets that would fit men seven or eight feet tall. As his army would retreat, he would leave these items for the pursuing army to discover. When the enemy would find the oversized gear, they would be demoralized by the thought

203 Kidner, 194.

of fighting such giant soldiers, and they would abandon their pursuit."[204]

Satan likes to play head games with us, too, often leaving us demoralized by fear or doubt. We assume Satan is bigger or greater than he really is. And the quickest way to thwart our enemy's psy-ops is to gaze upon the greatness of our God.

In this chapter we looked at an example of a crisis that was caused by the guilt of David. In that light we asked the question, "How should you deal with a crisis in which you bear some responsibility?" We found we must accept full responsibility for our guilt, and then let it go once we have confessed it to God. God can take a darkened sinner and make him as white as snow—it should cause us to worship.

We know that a crisis puts great strain on a relationship and even more so when one of the spouses bears some responsibility. I opened with the story of Karen being accidentally killed by a loaded gun the bedroom of her father. This is the type of thing that often destroys families. But this family and this father understood what it was to accept responsibility, plead for mercy, and moved on. As a result they survived the crisis. Let's pray more can do the same.

What are some steps you can take when you face a crisis in your marriage?

1. Every marriage will have at least one crisis that will put it to the test. Some of these tests are no fault of anyone; things like miscarriages, loss of a child, job loss, economic stress, etc. At such times we must learn that we cannot

---

204 Tim Downs, *Head* Games, Nashville: Thomas Nelson Publishers, 2007. Kindle edition.

always depend on our spouse for support, in that they are hurting as well. We must turn to God and draw our strength from him.

2. There may be times in your marriage when you or your spouse has created a crisis due to your own sinfulness, stupidity, or incompetence. In such cases the one who is guilty must look to David as your model by accepting full responsibility, repenting, and allowing God to restore your soul so that you can move on.

3. If you are the spouse who was not at fault, you must forgive yourself and let go of your anger, so you don't keep holding it against your partner. While caution and protection are in order, constantly reminding him or her of the offense does little to restore the relationship.

The British physicist Stephen Hawking emerged in recent years as a poster boy for atheism, especially in light of his heroic struggles against Lou Gehrig's disease. But the recent film about Hawking's life *The Theory of Everything* has been called a "God-haunted movie." In one of the opening scenes, the young Hawking meets Jane, his future wife, and tells her that he is a cosmologist. "What's cosmology?" she asks, and he responds, "Religion for intelligent atheists." "What do cosmologists worship?" she asks. And he replies, "A single unifying equation that explains everything in the universe." In another scene, Jane asks, "So, I take it you've never been to church?" When Stephen replies, "Once upon a time," she asks, "Tempted to convert?" Stephen replies, "I have a slight problem with the celestial dictatorship premise."

Later on in the film, Jane challenges him: "You've never said why you don't believe in God." Hawking counters, "A physicist can't allow his calculations to be muddled by belief in a supernatural creator," to which she responds, "Sounds less of an argument against God than against physicists." In one of her two published memoirs, the real Jane Hawking argues, "However far-reaching our intellectual achievements . . . without faith [in God] there is only isolation and despair, and the human race is a lost cause."[205]

David's Psalm 51 reminds us why. We are sinners and apart from the cleansing mercy of God, we are left in our guilt and sin, without hope. We and the human race are a lost cause.

---

205 Robert Barron, "The Theory of Everything: A God-Haunted Film," *Strange Notions blog.*

CHAPTER 18

THEY MAY NOT BREAK BONES
BUT WORDS CAN STILL HURT

Text: *James 3:1–12*
Theme: *Taming the tongue is vital to healthy communication in marriage.*

I was surprised and saddened when I heard some time ago that scholar Ruth Tucker was divorcing her husband due to domestic violence. Most of you probably don't know who Ruth Tucker is. She was a Ph.D. missions professor at Trinity Evangelical Seminary and is considered by many to be a leading expert on the topic. I have heard her speak several times over the years— once at seminary some years ago and another time at a conference I attended on Mormonism in Salt Lake City.

What made it surprising is not just the fact that she is a highly educated seminary professor but that her husband was, using her words, "an intelligent, articulate, well-educated minister who had served in two Bible churches, taught for six years at a Bible college, and edited books for two Christian publishers."[206]

---

206   Ruth Tucker, "Black and Blue Wife," *Christianity Today*, 2017.

Of her experience, she says, "During our marriage, my ex-husband hit me, squeezed my arms black and blue, yanked me around, threw me on the floor, and kicked me. But it wasn't until the last few years that his demeanor darkened, terrorizing me with his threats. During the last year of our marriage, I truly feared he would kill me, and it was then that I began writing a journal."

She later says, "Anyone who imagines that domestic violence is just the stuff of "ghettos" and "trailer parks" is wrong. Anyone who imagines domestic violence is just the stuff of unbelievers—people outside the church—is wrong. Anyone who imagines that the pastor in the pulpit could never be a perpetrator of domestic violence is wrong."

I have already told my story with my stepfather and in my case, the abuse was only verbal. For my stepsisters, on the other hand, it was physical as well. At least, until my mother intervened.

These are tough situations, and we struggle with how to reconcile them with the limited prohibitions of divorce that Jesus spoke to. The fear, degradation, and real dangers in some circumstances cannot be understated. Getting away from the danger is sometimes the only step to be taken.

While the Old Testament addresses it a few times, the New Testament never directly addresses the question of domestic violence—but it does speak about anger, and more specifically, the tongue and its power. Domestic violence starts with the heart and reveals itself in words and actions. Jesus speaks of this in Matthew 5:18: "But the things that come out of a person's mouth come from the heart, and these defile them." The point is that destructive works and physical violence generally go hand in hand.

In this chapter I want us to address the issue of the tongue and ask, "Why is it important to learn to control your tongue?" We will learn you are judged by what you say, and your words reflect what's in your heart and have consequences for good or for bad.

I. We will be strictly judged by what we say. (James 3:1–2)

"Not many of you should become teachers, my fellow believers because you know that we who teach will be judged more strictly. 2 We all stumble in many ways. Anyone who is never at fault in what they say is perfect, able to keep their whole body in check."

A. It is why many should not become teachers. Teachers use words to communicate ideas and not all ideas are equal. One of the greatest dangers of our contemporary culture is that it teaches that all ideas and beliefs are equal—no one is better than another. There are at least two problems with this philosophy. One, there is such a thing as objective truth. Something cannot be both true and false at the same time. Truth discriminates against falseness. Second, there is no way you can be intellectually consistent with this philosophy in that the moment I make a claim such as, "Jesus is the only way to salvation," then you must either accept it as equal and reject all other religions, or you must reject it and in doing so deny your philosophy—but you cannot have both.

Jewish culture understood that words and ideas have consequences. They understood that false ideas can lead to devastating consequences, so they guarded who could teach. The words of teachers shape the values and actions of a society and God judges him for the ideas that he teaches. That is James' point here. We will be judged by what we say.

Paul tells us in Ephesians that we are to "speak the truth in love." To quote others, "Truth doesn't care about your feelings." Jesus spoke words of truth and offended many, that is why they killed him. But His goal was never to offend. Speaking the truth in love is about using words to transform people into becoming more like Christ—and sometimes that is painful to the one who hears it.

B.   It reflects on your ability for self-control.

Sometimes we say things out loud that we later regret like the movie character who kept saying after an offensive comment, "Did I say that out loud?" It is a wise and disciplined man who uses his words guardedly and always with the right motives.

Pastor Scott Sauls from Nashville, Tennesse, illustrates this point. Sauls spent five years working with Pastor Tim Keller at New York City's Redeemer Presbyterian Church. He writes that there are many ways that he saw Keller model the gospel, but there is one thing that really stood out for him. He says:

"Tim [Keller] is the best example I have ever seen of someone who consistently covers with the gospel. Never once did I see Tim tearing another person down to their face, on the internet, or through gossip. Instead, he seemed to assume the good in people. He talked about how being forgiven and affirmed by Jesus frees us for this—for "catching people doing good" instead of looking for things to criticize or be offended by. Even when someone had done wrong or been in error, Tim would respond with humble restraint and self-reflection instead of venting negativity and criticism. As the grace of God does, he covered people's flaws and sins. Sometimes he covered my flaws and sins. He did this because that's what grace does; it reminds us that in Jesus we are shielded and protected from the worst things about ourselves. Because Jesus shields us like this, we should of all people be zealous to restore reputations versus destroying reputations, to protect a good name versus calling someone a name, to shut down gossip versus feeding gossip, to restore broken relationships versus begrudging broken people."[20]

II. The effects of what you say have great consequences. (James 3:3–6)

"When we put bits into the mouths of horses to make them obey us, we can turn the whole animal. 4 Or take ships as an example. Although they are so large and are driven by strong winds, they are steered by a very small rudder wherever the pilot wants to go. 5 Likewise, the tongue is a small part of the body, but it makes great boasts. Consider that a great forest is set on fire by a small spark. 6 The tongue also is a fire, a world of evil among the parts of the body. It corrupts the whole body, sets the whole course of one's life on fire, and is itself set on fire by hell."

A. It is like a bit in a horse's mouth. Think of how small a bit is in relation to the horse it directs. The horse is a large, powerful animal that could easily overcome us, but the small bit makes the horse move in the direction it does. Similarly the tongue is

---

20/ Scott Sauls, *Befriend*, Carol Stream: Tyndale, 2016 , 48.

a small part of our body but shapes the direction not only of our bodies but also of our lives.

B. It is like a rudder on a ship. The size of the rudder in relation to the ship is quite small but again, this small rudder determines the direction the ship will turn. So does the tongue.

C. It is like a spark in a forest. In recent months we have gotten news of dozens of forest fires in British Columbia and the States. They all start with something very small. In most cases it was a simple spark or flame that ignited dry timber. The damage that small flame caused destroyed the whole forest, took many man hours to fight, and spread over thousands of acres.

I have known husbands who lash out at their wives in anger and put-downs. Once they have vented, they are ready to move on. But their words created a spark that has set a fire in motion. The wife has not let it go and has not moved on. She can hold on to it for days and weeks, so don't be surprised, husband, if your outburst still has effects weeks later. The damage is not easily repaired. Nor can you blame your anger and words on others. Only you can control your anger and your words.

Remember, you are married to a very flawed person—and so is your spouse. While there is occasionally a place for stern words, they must be shaped by love. Being married to a flawed person means we must approach their flaws with wisdom and discernment. We must know what battles are worth drawing blood over—most are not. Remember the goal is always to strengthen the relationship, not destroy the other person. We can tear down or build up with our words.

Let me illustrate: In an article by Lori Hawkins in The Columbus Dispatch, he states, "When Apple Inc. set off a frenzy of activity with the debut of its iPhone 6 and 6 Plus, workers from Teardown.com lined up at 5 a.m. at stores across Austin to buy three devices. Then they returned to the company's offices, where engineers began disassembling the new products.

"'We took a screwdriver and tore them apart,' said one of Teardown.com's analysts. 'We wanted to know every detail of everything that's inside: who the supplier was for every component, wire, and screw, and how much it cost to make.' Over the next twelve hours, the battery, cameras, display, materials, and electronics were analyzed and priced, and the information was rolled into a spreadsheet.

"The 'quick-turn' report was shared with Teardown.com's clients, who include tech manufacturers, financial investors looking for market trends, and resellers who want to know how much individual parts cost. Attorneys use the reports for patent-infringement cases, and engineering teams study them for design ideas. Over the past fifteen years, Teardown.com has broken down more than 2,000 products, including tablets, digital cameras and camcorders, notebook PCs, and gaming consoles. Every product the company has dismantled, dating back to the first digital music players and GPS devices, is stored away in the company's morgue."[208]

Sadly, some people are like this in marriages. They make it their primary business to tear their spouse down rather than

---

208   Lori Hawkins, last modified 2014. http://www.pressreader.com/usa/the-columbus-dispatch/20141111/282561606419/9.

building them up. They take the efforts of others and seek to find fault. When done in marriages, it destroys them.

There is a third response to our question, "Why is it important to learn to control your tongue?"

III. What comes out of your mouth indicates what's in your heart. (James 3:7–12)

"All kinds of animals, birds, reptiles and sea creatures are being tamed and have been tamed by mankind, but no human being can tame the tongue. It is a restless evil, full of deadly poison. With the tongue we praise our Lord and Father, and with it we curse human beings, who have been made in God's likeness. Out of the same mouth come praise and cursing. My brothers and sisters, this should not be. Can both fresh water and salt water flow from the same spring? My brothers and sisters, can a fig tree bear olives, or a grapevine bear figs? Neither can a salt spring produce fresh water."

A. Taming the tongue is nearly impossible.

1. It is more difficult than taming an animal. People, who can be great at many things, may find watching what they say impossible. Their perfectionism becomes judgmentalism. It can lead to anger or gossip or comments that demonize someone. This reality should cause us to ask the question, "Why is it so it hard to control what we say?

2.   It is a restless evil that reflects our inward hearts. We are basically self-centered sinners and our words reflect what is in our hearts. The Bible speaks to this often.

Matthew 15:11 says, "It is not what goes into the mouth that defiles a person, but what comes out of the mouth; this defiles a person."

Matthew 12:34 says, "You brood of vipers! How can you speak good, when you are evil? For out of the abundance of the heart the mouth speaks."

Matthew 5:32 says, "But I say to you that everyone who is angry with his brother will be liable to judgment; whoever insults his brother will be liable to the council; and whoever says, 'You fool!' will be liable to the hell of fire."

Luke 6:45 says, "The good person out of the good treasure of his heart produces good, and the evil person out of his evil treasure produces evil, for out of the abundance of the heart his mouth speaks."

B.   To change what we say requires that we change what is in our hearts. If the words of a person express hate and anger, it means his heart is filled with hate and anger. Changing our words requires changing our hearts.

1.   These verses suggest that we cannot worship God with the same mouth that curses others. It is called hypocrisy, and we see it often and most of us have been guilty of it. A person comes to church on Sunday morning and sings worship songs, give testimonies, and shares how they love God. That very night and throughout the week they

treat their spouse with anger and contempt from the very same mouth. As James says, "My brothers and sisters, this should not be. Can both fresh water and salt water flow from the same spring?"

2. Worship must come out of a pure heart. The following story illustrates this.

A visual by Matthew Mitchell that I use to illustrate this point is that I hold up a bottle of water and then pour water out on the platform. Then I ask, "Why is there now water on the floor?" The answer is obvious—because there is water in the bottle.

Then I ask, "But why is there water on the floor and not Pepsi or Kool-Aid?" There is water on the floor because there had been water in the bottle. Similarly, Jesus said, "Out of the overflow of the heart the mouth speaks." What's inside us determines what comes out of us.[209]

When we are honest with ourselves, most of us know that something is intrinsically wrong with us and we need to change. But here is the most important point: only God can change our hearts. When we recognize that we are sinners deserving of punishment, then we know we have no hope unless we change. But the kind of change required is beyond our ability to produce. An evil heart cannot produce a pure heart simply by willing it to be so. Saltwater cannot produce fresh water.

This transformation of the heart is a central theme of scripture. Jesus used the phrase, "You must be born again." Changing the

---

209 Matthew Mitchell, *Resisting Gossip: inning the ar of the agging Tongue* Ft. Washington: CLC Publications, 2013 , 39-40.

heart is more than tweaking a few things—it requires total rebirth. Paul speaks of it as "dying with Christ and be risen to new life."

Corinthians 5:17–19 says, "Therefore, if anyone is in Christ, the new creation has come: The old has gone, the new is here!"

The fact that it is not our doing is revealed in Ephesians 2:8–9, "For it is by grace you have been saved, through faith—and this is not from yourselves, it is the gift of God—not by works, so that no one can boast. For we are God's handiwork, created in Christ Jesus to do good works, which God prepared in advance for us to do."

This handiwork should be expressed in our speech. Ephesians 4:29–30 says: "Do not let any unwholesome talk come out of your mouths, but only what is helpful for building others up according to their needs, that it may benefit those who listen."

In this chapter we addressed the issue of the tongue and asked, "Why is it important to learn to control your tongue?" We learned that you are judged by what you say, and your words reflect what's in your hearts and have consequences for good or for bad.

Just because a person is educated or even in ministry does not mean we can control the tongue. We saw that with our opening story of Ruth Tucker, a Ph.D. professor of mission, and her husband who was a pastor and successful author. His inability to control his tongue and actions reflected his heart—he was angry and bitter inside.

Domestic violence is a big issue in our culture. As we have seen, it starts in the heart, expresses itself in words, and is often followed by actions that include physical abuse. If we are to change domestic violence, we must change what is in the heart—and only the person who can do that is Jesus.

Let us look at some ways to put the points of this chapter into practical reality.

1. If you are being abused through domestic violence: Understand it is not your fault when a person loses control of their anger. Don't provoke it or feed it, as I have seen some do; but don't assume blame either. If your life is threatened, then get away from the danger and get protection. If a family is involved, call the police get a restraining order, and get the person out of the house.

2. If your anger gets the best of you, then remember you are the instigator of domestic violence—only you can deal with it—don't blame it on your spouse. You can learn to control what you say and what you do. If they have done something wrong or inappropriate, then confront them in an appropriate way. Violence against your spouse is never justified. Words intended to hurt never fix the issue. You must accept responsibility for your actions alone.

George Orwell's famous novel *Animal Farm* provides a parable about how we often treat each other in Christian community, families, and work settings. In Orwell's parable, farm animals rebel against the cruel farmer, but when they overthrow the farmer, and the pigs take charge of the place, they become even worse than the farmer.

Two pigs, Napoleon and Snowball, vie for leadership, and Napoleon eventually succeeds in exiling Snowball. But Napoleon's leadership does not bring prosperity and comfort. When the farm experiences a major setback, it's Snowball's fault, even though he no longer lives there. Snowball becomes a convenient scapegoat for Napoleon, so he can deflect criticism from his own poor leadership.

> Orwell writes:
> "Whenever anything went wrong, it became usual to attribute it to Snowball. If a window was broken or a drain was blocked up, someone was certain to say that Snowball had come in the night and done it, and when the key of the store-shed was lost, the whole farm was convinced that Snowball had thrown it down the well. Curiously enough, they went on believing this even after the mislaid key was found under a sack of meal."

Sadly, many of us humans suffer from this same "Snowball Syndrome." We blame our children, our spouse, our parents, our fellow Christians, our boss, or our employees. Sometimes it really is someone else's fault, but all too often we blame others without examining our own hearts. There's only one cure for the "Snowball Syndrome"—repentance and confession of sin.[210]

---

210 Collin Garbarino, "Desperately Seeking Snowball," *First Thoughts blog* 2013 .

CHAPTER 19

MONEY AND MARRIAGE

Text: *Matthew 6:19–34*
Theme: *Money issues in marriage are resolved when couples put the kingdom of heaven first.*

Let us read story that has been lived out in thousands of homes. "Making no effort to be quiet, Graham comes to bed. It's about 1 a.m. Anna has been asleep for three hours, but she's wide awake now. 'Anna,' says Graham, 'we're never going to make it if you keep spending so much money.' Stress squeezes Anna's stomach. She knows Graham has been working on their finances. She'd like to pretend she didn't hear him but figures she can't.

"She turns toward him. 'Honey, what can I do? I try not to spend too much. There are things that we need.' Graham sighs. "We need fifty dollars' worth of makeup from Dillard's? We need one hundred twenty dollars' worth of groceries a week? We need to buy new furniture for the living room and put up new curtains? These are not needs, Hon.'

"Anna stares at the ceiling. 'Okay, the furniture and the curtains may not be needs, but my makeup and—' Graham interrupts, 'Honey, you're beautiful. You don't need to spend that kind of money on makeup.' 'But that's what it costs. And I don't buy it that often.' She tries to snuggle next to Graham, but he pulls away. 'Are you kidding?' he says. 'I'm so stressed out, and you think you can just cuddle up and be cute and it'll all be okay. You've got to take some responsibility here, Anna. Things are not okay.'"[211]

As Graham and Anna have found, it can be a huge problem between husband and wife when one of them spends—or seems to spend—too much. In fact, if someone were to ask you what the number one reason is for couples falling apart, you might think sex, household chores, or the strain of bringing up children would top the list. However it's actually money that drives more couples apart. Three leading charities all cited money worries as the number one cause of conflict in a relationship. They said it was not lack of cash that was the main cause of strife, but issues around trust and values—basically, if you disagree about how to manage your finances.

Money problems surpassed other factors such as differing sex drives and poor division of labor in a survey of 5,000 adults, which was carried out by Relate, Relationships Scotland and Marriage Care. More than a quarter of respondees said family finances were the biggest cause of arguments with their partner, ahead of lack of compatibility 20 percent , poor work-life balance 17 percent , and differing interests 16 percent . Other common causes of dissatisfaction were alcohol consumption, jealousy, and rows

211   Sandra Lundburg, "Why Does my Spouse Spend so Much? *Focus on the Family*, 2017. https://www.focusonthefamily.com/marriage/money-and-finances/money-management-in-marriage/why-does-my-spouse-spend-so-much.

over the in-laws, while political differences, smoking and bringing up children all ranked surprisingly low in terms of relationship problems.[212]

In this chapter we will consider the questions, "How can you avoid allowing finances to damage your marriage?" We will find that finances become a major issue in marriage when one or both members of a marriage get too wrapped up in accumulating things, or they worry too much about financial matters. They are resolved when both parties put God first.

I. Both should focus on investing in eternal things. (Matt. 6:19–24)

"Do not store up for yourselves treasures on earth, where moths and vermin destroy, and where thieves break in and steal. But store up for yourselves treasures in heaven, where moths and vermin do not destroy, and where thieves do not break in and steal. For where your treasure is, there your heart will be also. The eye is the lamp of the body. If your eyes are healthy, your whole body will be full of light. But if your eyes are unhealthy, your whole body will be full of darkness. If then the light within you is darkness, how great is that darkness! No one can serve two masters. Either you will hate the one and love the other, or you will be devoted to the one and despise the other. You cannot serve both God and money."

---

212 Sophine Hine, The Number One Reasons Couple Fall Out," last modified March 3, 2016. http://www.goodhousekeeping.co.uk/news/the-number-one-reason-couples-fall-out.

A. Everything we value on Earth will pass away. Most of our existence will not be on this earth, and there is not one thing that you possess that you will take with you into eternity. Yet we fight and argue over things that have no lasting value whatsoever. You must start your discussions with this reality—"Everything you have will decay."

B. How we handle money reflects on the focus of our heart. The value we give to things says something about us. Things like a passion to get fancy new cars, larger houses, or the latest technological gadget says something about what is really important to us. We go into debt, we stress ourselves and lose sleep when we have to give up something of value to us.

C. You can't serve both God and money—you have to choose one.

Sandra Lundberg says, "You've probably heard a variety of reasons for overspending: deprived childhood, privileged childhood, depression, anxiety, the thrill of the hunt. All of these have one thing in common: a search for security. Consciously or not, the spender thinks something like, 'If I have this, I'll be in style.' Or, 'I'll be accepted.' Or, 'I'll be safe.' Or, 'I'll be okay.'"[213]

Buying things doesn't provide real security. It does nothing to change God's love for us. Due to the consumerism so prevalent in our culture, it's an ongoing battle for many people to let go of

---

213 Lundberg, 2.

the fleeting gratification of things for the long-term security of a relationship with God.

Several years ago construction workers were laying a foundation for a building outside the city of Pompeii. They found the corpse of a woman who must have been fleeing from the eruption of Mt. Vesuvius but was caught in the rain of hot ashes. The woman's hands clutched jewels, which were preserved in excellent condition. She had the jewels, but death had stolen it all. That's the bottom line in life. Worldly treasure is not a wise investment because you can't take it with you. Jim Elliot, a missionary who was martyred for his faith, understood this reality when he wrote in his journal, "A person is no fool to give up what he cannot keep in order to gain what he cannot lose." It's not foolish to give up what you cannot keep in order to gain what you cannot lose.

If you make eternity your focus, you can put your finances into perspective and reduce the tensions it creates in your marriage.

How can you avoid allowing finances to damage your marriage?

II. Trust God to provide for your essential needs. (Matt. 6:25–32)

"Therefore I tell you, do not worry about your life, what you will eat or drink; or about your body, what you will wear. Is not life more than food, and the body more than clothes? [26] Look at the birds of the air; they do not sow or reap or store away in barns, and yet your heavenly Father feeds them. Are you not much more valuable than they? [27] Can any one of you by worrying add a single hour to your life?

[28] "And why do you worry about clothes? See how the flowers of the field grow. They do not labor or spin. [29] Yet I tell you that not even Solomon in all his splendor was dressed like one of these. [30] If that is how God clothes the grass of the field, which is here today and tomorrow is thrown into the fire, will he not much more clothe you-you of little faith? [31] So do not worry, saying, 'What shall we eat?' or 'What shall we drink?' or 'What shall we wear?' [32] For the pagans run after all these things, and your heavenly Father knows that you need them."

A. You are more valuable to God than anything else he has created. One of the most difficult things to deal with is a loss of a job and the income that goes with it. It is exacerbated when you add debt to that mix. I have been there; I know. When you face such times, you must always remember—you are still of immeasurable value to God. Just as he has provided for us in the past, he will continue to provide. Even if we lose everything we own on Earth, we still have what really matters—a God who loves us and works all things for our good. Rom. 8:28

B. Worrying does absolutely nothing to resolve things. I can't think of anyone who has a better life because they are obsessed with worry because of finances. If you can devote yourself to more productive things, other than worry, you are far more likely to come out better.

Listen to these statistics on worry:

Forty percent of what we worry about never comes to pass.

Thirty percent of what we worry about happened in the past and can't be changed.

Ten percent of what we worry about relates to health. What's both funny and sad is that researchers have proved that worry actually makes your health worse not better!

Eight percent of worry is legitimate, but even then, worrying about it won't change

it! Your worry will not make the loan go through. Your worry will not make you pregnant or

"unpregnant." Your worry will not get rid of the cancer. Your worry will not pay the bills.

Jesus is telling you in this passage that your worry is useless.[214]

C. God knows your needs as much as you do. I am convinced that one of the reasons that God allows us to go through tough financial times is to get our priorities in order. God knows your need, but He wants you to know where everything we have comes from.

---

214 Bryan Loritts, "Why Worry," *Preaching Today*, last modified 2009. http://www.preachingtoday.com/sermons/sermons/2010/july/whyworry.html.

Recently I read a book titled *The God Guarantee: Finding Freedom from the Fear of Not Having Enough* by Jack Alexander. This book describes that "at the root of an ungenerous heart is not mere stinginess or greed but fearfulness. Accruing resources is often a way we try to take control of our own world and fend for ourselves because we fear we can't trust God."[215]

Alexander says, "The feeling of scarcity impacts every level of society. In a 2015 survey of American millionaires, more than half said they did not feel financially secure. Most reported they worried an unexpected change—a job loss, a market crash, or a failed investment—could affect their lifestyle at any moment. Fifty-two percent said they felt "stuck on a treadmill." At every level of wealth evaluated in the survey, respondents said they need double what they have in order to feel secure.

"And Christians today are not exempt from a scarcity mentality. They too worry about rising costs and stagnant incomes. Their time also is stretched to the breaking point in the digital age, and they are just as saturated as non-Christians with images and stories highlighting the hurt, brokenness, and lack in the world. They also have questions. Can God really meet our needs? How can we say God loves us if it seems as if he's not adequately providing for us? Sure, once upon a time God may have given his people manna to eat. But where is he today?"

This fear is fundamentally selfish. How can we worship and serve God if we are driven by the fear that we do not have enough, and if a crisis hits we will be destitute? This mentality says, "I do

215   Jack Alexander, *The God Guarantee: Finding Freedom from the Fear of Not Having Enough* Grand Rapids: Baker Books, 2017 , 28.

not really believe that God cares for me and will provide for me." In Acts 2, Luke clearly saw that the lifestyle of radical giving that characterized the infant church in the sharing of resources was proceeding from a heart that has been changed through the filling of the Holy Spirit.

How can you avoid allowing finances to damage your marriage?

III. Everything else falls into place when we seek God first. (Matt. 6:33–34)

"But seek first his kingdom and his righteousness, and all these things will be given to you as well. Therefore do not worry about tomorrow, for tomorrow will worry about itself. Each day has enough trouble of its own."

A.   The things we worry about most will be provided for. God is far more committed to our good than we believe. Look at what he did through Jesus. We see in God's free gift of salvation that God can be trusted. Jesus is more *precious* than anything else. 1 Peter 2:7 When we have him, we have the most important thing.

B.   Alexander continues, "This makes me wonder . . . If God, in his generosity, creativity, and abundance, chose to create humans with such intricate detail, why do we doubt he has the capacity to care for a single person? Does his provision cover seemingly irrelevant and useless things, like a bunch of stars millions of miles out of reach, but not the very beings he created in his own image? When we try to argue that God doesn't care, or we put him in a box we 'control,' we ignore the truth about his character. It's a mistake to write off God, believing he doesn't care about the details of either an individual life or the world as a whole. And it's a mistake to try to 'control' life without him."[216]

C. Stay focused on the problems of today—not what could be.

One reason it is so easy to fall into Satan's trap of the scarcity mindset that produces our fear is that we rarely make the time anymore to stop and appreciate all the blessings God has already showered on us and all the capacity for blessing others he has placed within us. Ironically, we can usually manage the day-to-day issues of life without too much pain—especially if we focus on these blessings. It is the imagined, awful scenarios that most likely will never occur that cause our anxiety. It is this "awfulizing" that cripples our marriages as much as anything else.

There is a Father who has blessed us and will continue to do so. But there is also an enemy, Satan. First Peter 5:8 tells us, "Your enemy the devil prowls around like a roaring lion looking for someone to devour." He will do everything to distract you, hurt you, and make you believe there is not enough, and that God does not really care for you. He will attack you in the places where you are most vulnerable. He will make empty promises and brew dissatisfaction in your soul and blatantly lie to you about God's

---

216 Ibid.

love and provision.[217] He plants seeds of fear and hopelessness for the future. But remember, "Greater is He that is in you than he that is in the world." 1 John 4:4

William Barclay offers a helpful word: "Those who feed their hearts on the record of what God has done in the past will never worry about the future. Worry refuses to learn the lesson of life. We are still alive, and our heads are still above water; and yet if someone had told us that we would have to go through what we have actually gone through, we would have said that it was impossible. The lesson of life is that somehow we have been enabled to bear the unbearable and to do the undoable and to pass the breaking point and not to break. The lesson of life is that worry is unnecessary."[218]

So, in a very real sense, financial anxiety can also be a spiritual battle. It is a battle of "Will I trust that God will provide for my needs not wants or will I succumb to my fears and anxiety."

Pastor Chip Ingram tells a story about when he and his wife were newly married. It was early in Chip's ministry, and there wasn't much extra money. They had a neighbor who was raising her young child alone after being abandoned by her husband. As rent came due one month, she confessed to Chip's wife that she did not have enough to pay the bill. The Ingrams felt burdened for her, wanting to help, but they barely had enough money in the bank to pay their own rent. After much prayer, they decided to pay their neighbor's rent instead of their own. As Chip tells the story, he and his wife had no idea how they were going to make ends meet. Rent

---

217 Ibid.

218 Barclay.

was due in three days, and they had only ten dollars in their bank account. On the third day, they received an envelope in the mail. It was from someone the Ingrams hadn't seen or talked to in years—a young man who had been blessed as a high school student by Chip's youth ministry. The man had been praying when he felt the Lord nudge him to send a check for the exact amount the Ingrams needed. God miraculously provided. [219]

While I don't recommend we make a habit of spending money we don't have, this story does illustrate that when we seek God first, He will provide. God reminds us over and over that none of this—not our money, not our health, not our families—is really our own. Everything is His and is part of His divine plan. And that same God promises to provide.

In this chapter we asked the question, "How can you avoid allowing finances to damage your marriage?" We learned that if we focus on investing in eternal things, realize God cares for us more than all of His creation, and seek his kingdom first, everything we need will be provided.

Many couples are like the one in our opening story. One spends too much and the other is fragile and worries too much. Both need to meditate on this passage and learn to overcome the fear of scarcity and to seek God's kingdom first. For the wife, it is to learn that stuff does not provide security, and for the husband, that worry fixes nothing.

Let us close with some thoughts on how we might apply what we have learned.

---

[219]   Chip Ingram, "Reimagine Stewardship," The Promises of God, *Application Teaching*. 2017.

1. If you spend more than you make, you need to ask yourself "Why?" I would suggest for many of you the problem is not lack of income but a belief that *stuff* is necessary for happiness.

2. If you always worry about money, you need to focus on putting God first in your life. With that comes the promise that all your real needs will be provided for.

3. Invest your time and resources in things that have eternal value. Remember there is nothing on this earth that you can take with you into the future.

In his book *The Life You've Always Wanted,* John Ortberg asks us to imagine a financial consultant sitting down with the apostle Paul. The FC says, "Paul if you look at this time chart, I think you'll agree with me that your spiritual life is doing pretty well but vocationally your tent-making has seriously fallen off and has led to some considerable downsizing in your financial portfolio. Let's take a look at the time log I asked you to keep since our last meeting."

This is how Paul answers. Second Corinthians 11:25–27: "Five times I received from the Jews the forty lashes minus one.25 Three times I was beaten with rods, once I was pelted with stones, three times I was shipwrecked, I spent a night and a day in the open sea, 26 I have been constantly on the move. I have been in danger from rivers, in danger from bandits, in danger from my fellow Jews, in danger from Gentiles; in danger in the city, in danger in the country, in danger at sea; and in danger from false believers. 27 I have labored and toiled and have often gone without sleep; I have known hunger and thirst and have often gone without food; I have been cold and naked."

It's hard for me to imagine what the financial consultant would say to all of this. But I do know this: God used Paul in a powerful way, and in putting God first, he has a reward in eternity that far exceeds anything he could ever obtain on Earth. He had his priorities right even if it meant some financial sacrifice to fulfill them.[220]

220 John Ortberg, *The Life You've Always Wanted: Spiritual Disciples for Ordinary People* Grand Rapids: Zondervan, 2002 .

CHAPTER 20

THE ADDICTIONS THAT DESTROY

Text: *Romans 7, 8*
Theme: *The Spirit of God frees a person from the addictions that destroy marriages.*

On Facebook the other day I ran across a post that reveals the heart of a young girl toward her father. It reads:

Dear "Dad,"

Don't worry, I'm fine. You were a good dad when you were clean. But you could never seem to stay that way. It seemed like even I wasn't enough to make you change, but sometimes I could tell I made you want to. The drugs and the addiction had far more control over you than the love you had for me. I have always tried to understand how you chose a high over your own daughters. How come I wasn't enough to make you stop using? At what point in this addiction battle do I just throw in the towel? I'm tired of the rollercoaster of addiction and I'm just the passenger. I'm daddy's little girl. And I'm watching daddy kill himself with this addiction. My heart goes out to everyone that's ever had to struggle with addiction.[221]

This sad reflection of a daughter is a commentary on how everyone hurts because of an addiction. And like her, they wonder, *hat is wrong with me that he would not love me enough to stop?*

David Sheff has written an outstanding book, titled *Beautiful Boy.*[222] The story is a personal narrative of battling with his son's methamphetamine abuse. Sheff reminds us that addiction affects those around the individual just as deeply as the individual. Just as more than one person suffers because of an addiction, more than one person must recover from the hurt and distrust. Sheff also points out that it does not help anyone to tiptoe around the issue—it cannot be ignored. He shows how facts and details—knowledge—is far more important than fear, doubt or denial. In the end it can be hopeful, life-affirming, and entirely rewarding.

These addictions also have a destructive effect on marriages, and we all have all seen it, heard the stories, or experienced it ourselves. The problem is that only the addict can make the changes needed to restore normalcy. Others, at best, can only intervene or keep from enabling the addict.

In this chapter we will address the question, "How can we overcome the addictions that enslave and destroy our marriages?" To address the question, we will return to a passage we addressed earlier in this book. We refer to it again because few passages of the

---

221   Facebook Post, Amber Rode, August 23, 2017.

222   David Sheff, *Beautiful Boy: A Fathers Journey through His Son's Addiction* Wilmington: Mariner Books, 2009 .

Bible speak to this issue of addictions so clearly. We will look at three things: 1. There is a moral, spiritual standard God calls us to live by; 2. The death and resurrection provide the path to victory; and 3. God has provided the Holy Spirit to do what you cannot do.

I.   There is a moral, spiritual standard that God gives for us in the law. (Rom. 7:14–24)

"We know that the law is spiritual; but I am unspiritual, sold as a slave to sin. ¹I do not understand what I do. For what I want to do I do not do, but what I hate I do. And if I do what I do not want to do, I agree that the law is good. ¹⁷ As it is, it is no longer I myself who do it, but it is sin living in me. For I know that good itself does not dwell in me, that is, in my sinful nature. For I have the desire to do what is good, but I cannot carry it out. For I do not do the good I want to do, but the evil I do not want to do—this I keep on doing. Now if I do what I do not want to do, it is no longer I who do it, but it is sin living in me that does it. So I find this law at work: Although I want to do good, evil is right there with me. For in my inner being I delight in God's law; but I see another law at work in me, waging war against the law of my mind and making me a prisoner of the law of sin at work within me."

A.   The law of God informs you of what sin is. While we all run the risk of being legalistic and self-righteous, the solution is not to eliminate all the rules and laws that seem to oppress us. There is a standard and God has revealed it in His Law. It reveals to us the essence of true holiness.

B. It reveals to you how far short of God's standard you fall. To paraphrase, he is saying, I get up in the morning, I set my face for what I know I should do—the Law gives me my rules, how to live my life. But by the end of the day, maybe halfway through the day, I have already sinned. The law is perfect, but we soon find out that we are not. When we measure ourselves against the holy standard of God, we find that not one person in this room can match up to it. The value in the law is not simply in revealing God's Holy standard but in revealing our weakness.

C. It is impossible for you to meet this standard through your own efforts. I believe that the heart of the addiction problem is that we are convinced we can fix this on our own. We are convinced that some slight tweaking of our thinking and behaving is all we need. The fact is we are powerless to deal with it by a sheer act of the will. Willpower is not enough, and to think otherwise is to deceive ourselves.

Richard Rohr puts it this way, "The experience of 'powerlessness' is where we all must begin. . . . It seems we are not that free to be honest, or even aware because most of our garbage is buried. So it is absolutely essential that we find a spirituality that reaches to that hidden level. If not, nothing really changes. It is not necessarily bad will or even conscious denial on our part. We just can't see what we are not forced to see. As Jesus put it, we 'see the splinter in our brother's or sister's eye and miss the log in our own' Matthew 7:4–5 . The whole deceptive game is revealed in that one brilliant line from Jesus . . ."[223]

The law reveals three things: 1. God's holiness; 2. Our sinfulness; and 3. Our powerlessness. Until we recognize our powerlessness, God seldom changes us. When we think of addictions we often think of drugs and alcohol but there are many others, some less visible, and are destructive in different ways, but they all require the same starting point to overcome.

One addiction that has become far more common since the invention of the internet is pornography. In years past pornography was outlawed and kept in hiding. But with the advent of the Playboy era, it became legal, more acceptable, more accessible, and more explicit. When I grew up it was hidden behind counters that could only be accessed by the store owner or found in an adult shop in a sleazy part of town. It would have been embarrassing to be caught there. Things have changed since then.

Now it is available to anyone with a cellphone or the click of a mouse. Ten percent of all visits to pornographic websites are from children under age 10 and 22 percent under age 18. Let that sink in. A whole generation is growing up with access to graphic material unheard of in years past. In addition, 68 percent of all men visit pornographic sites at least weekly, and pastors and Christian leaders are not immune. We are even seeing it among women. In one U.S. survey, 70 percent of fifteen- to seventeen-year-olds said they had watched porn. By the time they reached 20, the same study found it was almost impossible to find men who hadn't viewed the x-rated

223   Richard Rohr, *Breathing Under ater: Spirituality and the Twelve Steps* Cincinnati: St. Anthony Messenger Press, 2011 . Kindle edition.

material.[224] We have yet to fully realize the societal and spiritual ramifications of this reality.

In one sense I feel sorry for our young men today. They live in a sexually charged world unlike anything else in history. We all know the male is visually stimulated and women will never understand the power of the visual on the male sex drive. Think of it as a car that has its cruise control set at one hundred forty kilometers per hour. Every visual stimulus turns the cruise control switch on. Most men quickly learn to tap the brake to turn it off and, in the past, there were strong external and internal incentives to do so. But lately these incentives have been reduced and the cruise switch gets locked in the *on* position. There is often a long delay in tapping the break, sometimes requiring men to press it hard to bring it under control. Young women also suffer, because it objectifies them as sex objects. Young men begin to compare them to these images and are deceived into believing this is what these young women want. But what it also does is redirect men's sexual desire to pixilated images and not the real thing to be shared with a spouse. It is a recipe for disaster.

God's law tells us that viewing women this way is sin,[225] and many men who know this still struggle with throwing this monkey off their backs. Even if they want to stop, an addiction to it draws them in. There are some resources out now that were not available years ago to help men in this battle, but the embarrassment makes

---

224 "Is pornography changing how teens view sex?" last modified April 22, 2013. https://www.thespec.com/news-story/2550999-is-pornography-changing-how-teens-view-sex-/.

225 Matthew 5:27–28.

it hard for them to admit they need help and utilize them. Churches need to utilize these resources and encourage men to address it together—the days of silence on the topic have passed.[226]

How can we overcome the addictions that enslave and destroy our marriages?

II. The death and resurrection of Jesus provide what we need for spiritual victory. (Rom. 7:24-8:4)

"What a wretched man I am! Who will rescue me from this body that is subject to death? [25]Thanks be to God, who delivers me through Jesus Christ our Lord! So then, I myself in my mind am a slave to God's law, but in my sinful nature a slave to the law of sin. Therefore, there is now no condemnation for those who are in Christ Jesus, [2]because through Christ Jesus the law of the Spirit who gives life has set you free from the law of sin and death. [3]For what the law was powerless to do because it was weakened by the flesh, God did by sending his own Son in the likeness of sinful flesh to be a sin offering. And so he condemned sin in the flesh, [4]in order that the righteous requirement of the law might be fully met in us, who do not live according to the flesh but according to the Spirit."

---

226 Ministries that help men in this area are: "The Conquer Series," "Pure Desire," and "Every Man's Battle."

A. When we are in Christ, we are no longer condemned by the law.

One of the great problems with addictions is that we always live in defeat and feel condemned. We think God's love for us is contingent on how well we keep His law. The fact is God can never love you more than He loves you now. Because of His great love when we accept Jesus and walk in the Spirit, we are no longer condemned. But we are also called to "Walk in the Spirit," which is a supernatural resource every man can and must draw on.

B. To be in Christ, your old self must die and rise with him. The imagery is clear and powerful. Your old, self-centered, ego-driven self must die. So many addicts keep trying the same thing over and over only to find themselves defeated. They do not understand that their old self cannot fix the problem. That changes only when we are in Christ and by identifying with His death and resurrection.

As Rohr says, "We keep doing the same thing over and over again, even if it is not working for us . . . We really are our own worst enemies, and salvation is primarily from ourselves. It seems humans would sooner die than change or admit that they are mistaken. This thinking mind, with a certain tit-for-tat rationality, made the gospel itself into an achievement contest in which 'the one with the most willpower wins,' even though almost everybody actually loses by these criteria. That is how far the ego read: 'false self,' or Paul's word 'the flesh' will go to promote and protect itself. It would sooner die than change or admit that it is mistaken. It would sooner live in a win/lose world in which most lose than allow God any win-win victory. Grace is always a humiliation for the ego, it seems."[22]

C.   There is no place for ego in your spiritual battle—you cannot do it on your own.

I love the story Christ told of the Pharisee and the tax collector in Luke 18. It reads, "To some who were confident of their own righteousness and looked down on everyone else, Jesus told this parable: 'Two men went up to the temple to pray, one a Pharisee and the other a tax collector. The Pharisee stood by himself and prayed: "God, I thank you that I am not like other people—robbers, evildoers, adulterers—or even like this tax collector. I fast twice a week and give a tenth of all I get."

> 'But the tax collector stood at a distance. He would not even look up to heaven, but beat his breast and said, "God, have mercy on me, a sinner." 'I tell you that this man, rather than the other, went home justified before God. For all those who exalt themselves will be humbled, and those who humble themselves will be exalted.'" That theme of humility before God is found often in scripture. God exalts those who humble themselves before Him.

In preparing for this chapter I ran across this illustration that helps make the point that there is no place for ego. "Have you

---

22/   Rohr, 1/2.

ever listened to someone ramble on about something you know nothing about, yet you still try to contribute to the conversation?" says David Dunning, a professor at Cornell University. Dunning reflects on the issue of overconfidence through our predisposition to talk knowingly about things that we know nothing about. "There's actual science behind that phenomenon," he argues. He's recreated similar experiments in the lab, asking subjects about fictitious political figures, for example, or nonexistent cities—and gets much the same results as the late-night hosts [Jay Leno and Jimmy Kimmel] do. Dunning says, "What we find is that people are quite ready to start talking about things they can't possibly know anything about because we made that thing up in our office just the week before. Truly, our pride leads us to foolish places sometimes. Why are we so slow to listen and learn?"[228]

Similarly, if the out of control male sex drive, or other addiction, is one of his enemies, so also is his male ego. The same man who will not ask for directions when traveling is the same man who won't abandon his ego by thinking he can do it himself. He is doomed to fail in his quest for self-control. The ego always insists on the high moral ground. But as Jesus says, like the seed must die to give life, so must we. John 12:24

How can we overcome the addictions that enslave and destroy our marriages?

---

228   David Dunning and Justin Krueger, "Unskilled and Unaware of It: How Difficulties in Recognizing One's Own Incompetence Lead to Inflated Self-Assessments," *Journal of Personality and Social Psychology*, 1999, 77, no. 6, 1121-1134. See PDF at: https://www.avaresearch.com/files/UnskilledAndUnawareOfIt.pdf.

III. God has provided the Holy Spirit to do what you cannot. (Rom. 8:5–16)

"Those who live according to the flesh have their minds set on what the flesh desires, but those who live in accordance with the Spirit have their minds set on what the Spirit desires. The mind governed by the flesh is death, but the mind governed by the Spirit is life and peace. The mind governed by the flesh is hostile to God; it does not submit to God's law, nor can it do so. Those who are in the realm of the flesh cannot please God.

"You, however, are not in the realm of the flesh but are in the realm of the Spirit, if indeed the Spirit of God lives in you. And if anyone does not have the Spirit of Christ, they do not belong to Christ. But if Christ is in you, then even though your body is subject to death because of sin, the Spirit gives life because of righteousness. And if the Spirit of him who raised Jesus from the dead is living in you, he who raised Christ from the dead will also give life to your mortal bodies because of his Spirit who lives in you.

"Therefore, brothers and sisters, we have an obligation— but it is not to the flesh, to live according to it. For if you live according to the flesh, you will die; but if by the Spirit you put to death the misdeeds of the body, you will live.

"For those who are led by the Spirit of God are the children of God. The Spirit you received does not make you slaves, so that you live in fear again; rather, the Spirit you received brought about your adoption to sonship. And by him we cry, '*Abba*, Father.' The Spirit himself testifies with our spirit that we are God's children. Now if we are children, then we are heirs—heirs of God and co-heirs with Christ, if indeed we share in his sufferings in order that we may also share in his glory."

A. The Spirit enters you at salvation and unites you with Christ. Paul tells us in 1 Corinthians 12:13, "For we were all baptized by one Spirit so as to form one body." As a believer you already have the Spirit within you. But to cite Rohr again: "As hard as it is to believe, many formally religious people do not believe in the reality of Spirit in any active or effective way. They think it is their job to somehow teach, introduce, or 'win' Spirit, and they never get around to enjoying what is already and always there—and actively on their side." Walter Wink, a professor of biblical interpretation, calls it the mere "theological" worldview as opposed to the incarnational worldview, which is authentic Christianity. When all of you is there, you will know. When all of you is present, the banquet will begin.

B. The same powerful Spirit that raised Jesus lives in you. Ephesians 1:18–20 says, "I pray that the eyes of your heart may be enlightened in order that you may know the hope to which he has called you, the riches of his glorious inheritance in his holy people, and his incomparably great power for us who believe. That power is the same as the mighty strength he exerted when he raised Christ from the dead and seated him at his right hand in the heavenly realm." If the Spirit of God raised Jesus from death, can He not do the same for you?

C. The Spirit frees us by putting to death the deeds of the flesh. Galatians 5:22–26 says, "But the fruit of the Spirit is love, joy, peace, forbearance, kindness, goodness, faithfulness, gentleness and self-control. Against such things there is no law. Those who belong to Christ Jesus have crucified the flesh with its passions and desires. Since we live by the Spirit, let us keep in step with the Spirit."

We can also refer to Ephesians 5:18 which is the pinnacle of New Testament teaching on what we would call the filling of the Holy Spirit. Notice that it says, "Do not get drunk on wine, which leads to debauchery or immorality . Instead, be filled with the Spirit." The Greek term means to be filled, controlled, intoxicated, permeated, and thoroughly influenced. In Luke 4:28, the word "filled" is used to refer to those who are angry about Jesus' teaching. It says that "they were filled with wrath." They were thoroughly overcome with wrath. In Acts 13:45, certain Jews resented the success of Paul and Barnabas. And the New Testament says that "they were filled with jealousy." The Greek word is *Pleroostha* and means to be overcome by a power greater than your own. To be filled is to be controlled by something.[229]

Think of a glove. When you are washed clean by the blood of Christ, you are like a glove. A glove can't do anything on its own without being totally filled by a hand. The hand does all of the

---

[229]   James McDonald, "The Power Source," *Preaching Today*, 2012

work. The Holy Spirit comes into you and totally permeates you, just like a hand filling a glove. That's what it means to be filled.

The Holy Spirit has to have all of you. God is the source of the filling. We're the object being acted upon. God does the filling when we ask him to. You can't fill yourself with the Holy Spirit. "Be filled with the Spirit" is an invitation to allow the Holy Spirit to do what he is ready to do now. I want to challenge every single follower of Jesus to be continually filled with the Holy Spirit. Being filled with the Spirit is the only capacity God has given for you to live the Christian life in victory.

In this chapter we addressed the question, "How can we overcome the addictions that enslave and destroy our marriages?" We looked at three things: 1. There is a moral, spiritual standard God calls us to live by; 2. The death and resurrection provide the path to victory; and 3. God has provided the Holy Spirit to do what you cannot do.

The Facebook post by the young girl in our opening story illustrates what so many feel. How many wives would say the same thing? The damage that addictions cause in marriages can hardly be understated.

What can we do to help us overcome our addictions?

1. If you are married to someone who is an addict, I encourage you to do several things:

    a. Do not get caught in the trap of this young girl who thought that if her father loved her enough he would stop. All addictions are self-obsessed desires where a person does not even love themselves—much less others.

b. When a man is addicted to pornography, it is not about you. You may think, *hat is wrong with me? If I were pretty enough, or sexy enough, or a better wife he would not want to look at other women.* The reality is that it has nothing to do with you. The problem is his and only he can learn to deal with it. But you can confront him with it and expect it to be addressed.

c. If he tries to blame you, it says he has not faced up to his responsibility. Don't buy it and call him on it. Don't ignore the issue or be an enabler. It will not go away.

2. If you are addicted, then admit it and get help. There are support groups for alcohol and drug issues. There is no guarantee it will be easy and apart from God's enablement, there is little hope. I hope your church can offer something for men who struggle with pornography. At some level, most men have to deal with it, but few want to talk about it because of shame; and it is not something their wives can understand, leaving them defeated.

Author Ken Hempell tells this story: "Years ago while on an airplane, I read a fascinating but rather unpleasant story. It had all the qualities of a good mystery. A frantic 9-1-1 call brought police to a home. The caller had only been able to communicate that she needed help and was being killed. When police arrived, they found a bloody knife beside her lifeless body on the kitchen floor. Blood was spattered across the room, yet upon examining the body, they did not find a single cut or puncture wound ... [but] they noticed a trail of blood leading into the next room and followed it. Entering the room, they found a large dying boa constrictor.

"Apparently, the snake had been raised as a pet but on this day the snake had wrapped itself around the woman as she was cooking in the kitchen. For whatever reason she had allowed the snake to entwine her body in its coils, and once it began to constrict its muscular body around her, she sensed the danger. In a panic she grabbed a knife and began to slash away at the snake, and while managing to mortally wound it, she was killed in the process."[230]

This tragic story is a clear example of the power of sin in our lives. We often take subtle compromises into our lives as an innocent pet, thinking we can handle them without any real risk, and thus deal with sin flippantly, all the while placing ourselves in great danger.

Many feel like the snake of addiction has strangled them. But God provides help. Ask God to fill you with His Spirit.

---

230   Ken Hemphill, *The Names of God,* Nashville: B&H Books, 2001 , III.

CHAPTER 20

PARENTING: TRAINING UP A CHILD IN THE THINGS OF GOD

Text: *Ephesians 6:1–4, Deuteronomy 6:1–9*
Theme: *Parents must agree on the values and principles for childrearing.*

Imagine the following story:

It is bedtime at the Williams household and Lorna, the mother, tells her youngest child Devin to go pee before she goes to bed. But Devin has decided it is playtime and finds some reason not to obey, so Lorna tells her repeatedly that she must go. At the same time, the other child, John, is throwing pillows across the room while Lorna is trying to change him for bed. Lorna is getting frustrated because neither child is cooperating—so her voice starts to raise.

Thinking he is going to help the situation, her husband, Robert, yells from the shower, "You kids better listen to your mother or I am going to make you sleep downstairs tonight." The kids have heard his empty threats before and pay no attention to him, only adding to Lorna's frustration.

Some minutes later the situation escalates even more as Devin throws a tantrum and kicks Robert as he tries to dress her for bed after finally taking her to the bathroom. Out of anger Robert makes another empty threat and says, "Stop that Devin or I will make you sleep in the bathroom." His threats do nothing to improve the situation, and Lorna begins to use inappropriate language to express her anger at Robert for using threats that everyone knows will never be followed through on.

So now we have a multitude of problems that include kids that are misbehaving, a father who is using empty threats, and a mother who is angry and using words she should not be using. Lorna concludes from all this, "If there's one thing Robert can't stand, it's when I curse around the two little ones in the house. So we, inevitably, fight over that. I think yelling idle threats at the kids is terrible parenting and way worse than my language. He thinks my language in front of the kids is terrible parenting and way worse than his ridiculous threats. I get upset when he refuses to let the kids watch their show and puts on golf instead. He gets upset when John throws a tantrum and I give in. I get mad when he tunes everything out usually while watching...golf and ignores/doesn't intervene when the kids are fighting right in front of him. He gets mad when I don't have a whole lot of patience when the kids do things that kids do like make a mess right after I've tidied up . And so on."[231]

This is a true story except that the names and some of the details have been changed. In fact, the last paragraph is a partial quote with only the names and a few words changed. Yet you

---

231   This is an adaptation of a story by Lisa Van de Geyn, "We're fighting about our parenting styles" Today's Parent, July 29, 2013. https://www.todaysparent.com/family/parenting/fighting-about-parenting-styles/

could see a very similar story being played out in thousands of homes across North America every night before bedtime.[232]

Welcome to the world of parenting. In fact, it is one of the three major sources of marital conflict in an anachronism known as PMS: Parenting, Money, and Sex. Similarly, there are three main areas of conflict regarding parenting: sleep bedtimes , food what they eat , and discipline how kids are to be disciplined .

One of the reasons for parenting conflict is that each partner brings a parenting style into the family that often conflicts with the other. It is not just that men and women bring different outlooks on parenting, but they may also have different styles that are natural to them. The four main parenting styles are: Authoritative; Authoritarian; Permissive; Uninvolved.

The following graphs illustrate these four styles.[233]

Parenting Styles

	Low **Relationship** High	
High	Authoritarian	Authoritative
Low	Uninvolved	Permissive

(y-axis: **Expectations**, from Low to High; x-axis: **Relationship**, from Low to High)

232   Van de Geyn, Lisa, "We're fighting about our parenting sytles" Today's Parent, July 29, 2013. https://www.todaysparent.com/family/parenting/fighting-about-parenting-styles/.

233   Sydney and Shelby Trentzsch, "A Parent's Guide to Parenting," last modified April 24, 2014. https://my.vanderbilt.edu/developmentalpsychologyblog/2014/04/a-parents-guide-to-parenting.

The probability is that you can find yourself in one of these styles. The value of these graphs is that they help you visualize what you might not otherwise see and to provide for you a frame of reference to compare your style with that of your spouse. The limitation of these graphs is they cannot inform about what is the more appropriate style in any given situation. That is a discussion that goes beyond the scope of this chapter.

But the Bible gives us some fundamental principles of parenting that we should be able to agree upon and guide our interactions. To that end, in this chapter we want to consider the question, "What does the Bible teach us about the role of a parent?" In our response we will learn that the parents have a very important role because they are the primary instructors of their children and are to calmly but assertively train them in the things of God as their highest value and as a way of life.

I. The parents are the primary instructors of their children. (Prov. 22:6)

"Start children off on the way they should go, and even when they are old they will not turn from it."

A. It is the parents' God-given duty and right to raise their children. This is probably the most well-known verse in the Bible regarding parenting. While this verse alone does not prove that parents are the primary instructors of their children, when putting it alongside other key verses, the point becomes pretty clear. Every verse that speaks to the topic of parenting teaches and assumes that the parents bear the primary responsibility, and the right, of raising their children.

B.   The values a parent teaches will be with a child for life. This
     verse can also be translated, "Train up a child in his own
     way," meaning the parenting style must fit the child. Some
     need firm rules while some need more affirmation, some
     are sensitive, and some are strong-willed. The point is not
     every child is the same, and how you instruct must fit the
     child.

Also, this is not a guarantee, it is a proverb. Many a good
parent have raised a child in the way he should go, and the child
later rejects it. Taken as a promise this verse had let some people
down. But taken as a proverb, which it is, it provides wisdom and
guidance for the child's upbringing. As a rule even most kids who
rebel will return back to what they were trained in. But there will
be some who rebel and never return by no fault of the parent. The
odds of the kids picking up your values are very high, but there are
exceptions.[234]

The Preamble to the Canadian Charter of Rights and
Freedoms seems to affirm the intrinsic right of the parent in raising
their children. It contains a statement that "the Canadian Nation
is founded upon principles that acknowledge . . . the dignity and
worth of the human person and the position of the family in a
society of free men and free institutions." Canadian courts have
consistently recognized the importance of the family and the need
to protect parents from improper interference. The law is on the
side of the natural parents unless for grave reasons, endangering

---

234   Recommended: Joy Cage, *hen Parents Cry: How to Survive a Child's
Rebellion* New York: Berkley Press, 1993 .

the welfare of the child, the court sees fit not to give effect to the parents' wishes.[235]

In the charter we find that the parent has the right to custody and control of, to direct the education and religious training of, to discipline, and to make health care decisions regarding, his child. The protection of parental rights is based, at least in part, on a belief that parents will act to promote their child's interests. To protect these rights, therefore, is to promote a child's welfare. Most fundamentally, perhaps, parental rights are viewed as "natural rights." It is accepted as a basic tenet of our culture that parents have a "right" to control and care for their children.

In recent years both scripture and the present Canadian charter of rights are facing a challenge to its doctrine of parental rights. There is a growing trend in which state authority supersedes the parent in raising child. This is evident in Ontario's recent enforcement of 'Title 89' which has provided the blueprint for Alberta's "Bill 10."[236] At the National Conference of the Canadian Fellowship of Evangelical Baptists, these bills were cited, and churches were encouraged to offer a corporate response to this movement intended to undermine parental rights and promote its own sexual agenda in its place. Similar bills are being proposed in the U.S., and the

235   Nicholas Bala* and J. Douglas Redfearn, "Family Law and the Liberty Interest" Sec. / Canadian Charter of Rights. https://commonlaw.uottawa. ca/ottawa-law-review/sites/commonlaw.uottawa.ca.ottawa-law-review/ files/12_15ottawalrev2/41983.pdf.

236   "Bill 89 Pushes Gender Ideology in Child Services," last modified January 6, 2017. https://arpacanada.ca/news/2017/01/06/bill-89/.

church cannot stand by idly if these parental rights are being undermined.

Among other things, Bill 10 *requires* all Alberta schools Christian and homeschools included to allow and approve GSA clubs. It also adds the terms "sexual orientation, sex, gender identity, and gender expression" to the Alberta Bill of Rights. This list has never been part of this law. Rather, the following principle, "to promote the best interests, protection, and well-being of children" has sufficed—that is until now.

The phrase "religious faith, if any, in which the child is being raised" was previously listed for consideration in provincial guidelines in working with children, has been removed. Bill 89 also removes the requirement that a court determines, as soon as possible, the religious faith in which the child is being raised in the course of a child protection hearing. Most troubling, the bill removes the requirement for parents to be informed when their children are being taught about sexual orientation and the words "mother and father" are intentionally removed from the vocabulary.

When we evaluate Alberta's Bill 10 from a purely political-philosophical perspective, we see a Province that refuses to inform parents about what is being taught to their children, a Province that says there is only one way to deal with sexual ethics, a Province that maligns other points of view by demonizing critics, a Province that centralizes power in an education bureaucracy. It is totalitarian in its reach. Bill 10, and all the baggage it carries is something that could only be promoted by totalitarian type regimes.

What does the Bible teach us about the role of a parent?

II. Parents are to calmly train and instruct their children (Eph. 6:1–4)

"Children, obey your parents in the Lord, for this is right. 'Honor your father and mother'—which is the first commandment with a promise—'so that it may go well with you and that you may enjoy long life on the earth.' Fathers, do not exasperate your children; instead, bring them up in the training and instruction of the Lord."

A. Children who honor and obey responsible parents live longer and better lives. This promise is reiterated several times in Scripture, and if you look at the evidence, we see it is true. Kids who behave just do better in life. John Rosemond, author and child psychologist, affirms this and recommends parents give their children more "Vitamin N." The N stands for the word *No*. He points out that one of the major contributors to child misbehavior and depression is parental over-indulgence. It leads to its own form of addiction. [23]

B. Parents should provide firm guidance without exasperating their children. Notice the command, "Do not exasperate your children." We exasperate them by the way we treat them. We can do it through things like overprotection, favoritism,

---

[23] John Rosemond, "Is Your Child Getting Enough Vitamin N?" last modified November 14, 2016. https://www.prageru.com/courses/life-studies/your-child-getting-enough-vitamin-n

unrealistic or inconsistent expectations, no encouragement, making them feel unwanted, using love to manipulate, physical or verbal abuse. We can even do it by the extremes of permissiveness or by being too authoritarian.[238]

C. Parents are to train them to love and obey God. If I could identify one central value a parent needs to instill within his child, it is to love God. If they love God, everything else will fall into place. That is the one greatest thing I wish I had done a better job of as a parent. I allowed my sons to see too much of the "dark side" of professing Christians or, as a pastor, I could not protect them from it. We sent them to Christian schools, had devotions, read them Christian-based stories, and modeled our faith. But we couldn't undo the effects of the same churched people who attacked them at a very personal level. I have a wonderful relationship with both of them, but I cannot undo what happened.

My wife and I have always valued being a Christian presence for our sons. We made sure we were always a key part of their lives and we felt it was important. "Actress Sarah Drew, who has appeared on *Grey's Anatomy,* illustrates the importance of this when speaking about her new role as a mother: "The stay-at-home mom [or any mom] has the terrifying, holy charge of raising up little eternal beings into people who will encounter the world either through kindness and grace or with malice and indifference.

---

238 "Ways Parents Provoke." Accessed March 16, 2018. https://www.gty.org/library/articles/A325/ways-parents-provoke.

I cannot think of a more important job. And yet, our culture rolls our eyes at these women. Our culture says they've "given up" on doing anything [important] with their lives.

"The greatest thing motherhood is teaching me is how to be *present* . . . It's very easy for me to get buried in my phone. To check emails and texts and my Twitter feed . . . When I am not present in my life, I miss out on the beauty that is surrounding me. I forget to be grateful, and instead whine and complain about how things aren't going according to plan. Meanwhile, my son, who is fully present, is busy laughing with glee at the leaves he's chasing and at the game he has invented."[239]

When we are calmly and purposely present in the lives of our kids, we find unlimited opportunities to model and teach them about obeying and loving God.

What does the Bible teach us about the role of a parent?

III. Godly parenting is a 24/7 way of life. (Deut. 6:1–8)

"These are the commands, decrees and laws the Lord your God directed me to teach you to observe in the land that you are crossing the Jordan to possess, ² so that you, your children and their children after them may fear the Lord your God as long as you live by keeping all his decrees and commands that I give you, and so that you may enjoy long life. ³ Hear, Israel, and be careful to obey so that it may go well with you and that you may

---

239 Paul Pastor, "Mothering Beyond the Stereotypes," *Christianity Today* (2014 .

increase greatly in a land flowing with milk and honey, just as the Lord, the God of your ancestors, promised you.

⁴ Hear, O Israel: The Lord our God, the Lord is one. ⁵ Love the Lord your God with all your heart and with all your soul and with all your strength. ⁶ These commandments that I give you today are to be on your hearts. ⁷ Impress them on your children. Talk about them when you sit at home and when you walk along the road, when you lie down and when you get up. ⁸ Tie them as symbols on your hands and bind them on your foreheads. ⁹ Write them on the doorframes of your houses and on your gates."

A. The well-being of Israel and its people was tied to responsible parenting. This is an important reality that I believe is also true of North America. We especially see it in fatherhood relationships. When a father is daily involved in the life of his child, the child tends to do far better. I spoke in the prologue on the devastating effects of fatherlessness in our culture. We have seen it for years in the black community. In fact, this reality is one of the key reasons for me to preach this series on marriage. The break-up of marriages and the increase in fatherless homes have done immeasurable damage. The cure to many of our social ailments is tied to strengthening families and encouraging responsible parenting.

B. Good parenting teaches children to know and obey the *Shema*. The Shema was a key Jewish concept that every child was to learn early on. The Shema is stated in verses 4 and 5, "Hear,

O Israel: The Lord our God, the Lord is one. [5] Love the Lord your God with all your heart and with all your soul and with all your strength."

It is what Jesus said in response to the Jewish lawyer who asked Him the question, "Teacher, which is the greatest commandment in the Law?" He responded in Matthew 22:37–40, "'Love the Lord your God with all your heart and with all your soul and with all your mind. [38] This is the first and greatest commandment. [39] And the second is like it: 'Love your neighbor as yourself.' [40] All the Law and the Prophets hang on these two commandments."

C. Every means possible should be used to teach children to love God. This command Shema is so important to get across that parents, and especially fathers, should use every opportunity to instill it into the lives of their children. This means we must not only be present and engaged, but we must also be purposeful—it will not just happen.

Well-known Pastor Ray Ortlund, tells an interesting story that illustrates this point. He says, "Fifty years ago my dad and mom gave me a new Bible. It was my senior year in high school, the first week of two-a-day football practices, and I crawled home that day, bone tired. Mom made a special dinner for me, since it was my birthday, and Dad gave me a Bible with the following inscription: *Bud, nothing could be greater than to have a son—a son who loves the Lord and walks with him. Your mother and I have found this Book our dearest treasure. e give it to you and doing so can give nothing greater. Be a student of the Bible, and your life will be full of blessing. e love you. Dad 9/7/66* Philippians 1:6.

"As I read these wonderful words from fifty years ago, it never occurred to me to think, *Dad doesn't really believe that. It's just religious talk.* I knew he meant it, because I watched him live it. *He* was a student of the Bible, and *his* life was full of blessing, and I wanted what he had. It took me a few more years to get clarity in some ways, not surprisingly. But on this day so long ago, my dad said something to me that left a deep impression. It moved me then, and it moves me now."[240]

There should be no conflict on this topic in parenting. Both parents should be proactive in communicating and applying ways to instill the Shema into the lives of their children.

In this chapter we asked the question, "What does the Bible teach us about the role of a parent?"

We learned that the parents have a very important role because they are the primary instructors of their children and are to calmly but assertively train them in the things of God as their highest value and as a way of life.

Parenting is a wonderful but often difficult role that can lead to conflict in a marriage. Parenting takes intentionality and tremendous self-discipline, and both parents need to be engaged with the shared commitment to teach their children to love God.

Please, take a moment now to reflect on these principles for your marriage.

1. Men get out of your comfort zones. Your sons and daughters need you. They need not only that you be present but for you to model for them what it is to be "in

---

240   Ray Ortlund, "Fifty Years Ago Today," *Gospel Coalition* blog 2016 .

the process" of growing in their faith. You do not have to be perfect, but they must know you love God.

2. Do not abandon your right to parent your child to the state which does not value the Shema. The present leadership of our educational system is challenging those rights. We should not take them for granted.

3. There is no time off for parenting. It is a 24/7 commitment and it can wear you out. Seek Gods strength and guidance for the many times you will need it. Remember, God is even more concerned for your child as you are.

4. Understand both the strengths as weaknesses of your parenting style and ask, "How can I bring it in line with what God tells me about parenting?" If you are too permissive, force yourself to say no to your kids when they need it—help them set boundaries. If you are too authoritarian, you need to know that you have a far greater impact by firmly loving them than by just imposing rules that exasperate them.

A story by Roland Warren is a great way to close this topic on parenting. He reminds us that Mount Everest, Earth's highest mountain, has two standard routes used by most climbers. Both of them present a number of dangers, including freezing temperatures and hurricane winds. In addition, there are a limited number of months in the year and time periods during the day to safely scale the mountain. The greatest danger that has caused the most deaths is altitude sickness, which causes fluid on the lungs and swelling on the brain, making the person so disoriented that they can't think clearly. Warren goes on to say:

"Therefore, it's not surprising that even the most experienced climbers don't try to tackle Mount Everest alone. They hire special guides called Sherpas. The Sherpas are a unique people who, for generations, have inhabited the Khumbu Valley, the national park surrounding Everest. Because they have been living in the area for so long, they have developed a genetic ability to function at very high altitudes. Whereas most people start to have oxygen problems above eight thousand feet, they have an amazing endurance up to about twenty-three thousand feet. Since the Sherpa guides have trekked Everest many times, they are experts when it comes to knowing the weather patterns and the best time to climb.

"But these gifted Sherpa guides can do something else: with their uniquely trained and experienced eyes, they can help those in their care pause and take in the beauty of Mount Everest. You see, this mountain is not all danger. It's a delight as well, with many breathtaking peaks, vistas, and valleys that one can only see from its heights. That's why so many are drawn to it and would risk life and limb to plant their personal flag on its summit. And it's not surprising that the official Tibetan name for Mount Everest is Chomolungma, which means 'Holy Mother.'"

Parenting has much in common with climbing Mount Everest; children need their fathers, like inexperienced climbers need the Sherpas, to guide them and to help them avoid the perils and unwise decisions of life. But they also need their fathers to help them appreciate the wonders that await them on the upward journey to fulfill God's purpose for their lives."[241]

---

241 Adapted from Roland Warren, *Bad Dads of the Bible: 8 Mistakes Every Good Dad Can Avoid* Grand Rapids: Zondervan, 2014 , 176-178.

COMPARING LEGACIES

My mother is now in her late eighties and has fifty-four grandkids and great grandkids. Her mind is not as sharp as it used to be, and she does not remember them all, but she is fiercely proud of them and her legacy. The golden era of her life was when my father was living, and she was the mother of four children. In our talks she regularly reminisces about those days. She was the happiest in that setting and in her role as mother—whatever work she did was simply an extension of that role for her. All four of her children and her stepchildren are devoted followers of Jesus in part because she modeled for each of us what it is love to Jesus—even through the worst of times. In her twilight years, she prepares to leave this earth with a sense of fulfillment and accomplishment while welcoming the day she will be in the presence of God. She worked hard over her difficult life and throughout it all, she has lived for others and has no regrets. She was not perfect—she was strong-willed, strict but fair, and she had her own fixed ways of doing things that would sometimes frustrate her adult kids who tried to help her.

My mother represents the more traditional view of marriage and family that is now often portrayed as outdated and oppressive. We now live in an iWorld, in which legacies like my mother's are not valued and have become less common. In this world there are some who would criticize her having so many children as if a responsible person would have no more than one or two kids. Some might criticize her for not demanding her rights as a woman—as an equal among all. Some might claim she had missed opportunities because of her devotion as a mother. She was motivated and intelligent and could have advanced her career; she could have held political office, and she could have made something of her life as members of an iWorld would measure it . But my mother is insistent she would have lived her life no other way.

One of the premises of this book is that there are no utopias. That means it does not take much effort to find reasons to criticize the older, more traditional views of marriage. At various times and settings, women were abused and demeaned. There has at times been a quantifiable pay discrepancy between men and women. There were glass ceilings that limited advancement for women in the workforce and society in general. But in that context, my mother saw her role as more important than anything else she could do. And all her children admire her for it. These perceived injustices did not dominate her worldview.

I have argued that the iWorld has its own set of issues that are often minimized or overlooked. In other words, there are trade-offs. Sometimes in our quest to eliminate one set of problems intrinsic to a worldview, we must contend with another set of problems—some of which are equal to or worse than those you attempted to discard. This is no truer than in marriage. We might ask, "What will be the legacy of those who live with the values of an iWorld?" As we saw in the prologue, the statistics on the state of marriage and the consequences for this new view are already coming in—and, as we have seen, it does not look good.

In the introduction I referenced Robert Bork who wrote a book titled, *Slouching Toward Gomorrah*.[242] As I noted, he identifies the two major tenants of modern liberalism as being radical individualism and radical egalitarianism. He argued that radical individualism will inevitably lead to hedonism and radical egalitarianism will inevitably lead to tyranny. I think the evidence bears this out.

Radical individualism leads to hedonism because if the individual is autonomous, then there is no objective morality that guides his or her life. When we face the temptations and passions that are characteristics of all people of all times, then we have nothing to restrain us from acting on them.

On the other hand, radical egalitarianism leads to tyranny, because in the real world, things are not equal. There will always be some who are rich and some who are poor, some who are bosses and some who are workers, some who smart are some who are not so smart. To change that requires outside coercion to force equal outcomes. It will not happen on its own. Is it no wonder that every example we have of a socialist society requires totalitarian governments?

What is the legacy that the iWorld is most likely to leave us with regarding marriage? I believe it is shattered relationships and loneliness. An article written by Brian Jones[243] suggests that loneliness in America is connected to our democratic experiment

---

242 Bork pg. 22.

243 Brian Jones, "Is Democracy to Blame for the Loneliness Epidemic?" last modified January 16, 2018. http://www.theamericanconservative. com/articles/is-democracy-to-blame-for-the-loneliness-epidemic/?mc_ cid=b403a881b9&mc_eid=462acf1479.

where the emphasis on individuality is moving us away from one's family and community and is considered a sign of maturity. He cites Alexis de Tocqueville who observed over two centuries ago,

"Aristocracy links everybody, from peasant to king, in one long chain. Democracy breaks the chain . . . Each man is thereby thrown back on himself alone, and there is a danger that he may be shut up in the solitude of his own heart."

In his article, Jones explains, "According to Tocqueville's observation, the shift from aristocratic to democratic conditions is not merely a change of political forms. Democracy produces a set of psychological and even imaginative changes that cause democratic citizens to see themselves in a new way. The novel manner thus described is one in which citizens gradually come to view themselves as *separated* and *cut off*. The displacement from nature, family, place, and intergenerational bonds that once held citizens together is what gives rise to a democratic society."

In his blog on this issue, Mark Galli asks, "Can we mitigate this phenomenon at this point in our history? Social media, which promised to bring us together, has only made things worse. Can the church help our society here? Or is it caught in the same web of assumptions that democracy brings with it?" That is a question worth pondering. Frankly, most of like the freedoms that a democracy offers but we must also realize its limitations.[244] As George Washington said in his final address, "Democracy only

---

[244] https://mail.google.com/mail/u/o/#search/
galli+report/1610freocif99e14

works if you have a moral people and you can only have a moral people if you have religion"[245]

A key premise of this book is that God instituted marriage, and he gave us a design that, when modeled, moves us closer to His ideal. It is a design He created for our good and his glory. It is a design that reflects the relationship between Christ and His church. But in living out this design, it means we have to have the mind of Christ, which includes sacrifice and humility. And that may mean for us a voluntary suspension of certain rights and wants in order to move us toward something greater than ourselves.

---

245   George Washington, "Address of George Washington, President of the United States . . . Preparatory to His Declination," George and Henry S. Keating, Baltimore: pp. 22-23. In his Farewell Address to the United States in 1/96.

INDEX OF CHARTS AND GRAPHS

Chart 1- Divorce Rates, Center for Disease Control CDC , National Center for Health Statistics NCHS , 222.cdc.gov/nchs.

Chart 2- Ibid.

Chart 3- Swenson, Richard A., "Margin: How to Create the Emotional, Physical, Financial, and Time Reserves You Need," Navpress, Colorado Springs, 1992, p. 249.

Chart 4- Bureau of Statistics, www.nap.edu/read/18613/chapter14#35 see also, www.diastercenters.com/crime/uscrime.

Chart 5- http://www.pewsocialtrends.org/2014/03/07/millennials-in-adulthood/sdt-next-america-03-07-2014-0-05/.

Chart 6- "The Decline in Marriage Among the Young, Millennials in Adulthood", http://www.pewsocialtrends.org/2014/03/07/millennials-in-adulthood/sdt-next-america-03-07-2014-0-02/

Chart 7- Rector, Robert, "Marriage: America's Greatest Weapon Against Child Poverty", The Heritage Foundation, Washington DC, 2010, https://www.heritage.org/poverty-and-inequality/report/marriage-americas-greatest-weapon-against-child-poverty-o.

Chart 8- Ibid.

Chart 9- Roser, Mike, "Fertility Rates", 2017 https://ourworldindata.org/fertility-rate

Chart 10- Ibid.

Chart 11- Ibid.

Chart 12- Ibid.

Chart 13- Ibid.

Chart 14- Ibid.

Chart 15- Ibid
Chart 16- Ibid
Chart 17- Ibid.
Chart 19- "The Four Parenting Styles Graph", *Extension.umn. edu.* University of Minnesota. n.d. web. 9 Feb. 2012.